MY

MY LIFE OF MIRACLES

By Bob Walsh

MY LIFE OF MIRACLES

Editing by Margie Holly Walsh.

Photos provided by Bob Walsh.

Paperback ISBN: 978-1542865234

Amazon eBook ASIN: B01MSECXA4

Authored by Bob Walsh

Email: walsh516@aol.com

Published by PBJ Enterprises, Inc.

162 Liberty Street, Deer Park, NY 11729

United States of America

Printed and bound in the United States of America.

First Edition

CONTENTS

EXHIBITS

PRAYER TO ST. MICHAEL THE ARCHANGEL
Prayer for Protection from Evil Spirits

St. Michael the Archangel, defend us in battle; be our protection against the wickedness and snares of the Devil. May God rebuke him, we humbly pray and do thou, O Prince of the heavenly host, by the power of God, thrust into Hell Satan and all the evil spirits who prowl about the world seeking the ruin of souls. Amen.

AUTHOR'S NOTES

Catholic Congregation
for the Propagation of the Faith

The decree issued by the Catholic Congregation for the Propagation of the Faith (A.A.S., 58, page 1186, approved by Pope Paul VI on October 14, 1966) rules that Nihil Obstat and Imprimatur are no longer required for publications that deal with private revelations, apparitions, prophesies and miracles provided that nothing is stated that is in contradiction of faith and morals.

In that light, the author, a faithful Catholic in good standing with the Church, affirms that the contents of this book do not in any way contradict Roman Catholic faith and morals.

Respecting the Privacy of Others

The names of several people in this book have been changed to respect their privacy.

This Book is Based Upon Actual Events

The events described in this book are based upon true events that actually happened as vividly remembered by the author who personally witnessed them. For those who wonder how it is possible to remember details of so many events over so many years beginning in early childhood, the author provides a simple explanation.

"Anyone who has witnessed a miraculous act of God, the breathtaking beauty of an angel … or been accosted by an evil spirit … can never forget such experiences - no matter how young or unsophisticated he or she may have been at the time."

ABOUT THE AUTHOR
Bob Walsh

Bob Walsh is a devout Catholic, well founded and educated in the Catholic faith and in good standing with the Church. One of 12 children, he grew up in a small, four room apartment in the Yorkville section of Manhattan in the heart of New York City.

From his earliest days, it was evident that he was blessed with spiritual gifts involving healing because when he prayed, God healed … and did so often in quite miraculous ways. In time, those who encountered him regarded him as a "blessed child of God." While his childhood was filled with countless miracles … it was also filled with brutal, relentless onslaughts of the Devil. Its efforts to prevent him from using God's gifts continue to present day.

Family, friends and Catholic clergy expected Bob to become a priest when he grew up, but God had a different plan. He was called to minister to others as a member of the laity in life situations where priests had little or no access. Bob married his teenage sweetheart, Margie Holly, and together they raised their three children while he worked as a bank executive on Wall Street. When his parents died at an early age, Bob and Margie also raised his younger sisters.

Following a career on Wall Street, Bob served as a U.S. Goodwill Ambassador to Russia and Ukraine. On his trip there, he ministered to the poor, people in cancer hospitals, children in orphanages … and to political leaders … even in the Kremlin.

He was a prolife candidate for Governor of New York in 1994 and for U.S. Congress in 2000. In his parish of Ss. Cyril and Methodius in Deer Park, Long Island, New York, Bob has served as a Eucharistic Minister since 1978, a Director of the Respect

Life Ministry, a member of the Holy Name Society, a Catechist and a member of the Knights of Columbus.

In defense of children in the womb, Bob worked as a Board Member of the Life Center of Long Island, Board Member of the Legal Center for the Defense of Life, and a member of the Long Island Coalition for Life. He also served as a Board Member of Morality in Media (fighting pornography), a founder and Editor of the Catholic Chronicle Newspaper, Director of the Rockville Centre Diocesan Pastoral Assistance Program, and a Eucharistic Minister and Lector at St. Patrick's Cathedral in New York City.

Throughout his life, Bob has witnessed countless healing miracles including deliverance from evil spirits. He presents himself as living proof miracles can and do happen when people turn to God in faith. In 2009, he was diagnosed with two different types of malignant cancer and Hemochromatosis (referred to as "iron-overload") requiring a pint of blood be withdrawn every few weeks. Bob survived extensive surgeries to remove the deadly malignancies without chemo or radiation.

In early 2017, he was diagnosed with neuroendocrine cancer … a rare form of malignant cancer. As you will read, when it appeared one of the tumors was going to end his life, God interceded and miraculously removed the deadly tumor … but not the underlying cancer. Then in late 2018, a second lethal NET tumor appeared in Bob's digestive system. Once again, God miraculously interceded and removed the entrenched, deadly tumor just as He did a year before.

Bob continues to write spiritual books distributed worldwide, conducts presentations on religious subjects and leads healing prayer services for those suffering with afflictions of the mind, body and spirit.

DEDICATION

This book is dedicated to God and to all those who helped me see and follow the light of Christ in my life. I thank God for the gift of life, for the family and friends he sent my way, and for the spiritual gifts he entrusted to me. I thank Him as well for opening the gates of Paradise, and for blessing me with a guardian angel who has guided and protected me on my often perilous journey through life.

To my beloved parents, Ellen Marie Sheridan Walsh and Patrick Victor Walsh, I extend my heartfelt appreciation for their love, sacrifice, encouragement and guidance. My life is a reflection of them since they were the first to teach me about God, our Christian faith, how to love and be loved. Heaven is now all the more beautiful with their presence.

Much love and gratitude go to my seven sisters and four brothers, my first and lasting friends. They shared the joys, adventures, challenges and tribulations growing up together in our large, Irish American Catholic family. Like many who grew up in the Yorkville section of New York City during the 1940s and 1950s, we were poor in terms of worldly possessions but felt rich in terms of what matters most in life - God, family and country.

Special thanks go to my brother, Larry, my best friend growing up. Ever by my side, he witnessed many of the extraordinary events shared in this book. He, along with others who have shared life with me, provided additional facts and details describing events in this book.

To my beloved bride, Margie Holly Walsh, my soul-mate, I extend my heartfelt love and appreciation. She has shared life with me, hand-in hand, from our teenage years through the best and worst of times. Ever loving, hardworking and self-sacrificing, she has been a beacon of light and love for me, for our family, friends and others.

My appreciation goes as well to my wonderful children and grandchildren who grace my life in so very many ways.

Finally, I extend my heartfelt gratitude to the Blessed Mother, Saint Anne (Jesus' grandmother), St. Padre Pio[1], St. Paul (my patron saint), St. Patrick (my Confirmation name) and the many, wonderful priests, nuns, and holy men and women who have lighted the way for me on my spiritual journey. My heartfelt thanks and appreciation to you all.

May God's glorious light of love, peace and happiness shine brightly upon us all until the day we stand together in His loving presence with all the angels and saints in Heaven. Amen.

Bob Walsh

---

[1] On June 2002, Padre Pio was canonized a saint in Saint Peter's Square, Vatican City by Pope John Paul II.

PREFACE

In keeping with Christ's words in Luke 12:48, **"From everyone to whom much is given, much will be required,"** I felt strongly obligated to share many of the miracles I have been blessed to witness over the course of my lifetime. This book accomplishes that by providing a first-hand account, a unique "peek behind the curtain," into the reality of miracles … and the spiritual life that exists around us all.

From my earliest memories to present time, I have seen God bestow virtually every type of miracle to those who cried out to Him in faith. There have been so many, it is not possible to include them all in one book. And so, the miracles I share in this book are limited to those that stand out in some special way. To be sure, each confirms Christ's remarkable words in Matthew 19:26, "With God **ALL** things are possible!"

Unfortunately for me, the Devil was aware that God had bestowed certain spiritual gifts upon me including healing, evangelization … and deliverance. Since each gift is intended in one way or another to encourage people to turn toward God, Satan in its consummate hatred for God and all He loves, has relentlessly sought to interfere with God's plans for each of us.

In that regard, you may find some of the stories in this book disturbing since they describe in frightening detail what it is like to be tormented by the Devil and its legions of demons. I have included these events in this book to reflect the fact that all of us are subject to the Devil's wiles, wickedness, temptations and torments. None of us are exempt, perhaps especially those who are ordained … or are otherwise spiritually blessed by God.

Truly, the way God protected me when the Devil attacked is as miraculous as all the other amazing events I share. Throughout my spiritual experiences - both good and bad - I have learned two undeniable truths. When we have greater faith in

God than we have fear of the Devil, God **always** wins. And, secondly, the best way to navigate through life's many difficulties and challenges is to follow Christ's simple but profound advice to "**follow Him"** in terms of how we live.

My hope in writing this book is that it may help increase your faith in God and raise your awareness of the reality that miracles can and do happen when we turn to Him in faith. Ultimately, may my true life experiences help you recognize the reality of spiritual life - both good and evil - and follow Christ's advice to **follow Him** in all you do.

Chapter 1

MIRACLES REALLY DO HAPPEN!

How fortunate we are to have a loving God who blesses us with the gift of life and salvation and ministers to us at times in quite miraculous ways as we struggle through the many trials and tribulations in physical life.

At one time or another, we all cry out to God when we or our loved ones are overcome with sufferings of the mind, body or spirit. When I pray, I do so with great confidence in Christ's words that, "With God, all things are possible." I truly believe that He hears every word, every prayer, every time we call out to Him. He understands our pain and suffering, and knows what is best for us and those we pray for … and He answers our prayers in ways that are best.

That does not mean we always get exactly what we pray for … but it does mean God heals us in ways that are best for us and for our loved ones. Sometimes He heals in quite miraculous ways involving a physical healing … often He does not. Through it all, we are called to trust that God listens to our prayers and answers them.

This book is filled with stories of miracles of every type I have witnessed for the mind, body and spirit showing the reality that miracles really do happen. As you read them, you may be reminded of similar experiences you have had in your life.

You are in for a treat reading what I have witnessed.

Chapter 2

NATURE AND PROCESS OF HEALING

Healing is a loving act of God in which He purifies the mind, body and spirit. The fount of all healings is through Jesus Christ who reconciled our broken relationship with God the Father.

Jesus is the personification of all healing.

Christ came into the world to be our personal Savior, our Redeemer and healer. He is the personification of God's love for us living with us in the Eucharist.

He is the same loving, active healer today as in any other time in keeping with His solemn promise as recorded by Matthew 28:20, "And remember, I am with you always, even unto the end of time."

Many healings are, in fact, miraculous.

So what exactly are miracles?

To be sure … miracles are acts of love by God that are beyond our human ability to perform or to understand. They are personal expressions of God's love for us and are intended to bring us closer to Him. Some healings happen instantly but most occur over the course of Our Lord's time … just as many of our hurts and injuries develop over time.

Dramatic research conducted by Catholic healing ministers discloses some revealing facts. The majority of healings - said to be over 80% - take place gradually over the course of time as ongoing healing prayers continue. Nearly everyone who prays faithfully experiences a feeling of improvement. Some healings begin immediately during healing prayer and continue over the course of hours, days, weeks, months and even years. In certain cases, healing unfolds gradually even when there is no ongoing healing prayer.

Remarkably, some healing only begins and ends with the

healing prayers being said. Simply stated, when the healing prayer ends, so does the healing! When healing prayer continues, or resumes after a break in prayer, the healing process resumes. This form of ongoing healing prayer is often referred to as "soaking prayer."

As St. Paul tells us in the Bible, some people are blessed with a more powerful gift of healing than others. For those with a lesser gift of healing, deeper, longer healing prayer is often required before healing can be seen.

God usually heals through the intercession of others – through loved ones, the Church, healing ministers, doctors, the saints and others.

Sometimes when our faith or preparation is weak, God blesses the efforts of other faithful members of the Mystical Body of Christ to intercede on our behalf. There are several examples of this in the Bible confirming this. Consider God's words.

In Matthew 15:21, Jesus tells us, "A Canaanite woman from that region came out and started shouting, 'Have mercy on me, Lord, Son of David, my daughter is tormented by a demon.' But he did not answer her at all. And his disciples came and urged him, saying, 'Send her away, for she keeps shouting after us.' He answered, 'I was sent only to the lost sheep of the house of Israel.'

"But she came and knelt before him, saying, 'Lord, help me.' He answered, 'It is not fair to take the children's food and throw it to the dogs.' She said, 'Yes, Lord, yet even the dogs eat the crumbs that fall from their master's table.' Then Jesus answered her, 'Woman, great is your faith! Let it be done for you as you wish.' And her daughter was healed instantly."

Here is another example Jesus gives us. In Matthew 9:2, God tells us of the faith of four men who carried a paralyzed man up to a roof where they made a hole and lowered the man down in front of Jesus. Seeing **THEIR** faith, Jesus first forgave the man his sins when He said, "Take heart, son; your sins are forgiven."

Jesus then asked the surrounding crowd there, "Which is easier, to say, 'Your sins are forgiven,' or to say, 'Stand up, and walk?' But so that you may know that the Son of Man has authority on earth to forgive sins, Jesus said to the paralytic, 'Stand up, take your bed and go to your home!' And he stood up and went to his home!"

Yet another example is in Matthew 8:5 when God tells us of the Roman Centurion whose servant was paralyzed at home. The Centurion asked Jesus to heal the servant. When Jesus offered to go to the Centurion's home, the Centurion answered, "Lord, I am not worthy to have you come under my roof; but only speak the word and my servant will be healed."

The Bible then tells us that Jesus was so surprised by her faith. "He was amazed and said to those who follow him, 'Truly, I tell you, in no one in Israel have I found such faith. Go; let it be done for you according to your faith.' And the servant was healed in that hour."

When God reaches out and heals someone in our presence, rarely is there any thunder, lightning or earthquakes. However, sometimes He allows those praying for healing – and those being prayed for - to sense His healing Spirit as it descends. On occasion, this results in what is called, "being slain in the Spirit." That is, when someone physically collapses as the healing graces of God descend upon or around him.

For those who may not be familiar with saying healing prayer, a suggested way is found in Chapter 3 of this book. It is what I have used over the years in healing prayer services.

Chapter 3

HOW TO PRAY FOR HEALING

When you pray for healing, consider the many examples of healing that Jesus gives us as recorded in the Bible. In each of these, you can see the many common threads Jesus uses.

For example, in all the biblical stories describing miraculous healing events, it was **faith** that God responded to. Clearly, faith is the very spark that ignites God's mercy, love and generosity. Having said that, faith should always be preceded by granting forgiveness to others … and that includes forgiving ourselves … sometimes that is the most difficult to give.

Whenever I have prayed for God's help, I found certain phases of healing prayer to be key. Listed below are those steps in sequence in order of importance.

FORGIVENESS

The first step in healing involves forgiving everyone, everything … including forgiving ourselves. Consider what Christ tells us in the Bible especially how He tells us that when He forgives, **He also forgets what we did wrong!**

- In Paul's Letter to the Hebrews 10:17, God tells us, "Their sins and iniquities I will remember no more."
- In Isaiah 43:18, God tells us, "Do not remember the former things, or consider the things of old."
- In Isaiah 43:25, God tells us, "I wipe out your offenses; your sins I remember no more!"
- In Jeremiah 31:34, God tells us, "I will forgive their iniquity and remember their sins no more!"
- In Ephesians 4:32, God tells us, "Be kind to one another, forgiving each other, just as in Christ God forgave you!"

- In the one prayer Jesus taught us, the Our Father, He leads us to pray, "Forgive us our trespasses as we forgive those who trespass against us."
- Hanging on the cross, Jesus showed us how to forgive anyone, anything. He said, "Father, forgive them for they know not what they do!" When He said these words of forgiveness, He included all of us.

This first step is so important that Jesus tells us even if we bring gifts to the church but have unforgiveness in our hearts, we should put the gifts down and go make peace!

TELL JESUS WHAT YOU NEED

The next step in healing prayer is to clearly tell God what it is you want or need Him to do for you. Jesus shows us this in several stories recorded in the Bible. For example, in Matthew 9:27, Jesus shows us how important this is when He asks the two blind men what they want Him to do for them. Note that He did not ask them if they want to see. Jesus knows what it is that we need but He wants us to express faith in Him by saying it.

Make sure to ask for what is most important to you, and don't limit what you ask of Him. And while you have the opportunity, perhaps you should also ask Him to help others in your life who are suffering.

EXPRESS FAITH IN GOD

The next step in healing prayer is to express faith that God can and will help you in ways that are best. To illustrate, consider the following stories from the Bible showing the great importance of faith.

- In Matthew 9:27, Jesus asked the two blind men if they believed that He could do what they asked of Him – to cure their blindness. When they said, "Yes, Lord," Jesus replied, "According to **your faith**, let it be done to you!"

- In Matthew 8:13, a Roman Centurion asked Jesus to heal his paralyzed servant. He said, "Lord, I am not worthy to have You come under my roof, but only speak the word, and my servant will be healed." Jesus was so impressed with **the faith** of the Roman Centurion, He said to him, "Go, let it be done according to **your faith**!"
- In Mark 9:23, Jesus tells us of the father of a boy who was possessed since childhood, "All things can be done for the **one who believes**."
- In John 20:29, Jesus tells us, "Blessed are they who have not seen, **yet believe**."
- In Mark 5:34, Jesus tells us of the woman with blood flow for over 12 years. He said to her, "Daughter, **your faith** has made you well; go in peace, and be healed of your disease!"
- In Mark 5:36, Jesus shows us His great love for us and His understanding of our humanness as He tells us, "Don't be afraid … just **have faith**!"
- In Philippians 4:13, Jesus tells us, "We can do all things through Him who strengthens us."
- In Mark 10:46, Jesus tells us about Bartimaeus, the blind man sitting by the road who cried out, "Jesus, Son of David, have pity on me." He cried out so loudly that the holy men and women with Jesus told him to be quiet! But filled with faith in Jesus, Bartimaeus did not allow anyone or anything to keep him from crying out to God so he cried out even louder, "Jesus, Son of David, have pity on me." When he told Jesus that he wanted to see again, Jesus said, "Go, **your faith** has made you well."

Remember these examples of the importance of faith that

Jesus tells us about when you pray for healing. Let those Bible readings strengthen your faith so God can and will do whatever is best for you … and that He will do it in the very best way and at the very best time.

GIVE THANKS TO GOD!

This next step involves acknowledging what God did for you by thanking Him. Jesus shows us how important this is as He gives us the example of the one leper out of ten who were miraculously healed by Him (Luke 17:11). The one leper was the only one who went back to thank Jesus for healing him.

Jesus said, "Were not ten made clean? But the other nine, where are they?" Then He said to the one leper, "Get up and go your way; **your faith has made you well!"**

Tradition tells us this one leper who made time to go back and thank Jesus was then rewarded by having all that he had lost to leprosy returned to him! Make sure to make time yourself to appropriately express your appreciation for whatever God does for you.

THE GREATEST PRAYER

For us Catholics, this final step in healing prayer is the most important of all. It is uniting our healing prayers with that of the Holy Sacrifice of the Mass that is the greatest healing prayer of all. At every Mass, a miracle takes place when the priest consecrates the bread and wine into the Body and Blood of Our Lord and Savior, Jesus Christ. Following this most sacred of all moments, is one of the greatest healing prayers we can say, "Lord, I am not worthy that you should come under my roof … but only say the word … and my soul shall be healed." Amen!

Chapter 4

THE BEGINNING

My mother once told me about the amazing things that happened when I was born in Bellevue Hospital in New York City.

The nurses who handled me reported sensing something very different about me from the other babies in the nursery. In fact, reports circulated among hospital staff about the wonderful feelings of peace the nurses felt near me.

This, my mother told me, was actually the beginning of my extraordinary walk with God in a life filled with miracles.

It all began in earnest when a nurse who was suffering with arthritis was healed while she held me in her arms. Even though it is generally thought babies cannot see when they are first born, the nurse who was healed swore that I was looking right into her eyes as she was praying that God would heal her. As word quickly spread throughout the hospital, medical workers came to see 'the special child' in the nursery.

Soon, one of the nurses called a Catholic priest, told him what was happening and suggested he come to see for himself. When he did, the nurses allowed him to stand over me in the nursery. Nurses said the priest simply stood there, deep in thought, staring down at me as I peacefully slept.

When the priest began making the sign of the cross over me, the nurses said he suddenly stopped in the middle of the blessing and stood perfectly still. Something caused him to virtually freeze. After a moment, he completed the blessing.

The nurses asked if he thought there was anything special about me.

He haltingly replied, "Yes ... I did sense something special. As a matter of fact, what I sensed was something very good … and holy … about that child. In all my years as a priest, I have never experienced anything like it.

"While I was standing over him, I felt a glow of love … and goodness radiating from him! And as I was blessing him, he opened his eyes and looked right up at me! I know this sounds crazy, but I felt that he somehow understood what I was doing.

"Then I felt like I was blessed in return!

"Thank you for telling me about him. Before I go, I must speak with his mother."

As the priest made his way to speak with my mother, the nurses spread this latest news about me … and began to refer to me as their "blessed child."

When the priest shared his thoughts with Mom, she told him that the nurses had been telling her similar stories about her "special gift from God."

"He is my third child, Father," she explained, "but carrying him for nine months, I could tell there was something very different from my first two children. I could feel this child was special … I mean … in a religious sense.

"I could tell the child I was carrying was a holy child."

Unfortunately for me, Satan was also aware that God had, indeed, greatly blessed me. In its efforts to impede me from using God's gifts, the Devil wasted no time in launching its pursuit and torments ... beginning in the crib … as you are about to hear.

I remember being startled out of a sound sleep in my crib in the middle of a cold, dark night on January 25, 1946, my first birthday. A fearsome creature filled with pure hatred and consummate evil was slowly approaching. It radiated a nature hell-bent on tormenting and destroying anything of God … and it was coming after me.

It had just materialized off in the distance behind the apartment building where I lived since birth. Instinctively, I knew it was aware that I was conscious of its presence, its essence and that it was coming to inflict unspeakable harm upon me.

The apartment where I grew up during the 1940s and 1950s was a railroad-style apartment comprised of four rooms (five if you count the bathroom) located on the second floor of a brownstone tenement in the heart of the Yorkville section of Manhattan in New York City.

The rooms followed one another in a straight line, like cars in a train; hence its name, railroad rooms. Such apartments were quite common at that time throughout the east side of Manhattan. The kitchen, the first room in our apartment, looked out onto a darkened alley behind our building and the next.

Our family was quite poor but we were greatly blessed with devout, loving parents, Patrick Victor Walsh and Ellen Marie Sheridan Walsh. They ensured we were well educated in the Catholic faith and our rich Irish heritage and traditions. As the third oldest of twelve children in a four room flat, I never felt alone … until that night.

As the evil mass slowly approached, I sat perfectly still in my crib in this cold dark room shivering and worrying about why this terrible creature was coming after me. I could sense its essence; it was composed of consummate evil. It entered our home by passing silently and effortlessly through the large double-hung window located in the far right diagonal corner of the kitchen.

A feeling of helplessness swept over me. I felt so defenseless with no place to hide from it. I was so frightened I could not move, and dared not cry out for fear the evil thing would rush at me … and consume me.

The sounds of laughter and celebration from my first birthday party earlier that day now seemed so long ago. A pleasant vision from earlier events flashed before my mind's eye. As everyone sang "Happy Birthday," one candle on the cake burned brightly while another candle in the middle was left unlit. Mommy explained that it is a family tradition to leave one candle in the center unlit for good luck. The flickering of the lighted candle cast its light on the smiling faces of Daddy, Mommy and my older siblings, Paddy and Kitty.

The luxury of that joyful reflection quickly faded as I sat with my back to the end section of the crib that rested against the wall. Crème-colored wooden slats bordered all sides of the crib. Grabbing onto one of the cold, wooden slats to my right, I peered out into the darkened room where I saw Mommy and Daddy sleeping soundly in the bed to the right of my crib.

Against the opposite wall facing my crib was a four-foot wide closet with two large wooden doors on top and two drawers side by side on the bottom. To the left of the closet was a silver heat pipe that rose straight up through the floor and extended all the way up into a hole in the ceiling where it continued to the apartment above. It is up there by the ceiling that hundreds of roaches are always seen scurrying around. Mommy told me that pipes and radiators carry scalding hot water throughout the building from a furnace located down in the basement of the building.

To the left of the hot water pipe was a large double-hung window set in the wall at a forty-five degree angle to the rest of the room. This window overlooked an airway enclosed by the surrounding tenement buildings.

Off to the extreme right of my room was a pair of French-style glass-paneled doors each of which was two feet wide. There were thin curtains I could see through as they hung decoratively down the full length of each French door. These doors were to the left of Mommy and Daddy's bed; they led into the last room of our home, the living room, located at the front of our building. Beyond our living room, was the outside world of our neighborhood, Yorkville.

My three-year-old brother, Paddy, was asleep in a bed by himself in the next room to my left located between my room and the kitchen. As was the tradition of Irish families, the first-born, Paddy, was named after Daddy, Patrick Victor Walsh.

My two-year-old sister, Kitty, was sleeping at the other end of this crib that we shared. She was named after Daddy's mother, Catherine Marie Clarke Walsh.

Although surrounded by my family, I felt so alone in the utter darkness of our apartment home because I was the only one who was awake while the dark figure slowly approached. All sound in our home was gone as if something sucked it all out leaving an eerie, unnatural silence, a lifelessness permeating everything. Nothingness filled the air.

Why was this thing coming after me? I wondered. Where can I hide? What can I do? What was going to happen to me? I felt so defenseless against this monstrous entity. Since my crib was located against the wall next to the open doorway in the front of my room, it was not physically possible for me to look out through the rooms toward the kitchen in the direction of the approaching thing.

I sat perfectly still and breathed as quietly as possible as I listened intently and worried about what was going to happen to me. What was this bad thing and why was it coming to harm me? It continued to approach … moving very, very slowly.

It would soon be upon me.

In my mind's eye, I could envision it as it entered the next room, the second room off the kitchen where Paddy was still sleeping peacefully. Slowly, it glided past him without pausing. It obviously was only after me.

I looked over to Mommy and Daddy for help but they were still sleeping in the bed a few feet from my crib … completely unaware that some terrible presence has entered our home. Kitty also continued to sleep at the other end of my crib as the monstrous entity approached the open doorway to my room. I pulled the covers closer for protection and laid down.

I realized once again that this thing knew that I was aware of its presence and that I was terribly afraid of it. A sense of isolation, helplessness, and impending doom overwhelmed me. I was too afraid to cry out for fear of drawing more attention to myself.

I felt so vulnerable, so defenseless.

Why doesn't someone wake up and help me? Kitty stirred a little but did not wake up. Mommy and Daddy continued sleeping, unaware that an evil thing has entered our home.

Where I was in the crib, my feet and toes protruded slightly beyond my blanket and through the end slats of my crib. Too frightened to pull my feet back, I left them exposed and laid as still as possible while hoping the dark, threatening figure would think I was asleep.

Slowly gliding into my room, the “thing” paused at the foot of my crib and turned menacingly in my direction. A strange, unpleasant odor filled the room … and the air became much, much colder.

This loathsome creature was clothed within a charcoal black shroud composed of consummate evil devoid of any love or goodness whatsoever. It was bad … very bad … the essence of pure hatred and evil.

It was so black that it stood out starkly in the darkness of the room. Its head sloped directly down onto its shoulders as if it did not have a neck. There were no features, no hair, no ears, no eyes, no nose, no chin … no goodness. It was composed of pure, unadulterated evil.

Its head was only a foot higher than the end of my crib. It was peering down into me … encasing me in its vice of isolation and emptiness. I was so frightened. This evil creature remained suspended there, perfectly still, glaring down upon me.

I closed my eyes as I felt it was examining me, measuring me, reading me. I was so frightened, I was unable to move. The warmth of my urine spilled out from under my cloth diaper and flowed out onto my legs and the mattress sheet below.

Suddenly, sharp razor-like claws scratched my toes sending shock waves of pain and terror ripping throughout my mind and body! It had attacked me! I burst upright and screamed as I pulled my feet back away from the point of attack.

Quickly drawing away, I pulled myself up and looked toward the end of the crib. The black thing was still there! It had not moved. So what scratched me? Looking down toward the floor, I saw two eerie-looking eyes glaring in the dark right back up at me!

It was Blackie, our large jet-black colored family cat! Hissing menacingly, it was crouched as if it was going to pounce up on me in the crib. I cried out loudly for Mommy and Daddy to come protect me from our wicked cat and the evil thing at the foot of my crib … but they continued to sleep!

Worrying about Blackie distracted me for the moment from the evil presence. I discovered it was no longer stationed at the foot of my crib but I could sense it was lurking somewhere else nearby in the total darkness of my room.

In utter fear, I cried out to another presence I sensed was always around me - a presence of pure love and goodness. I cried out to it using my innermost feelings.

It understood.

In the very next instant, my room filled with a glorious white light that surrounded and immersed me in a blanket of love and safety. The monstrous evil spirit and Blackie the cat fled, chased away by the wonderful, good presence. Feeling safe and protected, I eased myself down confident that the evil thing - and our crazy family cat - could not harm me.

I would later learn that the evil entity was the worst of all creatures. It was a hate-filled demon dispatched from the very depths of Hell to hinder any good I might achieve in life … and to consume my life force … my soul … in the process.

My miraculous journey through life had only just begun.

Chapter 5

BLESSED CHILD OF GOD

After the terrifying encounter with a demon, I realized that I was born with a second sight … an extraordinary awareness of the spiritual realm of life including the presence of God, angels, devils and miracles. I understood the essence of good and evil.

My early life was so filled with supernatural events that I soon was regarded as a "blessed child of God." The people in my family at that time were amazed to learn that I could see angels and communicate with them … sometimes without spoken words. Unfortunately for me, I often saw demons as well, and could hear their hideous screams, sacrilegious remarks and threats.

As a child, I greatly feared the spiritual bullies, the demons, as they relentlessly tormented me. However, God and His angels protected me without which I might have perished. Years later, I would need every bit of that protection when powerful demons descended upon me with a fury that was hell-bent on carrying me away with them to the depths of Hell.

Born and raised in a poor, Irish Catholic family of 12 children, I had seven sisters and four brothers. We grew up in a small, four-room apartment on the east side of Manhattan, the Yorkville section in the heart of New York City. Back in the 1940s and 1950s when I was growing up, many families on the East Side had many children. We were all poor but didn't know it. In so many ways, it was a magical age, a wonderful place to grow up where it seemed everyone was guided by God, family and country.

Despite how poor we were, my parents made sure we received a sound Catholic education, received all our sacraments and lived our faith. The word of God in the Bible supplemented all this with what I like to call "travel advisories" to guide us on our journey along physical life.

My parents and extended family were among the first to notice there was something unusual about me … something spiritually good. They heard me speak of beautiful white lights, angels … and terrible "bad things." This was how my life began and continues to this day filled with miraculous experiences mingled with the Devil's torments and temptations.

My earliest recollections include relatives, neighbors and strangers coming to my home asking my parents to have me pray for someone who was sick. All this, in fact, seemed quite natural to me … including the times I heard that many of the people were healed in some miraculous way.

At the time, I assumed that this was something everyone did. I fully believed that whenever we pray, God heals the people we pray for. It wasn't until I started St. Monica's Catholic grade school that I realized this was not the case. That is when I learned that I was different … quite different … from everyone else. I also began to realize I would never enjoy a "normal" life like other children.

During my grade school years, things became increasingly more intense as the spiritual blessings and demonic torments continued unabated. At times when I felt completely overwhelmed, I would simply sit perfectly still, close my eyes and ears to the outside world … and focus entirely on the presence of God immersing me and all existence in His peace and serenity.

As my reputation as a "blessed child of God" spread beyond my neighborhood, I found myself besieged by all kinds of people from near and far. These were mostly people who needed God's healing, but there were also those who were simply curious … and then … there were those who clearly were agents of the Devil.

I also became the center of attention among Catholic clergy in New York's archdiocese - especially the nuns and priests of my parish, St. Monica's. As stories of miraculous healings circulated far and wide, some clergy were skeptical at first but in time joined others who were quite excited to have someone considered a "blessed child of God" right there in their very midst.

Unfortunately for me, they weren't the only ones who were so focused on me … the demons were even more so.

Chapter 6

MY FIRST MASS

"Hey, Bobby, for Christ's sake, what're you doing? Hurry up, or we'll be late for Mass," Daddy calls out from the kitchen.

The humidity has me sweating badly as I struggle nervously to get my striped polo shirt down over my head. Our apartment is always so hot during the summertime despite the fact that Mommy keeps the windows open in the front and rear to "get a cross-breeze" as she says going through our railroad styled apartment. I wish she did not do this because keeping the windows open also allows all the annoying flies to get in … and they have quite a nasty bite! Besides that, it is very rare that I feel any cross-breeze.

My shirt was so tight on me that my ears got pinched as I wiggled my head from side to side and pulled the shirt down with all my strength.

As I struggled, the demon taunt, "You're stuck in the shirt; you'll never get out. You can't breathe … you're going to suffocate!"

I fought until finally my head popped free through the opening. I took a deep breath of relief and tucked the edges of my shirt into my trousers.

"Do you know what day today is, Bobby?" Daddy asks.

I shake my head no, and wonder why he is asking.

"Today is July 9, 1950. I want you to remember this date because this is the day you're going to attend your very first Mass at St. Monica's!"

Daddy shouldn't worry about me remembering my very first Mass. I am five years old and will always remember my very first Mass as long as I live. Mommy and Daddy have told me so much about all the wonderful things that happen during Mass …

and now I am going to see everything for myself!

Daddy comes over and crouches down, “It’s swell how very much you care about going to your first Mass. I am very proud of you, son.”

Relishing the moment, he stares admiringly at me, but all of a sudden remembers the time, “Holy God, it’s getting late. We’d better get a move on or we'll be late for your very first Mass!”

Paddy and Kitty had declined Daddy’s offer to take them to Mass with us; they prefer to stay home playing. Daddy says Larry is too young to join us.

“He’d only make a ‘commotion’ being there and distract everyone.”

Mommy gives us a kiss goodbye before we hurry out into the cool, dark hallway outside the front door of our apartment. We quickly descend the three sections of winding stairs to the ground floor. At the end of the long hallway on the ground floor, I see the door that leads to the bright light outside our building. Daddy turns the doorknob, and for what seems like an eternity, he slowly opens the door. I burst through the door then push past the double swinging doors leading to the front stoop and the bright daylight.

“Whoa, slow down, Bobby!” Daddy calls out, “Hold your horses. It’s not **that** late. Take it easy; we have plenty of time to get there.”

Walking briskly, we pass a group of mothers gathered as usual with their baby carriages in front of one of the buildings on the street.

Daddy politely nods to them and greets them, “Good morning, ladies.”

They pause from their chattering only long enough to return his greeting before resuming their frenetic exchange of words. I wonder how they can hear each other since they all talk at the same time! Mommy says these ladies gather together like this every day.

Along our journey, we pass the gigantic all-girls junior public high school, P.S. 96, on York Avenue from 82nd Street all the way to 81st Street. As we approach 81st Street and York Avenue, Daddy tightens his grip on my hand as he tells me, "Bobby, always look both ways before you cross the street, even if the light is green. You know ... the light will not run you over, the cars will! Catch wise? Understand?"

"Yes, Daddy," I answer, grateful that he shares such important things with me for my safety and well-being.

Daddy says, "We have a lot of praying to do today, Bobby."

"Why, Daddy?"

"Besides praying for our family, we have to pray that God prevents another world war from breaking out. Our soldiers just got back from World War II, fighting the Nazis and the Japs, and now it looks like they'll be fighting the Koreans. This is terrible, Bobby. In a war, any war, thousands of people are shot, stabbed, beaten to death, starved to death, crippled for life!"

This is terrible.

"Who are 'Koreans,' Daddy?" I ask with difficulty pronouncing the word, Koreans.

"They are people who live on the other side of the world between Germany and Japan," he explains. "You see, there are bad people over there called 'Communists' who live in the upper half of Korea. Last Sunday they invaded the lower half of the country and killed people, and stole their food and belongings."

This greatly disturbs me. People are supposed to love and help one another, not hurt each other, "If it's their country, why do they hurt each other?"

Daddy smiles, "You'll understand when you grow up, Bobby. For now, let's just say it's because the Communists want to force everybody to live their way."

Daddy stops walking and looks to me, "For one thing, they don't believe in God, and they don't let people go to church like you and I are doing right now. They are afraid that people will have greater allegiance to God than to their Communistic way of life. We live in a great country, Bobby, where we can go to church and worship God without worrying about someone putting us in prison for the rest of our lives, or even killing us. Don't ever take our religious freedom for granted, son."

I nod in obedience and promise never to take our freedom for granted.

As we resume walking, Daddy adds, "On Tuesday, President Truman announced on the radio that he's sending our troops, ships and planes to South Korea to help the people there protect themselves. The President and Vice President Barkley have a tough job ahead of them. God help us; it looks like there may be another war."

I think about what Daddy said about war in a place far away from where we live. I'm relieved that it's not happening here. War sounds so terrible and frightening.

"Daddy, will you have to go there to fight the bad people?" I worry aloud.

"No, son. Fathers of families like ours have to stay home and take care of their families," he assures me. "That's how we fulfill our obligation to our country. Somebody has to take care of things here at home during war-time."

This is so comforting to hear. I don't want Daddy to go to some faraway place on the other side of the world where bad people would try to hurt him and possibly kill him.

As we cross York Avenue and continue on our journey westward up 79th Street toward St. Monica's Church, I gaze straight ahead toward the other end of the block. There I see a high, black wrought-iron gate that encloses a long set of stairs going up to what I know must be the church. The stairs jut straight out beyond the long row of three-story, brownstone tenements that line the right side of 79th Street from York Avenue all the way up to the black gate.

"That's St. Monica's up there, Bobby, by the gate and the stairs," Daddy points out.

My heart starts to beat rapidly.

"That's God's home," I say, "We're going to visit God in His home, just like we visit Nana in her home!"

Daddy chuckles, obviously amused by my comparison.

Suddenly, the sound of ferocious growling fills the air behind me. Even though I am still holding onto Daddy's hand, I am terrified by this unseen menace. My whole being focuses on what sounds like a fierce creature, a predator of some kind that has just cornered its prey, a tasty meal… me. My heart and mind explode with fear as razor-sharp teeth clamp on the back of my right leg above my ankle.

Sharp pain radiates from there all the way up my leg as I scream out in horror, **"Oooow!** Daddy, help me; something is biting me!"

Daddy's hand tightens like a vise over my left hand as he swirls around to confront the beast that is attacking me. With another scream swelling in my throat, I turn to discover that the fierce creature attacking me is a small but very angry, curly-haired dog! It is moving its head from side to side and backing up while its teeth are clamped on my leg! My eyes quickly follow upward along the dog's leash to where it is held by a well-dressed woman who looks startled by what her dog is doing to me.

As I try to pull away from the dog, I see Daddy's leg come swinging into view as his foot lands directly under the dog's belly making a loud "thump" sound. Daddy's leg continues upward thrusting the dog, leash and all, high into the air as the dog's sharp teeth let go of my leg! When the dog lands a few feet away, it is stunned and hurt.

As the dog whelps in pain, the lady is outraged by Daddy's attack, "Oh, my God, you terrible man! Why did you do that? My poor baby! Somebody call the police!"

The lady's shouting further alarms me. For the moment, I feel guilty that I have caused Daddy to hurt the dog in defending me. Now I am worried that the police will come and arrest Daddy for kicking the dog. Daddy surprises me by angrily shouting right back at the lady.

"Why don't you control your goddamned dog, lady! It bit my son! You go ahead and call the cops; I'll have **you** arrested for not controlling your dog!"

Daddy moves forward to kick the dog again, but the lady and her dog seeing Daddy charging, turn and run down 79th Street toward York Avenue. Daddy stands there glaring as the dog races ahead of the lady so fast that the leash is strained straight as an arrow.

Daddy is so upset saliva drips out of the corner of his mouth as he angrily shouts after them, "You'd better keep running. Son-of-a-bitch! She cares more for her freakin' dog than she does for my kid!"

Cupping his hands around his mouth so his voice will carry farther, Daddy thunders, "You and your goddamn dog better keep running!"

The lady and her dog reach the corner of York Avenue where they turn left and disappear from view. This is so uncharacteristic for Daddy to be so impolite and aggressive toward a woman, especially such an impressive-looking lady. He is usually very courteous. His actions demonstrate quite dramatically how much he loves me, and how protective he is of his family.

Daddy turns back to me and bends down to check my leg

and my slightly torn trousers.

"Are you all right, son?" he asks still quite agitated, "Are you cut? Let me see."

I look down at the area above my ankle and am greatly relieved to discover I am not cut or bleeding. It just looks red, and throbs painfully.

Although Daddy can see I am not seriously injured, he mutters, "Dog-loving, wacko woman!"

"I'm okay, Daddy," I say bravely even though I am still shaken by the dog's attack. I throw my arms around his neck and cling to him for reassurance. It occurs to me that this terrible thing happened to me on my way to church.

"Everything's all right now, son; the dog is gone. You're safe," he reassures me as I relax safely in his powerful embrace.

I hear the familiar growl of the demon as it lets me know that it followed me and agitated the dog into attacking me. I don't wonder why … I am going to my very first Mass. I remember that Mommy once said that the Devil can use animals to hurt and intimidate people. This attack was especially upsetting since I am deathly afraid of dogs.

"Can we please go to St. Monica's now, Daddy," I plead.

Looking in my eyes, Daddy says, "Just a minute, son; hold your horses. I have to tell you something first. Listen to me and pay attention."

Daddy points his finger in my face for emphasis, "Never, ever, go near any dogs … even if they are with their owners. Do you hear me? They are ALL vicious. Dogs can bite you and hurt you and if they have rabies disease, you will have to get eight giant needles right in your stomach! That is very, very painful! Do you hear what I am telling you? Understand? You stay away from dogs. Okay?"

"Yes, Daddy, I will."

He continues, "One more thing, if you are ever attacked

by a dog like that again, you kick the dog as hard as you can right in its nose or in its stomach, and then keep kicking it until it runs away. You yell at it too, loudly. Sometimes screaming at a dog can scare it away. Catch wise?"

I nod in agreement. My eyes wander over Daddy's shoulder to the front of St. Monica's Church where I see people climbing up the long stairs into the church.

Daddy also looks over and says, "Okay, let's go before we miss the beginning of Mass."

As we approach the church, it seems to get larger and larger until we are finally standing right in the very front by the center of the long stairs. My eyes scale up the long steps that span the entire front of the church. In front of the stairs to the right and left is a tall, black-wrought iron gate with long, sharp points along the top. When the gate is closed it extends across the entire front of the stairs. The gate is about one foot higher than Daddy and gives the impression that its purpose is to lock out unwelcome things. Especially bad things, I think.

I bend my head all the way back so I can look straight up the front of the church. The church is so high that it seems to reach into the clouds and heaven itself! Just beneath where the church comes to a pointed top, I notice there is a stained glass window that is difficult for me to see because of the bright sunlight glaring off the golden-colored, brick front of the church.

Rising above the top of St. Monica's Church are spires on either side of the top center area. These spires rise even higher into the sky than the center peak. I wonder about the significance of these spires. They are probably intended to point toward heaven where God lives. Daddy once told me that the spires are decorative but they also help people recognize where the churches are located in the city because the churches stand out clearly in the skyline thanks to the spires.

I know what Daddy said is true but I also think the spires

are intended to point upward toward God in heaven.

There are three sets of doorways leading into the church. At the top of the stairs directly in the center of St. Monica's Church, the entrance is comprised of two large red doors facing us. Each door has a half-panel of glass in the top section. The doors are set inside two other outside doors also red in color. These doors are wide open in a welcoming gesture. Similar sets of doors stand at each of the two side entrances at the top of the stairs in front of St. Monica's Church.

I feel so small and fragile compared to the church's mighty structure of brick, concrete, steel, and glass but I am thrilled to see a small window at the very top of this mighty structure. In a similar way, I reason, although I am small in terms of physical size, I know that I am far more important than any buildings no matter how big or grand they may be because I am one of God's children.

God gave me a soul enabling me to live, think, breathe, choose, see, hear, and to do things for myself which a building can never do. As one of God's children, I can also feel His love for me … something non-living things like buildings can never enjoy.

People scurry past us on the right and left as we climb the stairs, and quickly disappear into the church through the two swinging red doors at the top. I count each step as we make our way up, eleven steps in all. Daddy and I then pass through the large red doors and enter the cool, dark area on the other side.

I immediately sense the presence of a magnificent, all-consuming entity that is gentle, loving and kind. This presence is everywhere filling the entire church, transforming it into a deeply hallowed, holy place. From what Mommy and Daddy have told me in the past, I know that what I sense must be the presence of God in here.

"This area of the church is called the vestibule, Bobby.

You were baptized right over there," Daddy says as he points to a small room off to our far left.

We walk over to the small room and peer through its two full-glass doors. I can see a large white marble baptismal font standing prominently in the center of the room. A smaller font is connected to its right side.

"You know, that's where everyone in our family was baptized over the years," Daddy says sounding emotional, "That includes Mommy and me!

"Your godparents, Aunt Flo Porter, your mom's sister, and her husband, Vinny Porter, held you right over there, Bobby, only a few years ago. How do you like that, heh?"

There is a special kind of beauty in this holy place where I, my brothers and my sister, my parents and so many others became Christians. Right here! I can envision my Godparents holding me over the larger font while the priest poured the holy water of Baptism over my head. I can almost feel the cool water flowing gently over my forehead ... cleansing my soul of the original sin all of us are born with.

Sadly, that was the last time my godparents saw me. Aunt Flo and Uncle Vinny, and their daughter, Barbara, have never visited us at our home. I wonder why.

"Look at the floor tiles, Bobby. They're made of marble bordered with 'quatrefoils' which symbolize the four Gospels."

Daddy turns and leads me by my left hand through the set of glass doors to our right bringing us into the center rear area of the church. A sense of awe fills me as I gaze in wonderment about this cavernous, colorful structure inside St. Monica's Church. The sweet scent of incense delights my nose while hushed tones about me create an appropriate atmosphere of holiness and reverence for the presence of God in here.

Straight ahead of us is the front of the church. I recognize the large, white marble altar Mommy described so many times.

She explained that this is where Jesus comes to be among us during each Mass when the priest lifts the white, round host of bread and the cup of wine high into the air and offers them up to God the Father. A miracle takes place as the Holy Spirit of God descends upon the bread and wine transforming them into "the Body and Blood, Soul and Divinity of Jesus Christ" which we then receive in Holy Communion.

Mommy also told me that when Holy Communion is not distributed, it is stored in a sacred box behind the golden doors in the center of the altar. This sacred place is called the "Tabernacle."

To my right and left, I see dark wooden-panels behind the last pew where people are sitting as they wait for Mass to begin. The panels are four feet high, about one foot higher than me. At the end of each panel, there is a golden font attached right by the aisle. Each font contains holy water for people to bless themselves as they enter and leave the church.

Daddy dips his right hand into the font on his right, then makes the Sign of the Cross inadvertently splashing me with the holy water in the process. Using his right hand, he first touches his forehead, then his heart, then his left shoulder, and finally his right shoulder. Daddy nods to me to follow his example. Slowly, I repeat what Daddy did ... carefully avoiding spilling any of the holy water.

We make our way over to the left side of the church where we turn right by the last pew, and walk up toward the front. At the tenth pew from the Communion rail, Daddy stops and genuflects. I imitate him as best I can by bending my right knee until it touches the ground; then I stand up. We enter the pew to our left, kneel down on a padded kneeler, and say a 'prayer of hello,' as Daddy calls it, to God. After our prayer of hello, we sit down.

I look around these hallowed surroundings while my

hands examine the pew I am sitting on. The pews all look the same; they are shiny, hard to the touch, and made of dark brown wood.

To my right, I notice a small group of nuns sitting together in the front-right center section of the church. They are dressed the same in long black robes covering their entire bodies from head to toe. A white cloth is wrapped around their heads framing their faces and a large, stiff, white collar covers the upper chest area. Each nun has a large, silver- colored crucifix hanging in front over their hearts and brown rosary beads hanging down the right side of their bodies from the waist to just below the knee. Most of the older-looking nuns, the ones with lots of wrinkles, are wearing eyeglasses.

Mommy once told me that nuns are called "Sisters" because they live together most of their lives just like real sisters growing up together. She also explained that nuns live in the same home called a "convent." Like priests, nuns consecrate their entire lives to God, and so, they don't marry or have children.

"Look up there," Daddy says as he turns toward the back of the church and nods at the choir loft located high above the pews in the back of the church.

"There's Mr. Hughes and Mr. Kuebler at the organ; they play the music during Mass. Mr. Hughes usually plays the organ and Mr. Kuebler sings. That organ was built in 1906 but it still sounds like new."

My eyes sweep past them to study the gigantic, golden-colored organ pipes occupying the entire width of the loft's center section. The pipes stand out brilliantly in front of the dark-brown, wooden-panels behind them. They glisten in the bright sunlight pouring in through the large, colorful, stained-glass windows above them.

As Mr. Hughes begins to play the organ, beautiful, lilting sounds flow together and resonate throughout the church. Easing back against the pew, I am filled with a great sense of peace and belonging, the kind Mommy has told me about. She says we should enjoy such times because the bad times inevitably also come to all people, times of sadness and hardship. Mommy said this is what life is all about ... happiness and goodness, grief and sadness ... and the eternal struggle between good and evil.

I study the altar area in the front center of the church. First, there is a set of three steps leading up to the Communion rail. This rail separates the sanctuary from the rest of the church. The top step has a padded kneeler where people kneel when receiving Holy Communion. The rail itself is about three feet high and is made of white marble. In the center of the Communion rail, there are two golden gates that can be swung open when necessary.

About ten feet from the Communion rail are five marble steps that lead up to the center altar that is made of white marble. There are three shelves above the altar itself. Pretty flowers rest on the shelves. At the very center of the altar is the golden door of the Tabernacle where Holy Communion is reserved. Above the Tabernacle is a three-foot high golden crucifix with the figure of Christ hanging on it. To the far right of the crucifix, there is a large, white marble statue of an angel; and to the far left of the crucifix, there is another large, white marble statue of an angel.

Daddy tells me that the angel on the right is the Archangel Michael standing on top of the fallen angel, Lucifer.

A few feet above the golden crucifix, there is a five-foot white marble statue of St. Monica holding a cross. Above this statue is a spire that rises about ten feet higher. It has a plain white cross at its very top. Just behind this is a colorful, twenty-foot, stained-glass window that depicts Jesus hanging on the cross. Pictured at the foot of the cross is Mary, the Apostle John, and one of the holy women. To the left of this stained-glass window, there is another stained-glass window showing the nativity scene with angels floating in the air above the Holy Family and two shepherds. To the right of the center stained-glass window, there is another stained-glass window that shows Jesus ascending into heaven with the apostles looking on.

A bell rings from somewhere up front. Everyone suddenly stands up. Off to the right side in the very front of the church, there are two altar boys walking out with their hands folded in a praying position. Walking right behind them is a priest who is carrying a chalice covered by an ornate cloth. The altar boys are wearing white surpluses over long, black cassocks. The surpluses look like baggy shirts with short sleeves but no collars. The cassocks look like snug dresses buttoned up the middle from around the ankles all the way up to the neckline.

The priest is wearing a colorful, loose-fitting garment. They pause at the side altar where the altar boys genuflect and the priest bows. They now proceed to the center altar where they repeat the same actions. After making the Sign of the Cross, the altar boys kneel down. The rest of us in the church kneel down and listen to them praying.

I hear them praying certain words but they don't make sense. I can't understand what these words mean. It sounds like they are saying, "Ad Deum qui lae ti fi cat iu ven tutem me am."

Seeing my confusion, Daddy leans down and whispers, "They're praying in Latin, Bobby. The Mass is said in the Latin language."

This is confusing. Why is the Mass said in another language? I tug on Daddy's hand, and forgetting that I should speak softly, I ask in a loud voice, "Do you speak Latin, Daddy?"

Daddy quickly puts a finger to his lips and whispers, "Shush. Don't speak so loudly, Bobby. Nobody here understands Latin except maybe the nuns and priest. The rest of us follow along in this Daily Missal which covers the entire Mass."

He nods to the black book he is holding. Looking around,

I notice how most people are in fact also using a similar-looking book. But I still do not understand why Latin is used rather than English, so I ask again, "Why don't they say Mass in English so we can understand what they are saying?"

Daddy looks annoyed now as he snaps impatiently, "Shush! That's just the way it's always been. That's all! Latin is the language spoken around the world. Now stop asking so many questions and pay attention to the Mass. We'll talk about it after Mass."

I still don't think they should be saying Mass in a foreign language that no one understands.

Daddy shakes his head in annoyance and turns his attention back to the Mass up front. At different times, the organ plays very solemn but beautiful sounding music. This adds a special feeling of reverence to what is happening. I wonder if Jesus had music playing when He prayed in the temple. I bet He did.

Everyone stands up now as the priest walks up a winding staircase that leads to a white, marble pulpit about eight feet high up above everyone in the pews. We make the Sign of the Cross with our right thumb on our foreheads, our lips, and our hearts. Mommy told me that we Catholics do this whenever the priest is going to read the Gospel so that God's words that he reads will bless our thoughts, our words and our hearts.

I listen as the priest reads the Gospel, the living Word of God. When he finishes reading, we sit down and listen to what Daddy said is called a "homily," or a "sermon." That is when the priest explains what the scripture readings mean, and he gives us a special message to live by. His words sound impressive but I really don't understand what they mean to me.

When he finishes, the priest turns and climbs back down the stairs from the pulpit and returns to the center altar. Just now, a man serving as an usher comes down the aisle carrying a wicker basket attached to what looks like a very long stick. The usher reaches into each pew holding the basket in front of the people who put money in it. When he comes to our pew, Daddy digs into his right pocket and retrieves a dime that he deposits in the basket on top of other coins. Daddy whispers that this is how we help to support our church so it can pay its bills.

"What bills, Daddy?"

"The electricity, the … never mind!" he says annoyed, "It's just to help pay whatever bills the church has. Everyone gives whatever they can afford. Now please be quiet and pay attention to the Mass."

The sound of a loud bell clanging up by the altar fills the church and draws my attention to the priest who is now standing at the top of the steps in front of the altar with his back to us. He has his hands extended over the bread and wine as he is praying words in Latin too low for me to hear. Everyone in the church is kneeling.

A tingling sensation ripples all over me as I realize there is something quite extraordinary happening up at the altar. There are lots of angels and people in white gowns now surrounding the altar. I feel so much joy listening to the faint sounds of beautiful voices singing a glorious song of love to Jesus. The song doesn't have words, just sounds of love and praise.

I can hear each voice, and yet they blend together forming one beautiful voice. They must be the angels and holy people Mommy said come to every Mass when the priest extends his hands over the bread and wine and says a special prayer. There is an ever-expanding sea of these holy spirits filling the church.

Daddy whispers, "Watch closely, Bobby, the priest is going to raise the little white host of bread that has become the Body of Christ."

An altar boy, kneeling just behind the priest to his left, holds the bottom of the priest's garment so it doesn't touch the ground. The other altar boy rings the bell as the priest stands up and raises the consecrated white host high in the air. The priest returns the Eucharist to the altar, genuflects, and says another prayer, then holds up high the chalice containing the wine that has become the precious Blood of Jesus. The other altar boy again rings the bell.

I feel light-headed so I slump back onto the pew. The cool feeling of the wooden pew is helpful but I feel so weak. Daddy tells me to get up and kneel down but I tell him I can't because I feel dizzy. I am relieved that he allows me to continue sitting.

Daddy whispers that he is going to go receive Holy Communion so he tells me to stay in the pew and watch what he does. He gets up and stands in line behind other people in the aisle. Gradually, he makes his way up to the front where he waits behind people kneeling down at the Communion Rail. As soon as these people receive Holy Communion, they rise and return to their pews. Daddy walks up the three steps to the Communion Rail and kneels down becoming part of a long line of people kneeling at the Communion Rail waiting to receive the Eucharist.

Slowly, reverently, the priest distributes Holy Communion to each person by directly placing the consecrated Host onto each person's outstretched tongue. An altar boy accompanying the priest extends a gold plate under each person's chin to catch the Holy Communion if it accidentally falls.

The priest is now standing in front of Daddy. Reaching into the ciborium, the priest carefully selects one of the consecrated Hosts and places it on Daddy's tongue. Daddy makes the Sign of the Cross, then rises to return to our pew. His hands are folded together, palm to palm, in reverence to the presence of God within him.

I am happy I have seen Daddy receive Holy Communion. He looks so reverent and solemn as he kneels down next to me and buries his face in his hands. The organ is playing in the back of the church leading the congregation to sing a beautiful song, "Jesus, My Lord, My God, My All."

"Jesus, my Lord, my God, my all;
How can I love Thee as I ought?
And how revere this wondrous gift,
So far surpassing hope and thought?
"Sweet Sacrament! We Thee adore,
O make us love Thee more and more,
O make us love Thee more and more."

With Daddy in silent prayer, I feel so happy being here with him and so many other people who are praying, singing and celebrating the presence of God, the angels and saints among us.

Sometime after everyone has received Holy Communion, we all sit down. Another collection is being taken up now while more nice music is played on the organ. After the music stops, everyone in the church stands up. Facing the congregation, the priest gives us his blessing as we make the Sign of the Cross. He then turns and bows before the Tabernacle as the two altar boys genuflect. The priest turns to his right and follows the altar boys as they walk toward the sacristy off to the right side of the church. They pause before the altar on the right side and genuflect before the Tabernacle there. This is done out of reverence for Jesus within the Tabernacle.

I follow Daddy out of the pew, genuflect in the aisle as he does, then we turn and walk away from the front of the church where the Tabernacle is located. As we walk toward the rear of the church to leave, Daddy asks what I think of my first Mass.

"It was wonderful, Daddy!"

"What about what the priest had to say, were you able to follow and understand what he said?"

"Not so much," I answer honestly.

"What did you like best about the Mass?"

"I liked everything … especially the beautiful voices singing," I tell him.

Daddy laughs, "Beautiful voices! What beautiful voices? Some of those people singing sounded more like 'alley-cats' than they did people!"

Daddy laughs at his own joke, and is joined by an elderly couple walking directly behind us. They apparently were listening to our conversation. They obviously did not hear the same heavenly voices I heard during Mass.

I guess they also didn't see all the angels and holy people dressed in white robes either.

Chapter 7

BLESSED VISION

One of the earliest miracles I recall from my childhood happened when I was only six years old. Allow me to take you back to that extraordinary event.

I am so happy … we are going to visit Nana Walsh in her fifth floor apartment in the top floor of a brownstone apartment building on First Avenue near 81st Street in Manhattan. I enjoy walking the two blocks to Nana's, and once we get there, climbing up all those stairs that seem to go on forever to the fifth floor. Daddy says it is well worth the climb because they lead up to a place that is like heaven. Mommy always adds that Daddy says this because at the top of those stairs is his beloved mother, our grandmother, Nana Walsh.

She is so kind and gentle, always fussing over us. Surprisingly, this time when Paddy, Larry, and I reach her landing on the top floor, Nana is not standing there waiting for us as she usually does by her door on the right side of the hallway. Since her door is open, we rush in and see her sitting right there at the kitchen table smiling.

"Well, well, well, what have we got here?" she says playfully. "Three handsome Irishmen, that's what! Oh, you boys are gonna drive the girls crazy. Come over here and give your Nana a big hug and kiss, you handsome little leprechauns!"

There aren't too many places in the world I would rather be than in Nana's wonderful embrace. I love her so much, and wish we could see her every day. Soon when Mommy and Daddy arrive with Kitty and baby Geri, our joyful visit commences.

All too soon, our evening filled with Nana's delicious cooking, singing, stories and lots of fun comes to an end. She gives each of us a big hug and kiss and tells us to look out for one another.

Her words, "I love you," echo down the many floors of the building … and everlasting corridors of my memory.

Paddy already made it all the way down and outside Nana's building. That is when I remembered Daddy's words to hang onto the hand of my younger brother, Larry. Unfortunately, as he and I descended the long flights of stairs, Larry pulled his hand out of mine and bolted quickly down the stairs ahead of me!

"Larry, wait for me!" I cry out as loudly as I can. "Larry, please stop running! **Larry, please wait for me!"**

As I race down the old wooden stairs, the sound of the front door downstairs opening and closing brings panic to my already frenzied heart and mind. Will he wait outside the building? Paddy is there and may be able to grab him as he bolts out. But what if Larry doesn't stop, and what if Paddy can't grab hold of him?

If Larry runs wildly down the street, he will get lost because he is not familiar with Nana's neighborhood. He may never be able to find his way home. I may never see him again! When I reach the bottom and run outside, I discover that my worst fears have come true. Paddy is standing there looking up the avenue. There in the darkness of the night to my left, we see Larry running away along First Avenue heading toward 82nd Street where we live.

I call out to him at the top of my voice but the noise of the traffic on First Avenue drowns out my words. I watch in horror as Larry reaches the corner, turns right without hesitating and races straight out onto First Avenue … in front of onrushing cars that are speeding toward him!

My heart feels like it is going to explode from fear that my little brother may be run over and killed by one of the cars. I am overwhelmed with a profound sense of fear, desperation and helplessness. Realizing there is only one thing I can do, I concentrate all my consciousness into a soulful plea to almighty God. In that moment, I feel completely detached from my physical surroundings as I cry out to God to please protect my baby brother from getting hurt.

Frozen in fear, Paddy and I watch as Larry speeds halfway across First Avenue without being hit … but there is a long tractor-trailer thundering along the far side of the avenue heading directly for Larry! With wheels as tall as us, the tractor-trailer roars ahead without a break in its speed. The driver apparently doesn't see Larry!

I cry out to God, "Please don't let that truck hit Larry!"

As I watch in terror, the cab of the trailer passes right in front of Larry who continues to run. Bending over, Larry runs under the mid-section of the long trailer section! After the tractor-trailer continues on its way up First Avenue, I look on in great fear to see if Larry's body is lying in the street all mangled and lifeless in the wake of the enormous truck.

Focusing through the darkness of the night aided only by the light cast on the area by the corner lamppost, I can see that Larry's body is **NOT** lying there in the street! Other worries quickly flash through my mind. Is his body being dragged along First Avenue under the huge truck? Or, is he somehow caught up in the undercarriage of the trailer?

In that moment, I also realized that it was entirely possible that God heard my cries and spared Larry's life!

A visual inspection of First Avenue farther on discloses that Larry is **not** lying in the street, and common sense tells me that he probably is **not** stuck underneath the tractor-trailer. This can only mean that he miraculously made it safely across by running under the long section of the tractor-trailer without being run over!

Tears flow down my face as I cry aloud, "Oh, my God, thank you, thank you! Thank you for protecting my little brother from being killed by that gigantic truck!"

A feeling of relief and indescribable gratitude wells up within my heart and soul.

"Where is Larry?" Daddy shouts angrily as he arrives and looks up and down First Avenue. "Where is he? Why the hell are you boys just standing there? Answer me, where is your little brother? Did he run away?"

Before I can answer, Daddy slams me across the back of my head practically knocking me over as a sharp pain cascades throughout my head.

"What did I tell you about holding Larry's hand? Didn't I tell you not to let go of him, to hold onto his hand? Which way did he go?"

"He pulled away from me, Daddy, and ran down the stairs. I couldn't catch up to him. He was too fast. When I got outside, I saw him run across the avenue but the truck didn't run him over!"

"Oh, my God! What truck? Did Larry get hit by a truck?" Daddy cried.

"No," Paddy answers, "He ran across the avenue and ran down 82nd Street."

"Jesus Christ almighty! Can't I depend upon you boys to do anything right?" Daddy complains.

"Why the hell didn't **you** stop him, Paddy?"

"I couldn't. He ran right past me," Paddy answers looking worried that he, too, might be hit by Daddy.

"Why didn't you run after him?" Daddy asks.

"You told me to stay by the front of the building, Daddy," Paddy explains.

"Jesus Christ, I can't believe you kids," Daddy continues. "Would you stay standing there in front of the building if a truck was coming right at you? Don't answer that!"

Staring out into the dark of the night, Daddy says, "Where

could he be now? Son of a bitch, I'm going to give him the beating of his life when I get my hands on him!"

Mommy now arrives out of Nana's building with Geri in the carriage she just retrieved from the back of the hallway. She looks terrified when she hears that Larry has run away into the night.

"Patsy, please go run ahead and see if you can catch up to him before he gets too far," Mommy cries.

"You're right," Daddy answers, "Keep an eye on the rest of the kids."

I watch as Daddy rushes out between the parked cars, carefully looks both ways, then begins to run very fast across First Avenue. At the corner, he turns right onto 82nd Street and disappears. Mommy gathers us close to her and instructs us to pray that God will help us find Larry.

As we start our worried journey home, Mommy tells us, "Hold onto the handlebar of the carriage, and keep your eyes peeled to see Larry."

Mommy asks me to explain what happened, so I tell her how Larry ran away from me, ran past Paddy and then ran under the gigantic tractor-trailer but didn't get run over.

With a horrified expression, Mommy snaps, "That's it! Don't tell me anymore; I don't want to hear any more! Just pray!"

Off we go, heading toward home. Mommy is walking so fast we can barely keep up with her. As we hurry across First Avenue at 82nd Street, I look ahead and see Daddy AND Larry in front of St. Stephen of Hungary Catholic Church in the middle of the block on the right side. It looks like Daddy is holding onto Larry and hitting him! He is shouting something but I cannot hear what he is saying.

Suddenly, Larry breaks free and runs off into the darkness with Daddy in hot pursuit after him once again!

The rest of us quickly walk down 82nd Street. As we pass St. Stephen's Church, I am comforted because I can sense that Jesus is in there in the tabernacle. I ask Him to please to help us find where Larry has gone.

A feeling pours over me indicating that God will help me find Larry so I tell Mommy and Paddy, "Don't worry, God is going to help me find where Larry is!"

Wiping away tears, Mommy says she hopes so.

Passing each of the darkened hallways, I peer in to see if Larry is hiding there from Daddy. He is not. I can only hope that Larry has run safely back home to the building where we live and is waiting there for us. I also hope that Daddy gets over his anger. In this moment of fear and worry, I realize that despite all the miracles I have witnessed in my young life, there is no way that I, by myself, can ever know where Larry has gone. I more clearly realize more than ever before that God, and God alone, is the only One who can create a miracle.

Realizing that only God knows where my little brother Larry has gone, I implore Him to let me know. Nothing comes to mind right now, but I understand that God WILL let me know … when it is the right time to tell me. I just must be patient, believing and trusting that He knows best.

We reach York Avenue and wait for a green light. It seems like it takes the light forever before it finally turns green. After crossing, we soon come to a street where halfway down the block there is a lamppost stationed in front of a tall, brownstone building. Shedding light on the immediate area, it illuminates a solitary figure walking in front. It is Daddy pacing back and forth, peering out into the darkness of the night … quite apparently still looking for Larry.

"I wonder if Daddy found Larry and made him go home upstairs already," Paddy says hopefully.

"I don't think so," Mommy says dejectedly, "It looks like

Daddy is still looking for him."

When we catch up to Daddy, I can see that he is very upset and worried. Together, we continue our worried journey toward home.

Daddy confesses, "I caught him by St. Stephen's Church, and gave him a good whack on the head but the son-of-a-bitch ran away again down the block somewhere."

"You hit him?" Mommy says incredulously. "What the hell is the matter with you, Patsy? Why did you hit him? Didn't you realize that he would only run away again?"

"I don't want to hear that right now, Ellie. I chased him down here but he disappeared in the dark. I asked the old lady if she saw anything from her ground floor window but she said that she just got there and didn't see anyone."

I turn to see the old lady still peering out shyly from behind her shade in the ground floor window to the left of the front stoop.

Mommy and Kitty are crying.

"Don't worry, we'll find him," Daddy assures us.

"I am worried, Patsy; its dark out and there's no telling where he might be right now. He's probably lost and scared to death, and doesn't know how to find his way home. And who knows what perverts may be out tonight looking for little kids like him! Why the hell did you hit him?" Mommy bitterly complains.

"All right, all right, please stop, Ellie. We'll find him. I promise," Daddy persists.

"Let's get the baby and the carriage up into the apartment, then I'll go out looking for him. Kitty you come upstairs with Mommy. Paddy, you and Bobby stay down here and keep your eyes peeled for Larry. If you see him, whatever you do, do not chase him! Just tell him to stay put where he is until I get back."

Paddy and I continually look up and down the street straining our eyes in the hopes of seeing Larry somewhere in the darkness … but he is nowhere to be seen. Except for an occasional person walking here and there, the streets are deserted, dark and deadly quiet. Overwhelmed with guilt and despair, I sit down on the ice-cold concrete steps of my front stoop and call out to God once again and beg Him to please let me know where my little brother Larry is located.

My guardian angel's familiar voice gently flows into my mind, "He is down by the river."

This is immediately followed by a vision of Larry sitting on top of a large, curved concrete structure located down by the East River! He appears to be completely relaxed taking in the beautiful, panoramic view. The sound of Daddy's heavy footsteps behind me disrupts my vision. As Daddy appears by my side, his face displays fear and concern, so uncharacteristic for him. In fact, I don't recall ever seeing him like this.

"Did you boys see Larry?" Daddy asks.

"I saw him, Daddy," I quickly say with certainty as if Larry was standing right here in front of the building with us.

Daddy quickly asks, "Where? Where did you see him?"

I realize that Daddy probably will not understand that my guardian angel just told me where Larry is right now … but I decide to tell him anyway.

"My guardian angel just told me that Larry is down by the river. Then I saw a picture of him in my mind … sitting on top of that big concrete thing down by the East River."

As I answered, I pointed off in the darkness toward the river.

"What're you talking about? You can't see that area from here; it's too far away," Daddy says incredulously. "It's physically impossible to see that area by the East River from here!"

"But I **can** see him, Daddy. Larry IS down there right now. We should go get him before he runs off again," I say with a sound of urgency.

Paddy's eyes dart back and forth from Daddy to me as Daddy stares at me before looking again in the direction of the river. It is clear from his expression that he doesn't understand but is so desperate to find Larry, he is willing to try anything … to believe anything.

Turning in the direction of the East River, Daddy says, "You really can see him down there by the river, heh?"

"Yes, Daddy, I see him very clearly in my mind's eye! He is down there right now!"

"Well, miracles do happen with you, don't they, kid? Let's go!" Daddy says eagerly.

"Let's hope he's there," Paddy says.

With Daddy between Paddy and me, we trot down the street as we head toward the East River. It is interesting how a little hope can so quickly lift your spirits and attitude. There is a feeling of confidence and eagerness about us now as we reach East End Avenue, look both ways then quickly proceed across the intersection. Soon, we are close to the area where I saw Larry in my mind's eye.

Suddenly, Paddy excitedly whispers, "There he is, Daddy! Larry **is** sitting on top of that concrete thing!"

Paddy is pointing toward the other end of a short street between us and the wide promenade walkway that overlooks the East River.

In a low voice barely audible, Daddy says, "Shhhh, be quiet! If that IS him, we don't want to scare him off. Let's walk slowly up to him … nice and easy. Don't say anything to him … but if he starts to run, we have to run as fast as we can to get him before he disappears again. Okay, boys?"

"Yes, Daddy," Paddy and I whisper at the same time.

Calmly and quietly, we walk up the street that is about one hundred feet long. I turn in time to see Daddy's face transform from one filled with fear and distress, to one of great relief as he apparently sees Larry sitting there … just as I said.

Larry smiles widely as he looks at the three of us calmly walking up to him. Saying nothing, he just sits there with his knees pulled up to his chest and his arms wrapped around his legs. Strangely, no one says anything as we stand there together looking back and forth at one another.

Daddy, with his hands on his hips, and a smile of great relief on his face, asks Larry, "What are you doing up there, 'LaLa?"

"LaLa" is Daddy's affectionate name for Larry whenever Daddy is happy about something involving Larry. I guess he is happy we found Larry, and that he is safe and sound.

Larry shrugs his shoulders and answers, "Just watching things."

"Just watching things, heh," Daddy says, "Come on down, son. I'm not going to hit you; I promise. I just want you to come home now with us. Okay?"

Daddy encourages Larry to come down by extending his hands outward to help him climb down. I am surprised and relieved to see Larry eagerly grab Daddy's hands and stumble awkwardly down the rounded concrete structure to the safety of the ground where they exchange a really big hug.

I am so happy we found Larry … safe and sound. Paddy and I go over and put our arms around Larry's shoulders. The look on Larry's face tells us he is quite pleased with all this attention.

"You scared the hell out of us, Larry," Daddy tells him. "We didn't know where you ran off to. When did you tell Bobby that you were going to come down here?"

Looking up at Daddy with a confused expression, Larry says, "I didn't tell Bobby."

"Then how did Bobby know that you were down here,

heh?"

Larry looks at me, and shrugs his shoulders.

Daddy must realize this is another miracle because he knows that no one can see all the way down here in the middle of the night from our front stoop so far away. It is impossible … at least physically.

At the corner, Daddy asks, "Larry, weren't you afraid that you were lost?"

"A little … but then I knew that Bobby would find me because God tells him things. So … I just knew that God would tell Bobby where I was lost."

I once again thanked God for interceding on my behalf in such a miraculous way. What a pleasure it was to walk home in the utter stillness of the dark night with Daddy, my older brother, Paddy, my little lost brother, Larry … and our guardian angels.

What a beautiful moment in time. Thank you, God.

Chapter 8

THE OLD LADY

One Sunday morning, Paddy, Kitty and I were getting ready to go to the weekly nine o'clock school Mass at St. Monica's.

Mommy gave each of us a nickel to put in the collection basket at Mass. Then she gave Paddy a few dollars and told him to go after Mass to buy the "Sunday Daily News" and the "Daily Mirror" newspapers, and then stop at the bakery on the way home to buy the usual dozen and a half rolls for breakfast.

I was envious of Larry who was allowed to stay in bed, warm and snug, sound asleep under the blankets. How lucky he is, I thought. He can stay in bed while we have to get up early in the morning and go out into the cold morning air for a long walk to St. Monica's Church. But then … we get to attend Mass.

Then I felt sorry for Larry because Mommy and Daddy only took Larry and Geri to Mass twice a year on Easter and on Christmas. They say that is their yearly duty as Catholics.

This was not correct. Sister Pascaline once told my class that many of the older Catholics believe this, but they are wrong! She said that everyone is supposed to go to Mass every Sunday, and if they really understood what Mass is all about, they would want to go every day!

"When we go to Mass, we aren't doing God a favor; it is God who does us a favor," Sister explained.

Paddy, Kitty and I made our way the three blocks to St. Monica's on 79th Street. The brightly sunlit streets of Yorkville at this time on Sunday morning were deserted except for kids like us on their way to the nine o'clock school Mass.

Upon entering the church, we split up and went to where our respective classes were located in the church. We were required to sit together with our classmates at this Mass. Sister

Pascaline marked her little black book to show who attended the nine o'clock Mass. All the nuns did this for their respective classes.

At the nine o'clock school Mass, the nuns could always be found sitting in the last pew behind their class in their appointed area of the church. Kneeling down in the customary manner, I blessed myself by making the Sign of the Cross. As I then sat down, however, I saw an old lady only a few feet away who was limping toward me.

I had seen her in church a few times before. Her pale white face was soaked in more pain and sadness than the last time I saw her. Judging by her shabby clothing, I could tell that she was very poor, perhaps even homeless.

Other schoolchildren noticed her and began to whisper and gesture in her direction. As she hobbled over toward me, I could see her deformity more closely. It prevented her from standing erect. Her arrival at my side caused a great commotion among my classmates and resulting in Sister Pascaline arriving to intervene.

"Excuse me, madam," Sister said politely, "I am sorry but these pews are reserved for the school children only. You cannot sit here; you can sit in the pews in the sides of the church."

The lady surprisingly ignored what Sister Pascaline said so Sister repeated what she said but the old lady was not listening to her. The old lady had her eyes set on me with such a sad, pleading expression. Sister Ramon, the seventh-grade teacher came over to see if she could do anything to help but the lady ignored her as well.

"Please pray for me, sonny; I am so sick," she pleaded as she reached her thin, bony hands out to me.

Her haunting eyes reflected deep suffering in her spirit, not just her body. A great compassion for her welled up within me as I saw and heard only her now. I reached out and gently held her hands. In that brief moment, I closed my eyes and cried out to Jesus to have mercy on her.

"Please heal her, Jesus," I prayed, "mind, body and spirit."

An exhilarating shower of graces poured over me and traveled directly onto the old lady causing her to flinch. It was clear to me that God was rewarding her faith in some way. By that time, we were surrounded by nuns and some adult parishioners.

Sister Ramon, who was regarded throughout St. Monica's as quite athletic, told the lady she must leave! "If you need help, I will help you," Sister promised.

To everyone's surprise, the elderly lady abruptly stood straight up and shouted, **"I am cured! I am cured! God has healed me!"**

Her words reverberated throughout the hallowed walls of St. Monica's Church stunning everyone present. A miracle had taken place right in front of everyone looking on. God rewarded the faith of this poor old lady by curing her right then and there! She was now standing up straight as an arrow as if nothing was ever wrong with her! More wonderful than the cure of her physical ailment, I sensed God had also healed her broken spirit.

The nuns were stunned; they did not know what to say or do. Everyone had seen how badly crippled this lady was only moments before when I held her hands and prayed for her. Now, she was standing perfectly straight as she proclaimed that God miraculously healed her!

"Thank you, God, thank you!" she cried.

Sister Ramon exclaimed, "Oh, my God … oh, my God! Praise be the Holy Name of God!"

Sister Ramon gently asked the lady to go to the back of the vestibule where she could more appropriately thank God during the Mass. She nodded okay. Although the old lady was still clothed in rags, her whole countenance now exuded joy and happiness as if she didn't have a worry in the world.

Looking at me, she cried out, "Thank you; you're an angel of God. Thank you."

After the ushers politely escorted the lady to the back, I turned to see all my classmates and nuns looking at me - apparently bewildered by what they had just witnessed. Sister Pascaline came to my side and asked if I was all right.

"Oh, yes, Sister; I feel wonderful! God healed that lady!"

"Yes, Robert, I saw. That was amazing. You showed great courage and compassion for that poor lady. That was a wonderful example … for all of us.

After Mass, I met Paddy and Kitty as planned outside the church in front of the center steps. They were anxious to hear details about what happened with me and the old lady.

After telling them, Paddy scoffed, "You didn't heal that lady, Bobby. You can't heal anyone; you're just a kid."

Kitty protested, "That's not nice, Paddy; leave Bobby alone. He's a good boy."

"That's all right," I said. "Paddy is right. I cannot heal anyone; only God can heal people. All I do is ask God to heal them."

Paddy's comment reminded me that is how other people think about me, but there is nothing I can do about that. It is God alone who acts in ways and times **HE** believes are best for the good of those who cry out to Him. I am just an intermediary who is blessed to witness the healing graces of God descend upon those He heals.

Sadly, many people reject the reality that God can and does intercede in miraculous ways. That is because they try to fit the limitless capacity of God into their limited human understanding. No one can do this.

News of what happened with the old lady in St. Monica's

Church spread quickly throughout St. Monica's parish and the surrounding neighborhood. For the rest of that school year, I found myself the center of attention, a subject of great curiosity for old and young alike.

Some children took great joy in teasing me by bowing in front of me and begging me to heal their imaginary ills. I suspected the Devil was behind much of that teasing, enjoying every moment of my discomfort. Its hope was that I would allow my feelings to be so hurt that it would discourage me from praying for people.

That didn't work then … and it doesn't work now either!

How sad it is that so many people, young and old, do not realize the limitless love and mercy of God that awaits them if only they would turn to Him in faith.

How sad it is also that given the choice, so many people choose to be mean and hurtful, rather than being kind and helpful.

Worse yet, how frightening it is that so many people do not believe that demons really do exist and, in fact, do everything they can to mislead and hurt every single one of us in any way they can.

Chapter 9

THE "KID SAINT"

In the weeks following the miracle involving the healing of the old lady in St. Monica's Church, my reputation as a "blessed child" expanded. People who knew me began to treat me with deference - but not all did.

One of my classmates explained, "Everyone knows you are different, Bobby. A lot of us think you're a 'kid saint."

Sadly, boys were not among this group. They seized every opportunity to tease me, often calling me, "Saint Robert," and asking me to pray for healing of some make-believe illness.

Not everything that resulted from being regarded as a blessed child was hurtful. In particular, the nuns at St. Monica's school understood much of what I was going through thanks to the stories circulating around the parish about some of the remarkable things that happened after I prayed for someone. I often found myself being asked by the nuns to provide details of the latest healing event.

But I never tired of re-telling the same story over and over again because this reminded me of God's remarkable love and mercy for those who cried out to Him in faith. Not surprisingly, stories of miracles greatly moved the nuns and priests, but that was not all that impressed them. Other more subtle things also impressed them.

For example, whenever I was asked questions involving spiritual matters, my replies displayed an extraordinary understanding and knowledge far beyond my age. Another example was when the teacher in my first grade, Sister Pascaline, asked everyone to draw a picture of anything that made us happy, anything that we liked. While my classmates drew pictures expected of seven-year old children, I drew something spiritually profound.

I drew a picture of three crosses on top of a hill with seven streams of water flowing down from the center cross into a stream at the bottom filled with fish of different sizes and colors.

When Sister Pascaline asked me to explain what my picture represented, I matter-of-factly told her that the three crosses represented the scene at Calvary, and that Jesus was the one on the center cross. The hill represented the Church. The streams of water flowing down the hill from Jesus' cross represented the seven sacraments. The stream of water at the bottom of the hill represented the stream of life. The fish in the stream represented all of us being nourished by the seven sacramental streams of water.

Needless to say, Sister Pascaline was quite impressed ... and couldn't wait to share this latest story involving the "blessed child" with other nuns in their convent.

Of all the nuns, a fiery-spirited Irish nun, Sister Cecil, understood me better than the others in St. Monica's. She was especially protective of me, and regularly sought me out to encourage me and to inquire how I was doing.

Once during a particularly difficult day, she took me aside and said, "Listen here, Robert, God has blessed you with spiritual strength, wisdom and understanding to accomplish whatever it is He wants of you. And He never gives you more than you can handle! So stay strong!"

It seemed whenever things were especially difficult for me, Sister Cecil would be there to whip out her wonderful Irish wit and humor, occasionally calling me "Saint Robert" herself!

Whenever I served as an altar boy, people came into the sacristy before Mass to ask me to pray for someone. This intrusion understandably bothered the priests but Father Kelly, often interceded on my part with his fellow priests. In time, the priests heard of miraculous healings that followed my prayers and so, in time, they, too, came to recognize that the Hand of God was involved in an extraordinary way. They no longer complained about intrusions in the sacristy. In fact, some of them also began to ask me to pray for special intentions.

The best comfort came from my parents, and my spiritual advisor, Father Kelly. I constantly thanked God for blessing the wonderful people who looked after me, protected me, comforted and guided me on my spiritual journey.

Chapter 10

MIRACLE AT CONEY ISLAND

One of the most uplifting, joyful miracles in my childhood happened when I was eight years old. Allow me to describe that wonderful, remarkable event when I personally witnessed the great love and utter mercy of God.

Standing next to Mommy, I watch as she holds up a crisp, new-looking twenty-dollar bill and exclaims, "Hooray! Look at this! Now we can afford to go to Coney Island and the world famous Steeplechase Amusement Park!"

Her words set off a frenzy of loud cheering. We have been hoping for so long that our family might someday get enough money to go to Coney Island and go on the great rides at Steeplechase which Mommy has told us so much about.

Mommy announces, "We'll go on Saturday, June 20th, because that will be Daddy's 37th birthday. You know, Coney Island and the Steeplechase are two of his favorite places in the whole wide world!"

When the appointed Saturday arrives, everyone gets up early and gulps down our favorite breakfast of Kellogg's corn flakes with bananas and milk. We already have our bathing suits on under our clothes just as Mommy instructed to save time at the beach.

Daddy reminds Mommy to put lots of sun lotion on each of us since we are not accustomed to being out in the hot, blazing sun all day. With a bag of bologna sandwiches packed for lunch, we eagerly start out on one of the most exciting trips we have ever taken. The sun is shining brightly; it is already very hot out as we trek along the streets of Yorkville at a fast pace on our way to the IRT Lexington Avenue subway station at 86th Street and Lexington Avenue.

At the train station, Daddy carefully lowers the baby carriage one step at a time until he finally reaches the turnstiles on the level below the street. He tells all of us kids to duck under the turnstiles since we are all young enough to ride for free.

Riding the subway is big part of today's treat because we had never been on the subway before. We wait for the train with our backs pressed hard against the cool, ceramic-tiled wall – as far back from the edge of the platform as we can go. Soon there is a rush of wind blowing in our direction from the left. Daddy says the wind is being caused by the subway train coming toward us from that direction.

He explains, "Listen, kids. The wind is a sign that the train is coming because it pushes the air in front of it. You all understand? Listen … you can also hear the train coming."

Sure enough, within moments, I feel the platform rumbling as the subway train approaches. I am actually frightened by the ferocity of the sound and rumbling caused by the subway train as it explodes into the station and causes hurricane-type winds to blow strongly around us! Each car whizzes by, car after car, until the train finally slows down and comes to a loud, screeching stop. As the doors slide open sideways, Daddy and Mommy rush us into the train.

"Step over the gap between the train and the platform," Daddy cautions us.

I am so frightened that I might slip down into that opening, I take extra-long steps over the gap. Safely inside, we sit down just as the train jerks to a start and slowly begins to rumble on its way out of the lighted 86th Street station. Soon it bursts into the pitch-black darkness of the subway tunnel. The roar of the train now sounds much, much louder. All this is so scary; it reminds me of how evil creatures torment me.

I am intrigued by the golden-colored, straw-like seats in the train. They are slick to the touch and make funny squeaking noises as we bounce on them caused by the train racing along through the darkened tunnels. The train shakes violently creating deafening, screeching noises as it speeds wildly on its way at a breakneck speed. There is a refreshing breeze blowing in from open windows on the subway car.

When we reach a certain station, Daddy has us get off and walk to another part of this large train station where we get on what he calls the "D" train.

"This train is going to take us all the way to the last stop, Coney Island – Stillwell Avenue, where we will get off."

After riding on the "D" train for a long time, Daddy calls out, "When you see a giant, round tank that is the size of a large building, we'll almost be at Coney Island! When you see the sky-high "parachute ride," **then we will be there!"**

Soon, just like Daddy said would happen, the train bursts out of the darkened tunnel and rushes into the bright sunshine of the day. Our subway car is filled with cheering children as the giant parachute ride comes into view off in the distance. We are almost at the world famous Coney Island. I am so excited!

At the last stop, we follow the crowd walking down a long, wide ramp that leads to the street. My sense of smell is pleasantly greeted with the scent of hot dogs, French-fried potatoes, cotton candy … and the unique scent of the Atlantic Ocean filling the air. My ears are filled with exciting carnival-like sounds coming from rides, children laughing and people working at the game booths calling out to passersby inviting them to come over and play.

What an interesting, colorful, thrilling place this is!

On our way to the boardwalk and the beach beyond it, Daddy points out another very famous place.

"Over there, kids … that's 'Nathan's' on Stillwell Avenue. That's where they serve foot-long hot dogs!"

Mommy adds, "You know … Nathan's is known all over

the world."

"Wow, foot-long," Paddy exclaims.

Daddy insists, "Let's stop and buy one of those hot dogs and one of those crinkled, French-fried potatoes they serve in white cone-shaped paper cups."

Standing by Nathan's street-side counter, each of us takes a turn taking a bite out of the foot-long hot dog, and then a few of the crinkled fries. Both are absolutely delicious … even better than they smell!

"Hey, kids," Daddy says excitedly, "let's take a quick look at the 'Cyclone.' It is the scariest roller-coaster ride in the entire world!"

As we walk up the block, I look up and watch as the Cyclone roller-coaster haltingly climbs up to the very top of the tracks. It makes a loud "clickity-clackity" noise as it slowly rises. Pausing for just a second at the very top, it then goes over the top and races straight down on the other side at a phenomenal speed! People on the roller-coaster are screaming at the top of their voices as the ride wickedly whips up and down and around the tracks making its distinctive "clickity-clackity" sounds while racing at lightning speed.

I wondered why anyone would want to go on a ride that is so incredibly rough and dangerous.

Along our way to the beach, I am fascinated by a small booth where there are two women dressed like gypsies sitting outside at a table.

They are calling out to people passing by, "Come have your fortunes told! See what the future holds for you!"

This doesn't make sense to me because I know only God knows the future. How can they possibly know what only God knows?

As we pass them, they suddenly stop calling out and stare at me. They are actually sneering at me! I wonder why … until I sense an evil force around them. What strikes me as strange is that I do not see a black outline around their heads. That usually indicates a person who is living a very sinful life … or sadly, even worse … someone who has given himself over to the Devil.

I silently ask God to protect me and our family.

Daddy shakes his head in disgust and shouts out loudly so the ladies can hear him, "Going to a supposed fortune-teller is stupid because only God knows the future, not the angels nor the saints, and certainly not the Devil! That's why going to a fortune-teller is against our religion; it is a sin to do so!"

I could actually feel the anger and hostility emanating from the ladies toward us.

At the top of the ramp, we cross over to the other side of the boardwalk where we stand for a while looking out over the heavily-crowded beach. I have never seen so many people in one place at one time … except in visions I have had of heaven.

Daddy confirms my feeling, "Ellie, I've never seen so many people here before! There have to be at least one million people here today! Let's leave the baby carriage up here by the railing; we can keep an eye on it from where we settle on the beach."

Mommy agrees and tells us to sit down on the wooden boardwalk to take off our shoes, socks and pants. After I take off my shoes, I discover to my utter dismay that the wooden boardwalk is boiling hot from the sun! Wearing only my bathing suit, the rest of my body is now exposed to the boiling hot sun.

Leaving the baby carriage behind on the boardwalk, we make our way down to the beach where I have another unpleasant surprise. The sand is also red hot and is filled with hundreds of tiny, cracked seashells that hurt the tender underside of my feet. Walking gingerly and quickly picking up my feet minimizes the pain. Fortunately, Mommy decides to settle down at an open area halfway to the water's edge where the Atlantic Ocean's waves are constantly crashing onto the beach.

Pulling out an old white bed sheet, she spreads it out on the sand, then tells us to sit down on it so the wind can't blow it off the sand. She doesn't have to tell us twice; we are all anxious to get off the painfully hot sand.

"Try not to get sand on the sheet, kids," she pleads.

The baby, Geri, is thrilled running her hands through the sand from where she sits on the edge of the sheet. My nine-year-old sister, Kitty, is sitting next to her showing her how to build a "sand castle." It looks more like a "sand hut" to me.

My older, ten-year-old brother, Paddy, and younger, six-year-old brother, Larry, and I begin digging a huge hole in the sand. I am curious to see how deep down we can go. Much to my surprise, a little water appears at the very bottom.

After a while, Daddy invites Paddy, Larry and me to go down to the water with him. Kitty and Geri are content to stay with Mommy. As we make our way to the water, Daddy reminds us to watch where we are walking so we don't step on any of the countless sunbathers lying on their sheets.

Down by the water, we hold hands as Daddy warns us not to go too far out into the ocean. I am shocked to discover the water is absolutely freezing! Even though I am shivering, I inch farther into the ocean along with the others until we are in up to our waists with the water splashing wildly up into our faces. The ocean water tastes very, very salty. The sand under my feet is playing games with my balance as it constantly shifts under the movement of surging and withdrawing waves. My feet sink straight down into the sand while the rest of my body is wickedly pushed and pulled by the powerful waves.

I am relieved when Daddy finally says we are going back to our blanket on the beach. It's a struggle to walk against the water as it pulls me backward toward the ocean as if it is trying to prevent me from leaving. My legs feel much lighter when I finally break free from the ocean's powerful grasp.

The sand feels deliciously warm under my feet but the rest of me shivers as the wind blows against my wet body. When I get back to the sheet, Mommy throws a warm towel over my shoulders and tells me and the others to sit down so we can eat our lunch.

As she unpacks and distributes a bologna sandwich to each of us, I sense there is great sadness nearby. Looking in that direction, I see a sad-looking boy staring at me from where he sits on a sheet immediately to our right. Behind him are his mother and some kids busy doing various things. No one appears to be paying any attention to him. Smiling, I offer him a bite of my bologna sandwich but he shakes his head no and continues to stare at me.

I have the distinct feeling he wants me to talk, so I say, "My name is Bobby; what's your name?"

"Johnny," he eagerly answers with a smile.

I go over with my bologna sandwich and sit next to my new friend, Johnny.

"We're going to go on the rides at Steeplechase after lunch," I tell him. "Are you going there too?"

Johnny looks down at his legs and says in a barely audible voice, "I can't go on rides … I can't walk like other kids."

I now notice how very thin and frail his legs look.

"Why can't you walk like other kids?" I ask.

"I don't know. Mom and dad know, but they tell me I'm too young to understand."

"Bobby," Mommy calls over to me, "hurry up and finish your sandwich; we have to leave soon."

I tell her okay, and chomp away on my bologna sandwich. As I do, I ask Johnny what he CAN do … and what he likes.

He tells me that he likes to read, watch television, listen to music on the radio … and he especially likes Christmas.

"Why Christmas," I ask.

"Because every Christmas, I ask God for a special present … to be able to walk … and even run like other kids."

This is good news … he talks to God.

So I tell him, "You know, Johnny, you don't have to wait until Christmas to ask God for that gift. You can ask Him at any time of the year."

"I can?"

"Sure. Why don't we ask Him right now to give you that gift. Let's close our eyes, and ask Him right now. What do you say?"

Johnny excitedly says, "Sure, let's do it … even though it's not Christmas!"

As Johnny closes his eyes, I do as well and focus all my love and attention to God as I pray, "Dear God, PLEASE send your healing graces down upon Johnny right now so he can walk and run just like other boys do. Thank you, God. Amen."

The familiar tingling sensation pours over and through me indicating that God has heard and answered my prayer. I just don't know if that includes a physical healing for Johnny, but that's okay … I know that God ALWAYS does what is best.

"Okay, guys, let's go," Mommy's voice abruptly snaps me back to the present. "It's time for us to head for Steeplechase Amusement Park!"

I tell Johnny goodbye and promise to keep praying for him. He says he will do the same for me. How wonderful! After I pray for people, very few say that they will pray for me!

Daddy leads the way over the scalding hot sand to the wooden boardwalk where we sit down to finish dressing. I brush the sand off my feet then put on my pants, socks and sneakers. All of a sudden, there is a big commotion with lots of yelling and it sounds like crying coming from the area on the beach we just left.

Daddy says, “Oh, oh, it sounds like a wild fight has broken out with all that yelling going on. The heat probably got to some of the people.”

“I don’t think so,” Mommy clarifies as she points, “Look, Patsy. All that noise is coming from those people chasing that boy who’s running crazy all over the beach? Isn’t that the boy Bobby was talking to on the sheet next to us?”

Sure enough, I look out onto the beach, and see little Johnny running so fast that no one can catch him! Wow! I guess Johnny got his Christmas present a little early this year. Thank you, God!

Chapter 11

PENNIES FROM HEAVEN

Mommy looks surprised, "Patsy, what are you doing home so early?"

"I got bumped off today, Ellie, and I don't know when I'll be able to get back on. Sounding so depressed, he adds, "It may be a week or two … maybe even longer."

Watching him nervously puff on a Chesterfield cigarette, I recognize this as an indicator of how he greatly concerned he is.

"Geez, Patsy, of course, this has to happen just when we need extra money with the kids going back to school. They need some clothes, shoes … and there are all the book bills. It seems these layoffs always come at the very worst time."

"I know, I know, Ellie. We'll have to skimp by and pray that I get back on the job soon."

Mommy reaches for a Chesterfield cigarette evidencing her concern. The two of them smoke way too many cigarettes! Daddy says he smokes two packs a day; Mommy says she smokes "only" one pack.

Only one? I think even **one cigarette** is too much. Smoking must do terrible things to the lungs. You can't inhale all that smoke directly into your lungs without it doing some terrible damage. The lungs are not made to deal with poisonous smoke. I wish Mommy and Daddy would stop smoking but every time I ask them, they tell me that if smoking was so harmful, the government would not allow tobacco companies to sell cigarettes.

Even if the government says it is not harmful, I still think it is very harmful to the body.

"The last time you were out, you were out for nearly two weeks," Mommy reminds him, "We couldn't pay our monthly bills. It took us a **long** time to catch up. Remember?"

"Yes, of course I do."

Mommy worries more about paying the bills than Daddy does. This might be because Daddy usually gives his pay on payday directly to Mommy so she can pay the bills. She does so by going to the different bill-paying locations in Yorkville. Daddy keeps a little money in his pocket for carfare and lunch. Mommy says this arrangement is quite common among families throughout Yorkville where we live.

"Well, there's no time like the present to 'stretch the dollar' as far as it will go, and to start cutting corners again," Mommy says encouragingly.

"We need some milk, bread and eggs, so I guess I'll ask one of the kids to go to grocery store and get it on trust. Thank God for Adam, the owner of the grocery down the block. He's been so helpful to us and other families in the neighborhood. Every time someone gets hit with hard times, he's always been there to provide groceries on trust until they get back on their feet. I don't think Adam has ever turned anyone away. He's such a good man."

Daddy responds, "Yeah, but when people are on 'trust' with him, he doesn't let them get cigarettes or beer."

"That's because those are not 'essentials,' Patsy," Mommy explains. "When you have to cut corners, you cut out the beer and cigarettes first before anything else. I'm sure Adam does that to help people discipline themselves during hard times … and avoid running up a big bill they may later regret. Otherwise, he gives people the food they need to help tide them over."

"Yep, you're right, Ellie. That's why everybody sees to it that they pay Adam back every penny they owe him as soon as they can."

The process of "trusting" customers down on their luck is yet another common practice among the people of Yorkville where owners of small grocery stores help their regular customers when times get financially tough.

And so, I go to the grocery store to get the food we need now on trust. Mommy writes out a list of groceries for me to give to Adam … assuming he'll give us trust as usual. As I walk to the store, I think of how I will ask him to trust us for the groceries we need.

As I enter the store, I see Adam standing at the counter as usual so I say, "Hello, Adam, how are you today?"

Smiling, he answers, "I'm fine, young man. Thank you. What can I get for you?"

"Well, we need some groceries … but my father just got laid off today so my mother told me to ask you if you can trust us again for a while until Daddy gets back to work. We promise to pay you back everything."

Adam blinks and says, "Sure, son. What is it your Mom wants?"

I give him the list, which he uses to retrieve the items Mommy wrote down.

Carefully loading them into a cardboard box, Adam then reaches under the counter, pulls out a notebook, and says, "I'm writing the amount your family owes in my book. I'll keep a running account until you can pay it back."

He actually looks happy that he is able to help by "trusting us."

"You can tell your mother she can send any one of you kids and simply tell me to 'put it on the bill.' Okay?"

I nod okay and thank him.

I slide the box of groceries off the counter and turn around to leave. At the door, I realize that I cannot open the door because my hands are tied up carrying this heavy box. Before I can figure out what to do, Adam suddenly appears and reaches around me to open the door.

"Have a good day, Sonny," he says cheerfully.

Wow! He even opened the door for me! He may never become rich running his business like this, but his kindness and generosity certainly are earning him treasures in heaven.

As Jesus said, "What you do for the least of My brethren, you do for Me."

That means when he helps others, he's actually helping Jesus. Therefore, his reward will be **MUCH** greater than any money people might give him.

When I tell Mommy and Daddy of Adam's kindness and his promise to let us put groceries on the bill, they both look greatly relieved.

"That's swell," Daddy says.

Mommy adds, "Bobby, please say a prayer that God will help Daddy get back to work quickly!"

"Okay, Mommy, I will go pray right now."

I go into the room off the kitchen and lay down on the bed. With my eyes closed, I clear my mind of everything and think only of God.

"Dear God, please help Daddy get back to work. Mommy and Daddy are so worried about all the bills we have. Can you please send them some money to help? Thank you, God, for whatever You do to help us. Thank you also for the gift of people like Adam, the grocer, who helps when things are difficult. Please bless him, Lord, and if **he** ever needs help from others, please send someone to help him. Amen."

As soon as I finish my prayer, a surprising vision forms in my mind. I see my entire family going for a walk during which someone in our family finds a big roll of money! I feel certain this is God's answer to my prayer for help with our family's money problems. He wants our entire family to go on a walk of faith to find the money we need.

I jump out of bed and run out into the kitchen and eagerly

tell everyone, "God just showed me a vision of our entire family going for a walk and one of us finding a big roll of money to pay our bills!"

Mommy and Daddy look at each other and smile. Having previously witnessed many miracles in my life, they don't hesitate to quickly get our family organized to go for a walk … a walk of faith … right now!

Mommy calls out to everyone, "We're all going for a walk because Bobby says that God is going to let one of us find a big roll of money!"

"Let's go, shake a leg!" Daddy urges everyone.

When everyone is gathered by the front door for our walk together, Mommy says, "Now remember, Bobby said God gave him a vision showing one of us finding a roll of money so I want you all to keep your eyes pinned to the ground to find that money!"

Daddy leads the way out of the apartment into the darkened hallway followed by Paddy, Larry, Kitty holding Geri's hand, me and then Mommy. It looks so funny seeing everyone looking down at the floor as they walk … all eager to be the one who finds the money God sends to help our family.

All of a sudden, Paddy steps on something causing him to stumble and stop in his tracks.

Quickly bending down toward the floor, he rises holding up a thick roll of money in his hand!

Paddy shouts, **"I found the money; I found the money!"**

Daddy rushes to Paddy's side as Paddy proudly hands the roll of money to him. With his eyes wide with amazement, Daddy counts the money.

"My God, Ellie, there's over two hundred dollars here! That's more than enough to pay all our bills!"

A cheer goes up from everyone!

Mommy cries, "It's a miracle! It's a miracle! Thank you,

God. Thank you for helping us."

How wonderful and amazing it is that God answered my prayer this way. It required our entire family to go on a walk of faith trusting that God would reward our faith and help us in such a remarkable, implausible way. I guess that puts us in the good company of St. Peter who God also asked to take a walk of faith.

The only difference, of course, is that God asked us to walk on land.

Chapter 12

CENTRAL PARK ANGEL

As soon as the snowstorm subsided, my brother, Paddy, and I happily grabbed our sleds and hurried out of our apartment on our journey to Central Park to go sled riding. With the wind strongly whipping around us, we had to drag our sleds behind us as we eagerly made our way toward the 79th Street entrance on the eastside of the park.

"Walk behind me, Bobby," Paddy called out. "I'm making a path through the snow so it'll be easier for you."

Paddy is my older brother by two years; he's 11 years old. He's always looking out for me. As the oldest boy in our large Irish Catholic family, he is named after our father, Patrick Victor Walsh. Paddy proudly embraces his role as the leader of his brothers and sisters.

We had to lean slightly forward to push through the snow and fight off the wicked wind blowing snow and ice-cold air at us. Eventually, we travelled the seven blocks to Fifth Avenue where we crossed over, entered the park and went right over to "Cherry Hill" located to the left of the park's entrance. This hill was among the most popular places in the park for sled riding. Not surprisingly, there were already a great many kids sledding there.

After going down the hill a few times, an older boy told us there was another, much better hill for sledding.

"It's called "Pilgrim Hill," he said and then showed us the way a little farther south in the park.

Some other kids joined us as we went south along the path. After a short walk, we arrived at Pilgrim Hill. Looking up at the top, I discovered why it is called Pilgrim Hill. At the top, there was a large metal statue of a pilgrim. The hill itself didn't look as long as Cherry Hill but it certainly was steeper and had more bumps on it to make for some elevated sled-riding when you go over one of them.

Pilgrim Hill wasn't too crowded so up and down we went for what seemed hours. Like so many things in life, the climb up to the top was always more difficult and slower than the fast, much easier ride back down to the bottom.

It was starting to get colder and darker so we decided it was time to head home but Paddy wanted to go down Pilgrim Hill just one more time. Standing at the bottom of the hill with my sled off to the side, I watched as Paddy came flying down the hill. Near the bottom, however, Paddy's sled hit a large bump and went flying high up in the air … sled and all. When he came down, he crashed right into a wooden barricade that was located at the bottom of the hill!

This made a loud, scary crash noise. I could see right away that Paddy was injured as blood spurted out all over his face from a nasty-looking gash above his left eye! Some men came running over to help but no one knew what to do. I knelt down on my knees next to Paddy who just sat there in the snow stunned. I put my hand on his shoulder as I quietly, urgently, called out to God for help.

"Somebody please help my brother!" I called out trying not to show how frightened I was for Paddy.

"How bad is it, Bobby?" Paddy asked clearly sounding like he hoped I would say it's not bad.

"Oh … it's just a nasty scratch, Paddy," I answered trying to sound as matter-of-fact about it as I could.

I was so worried for Paddy as I watched the blood slowly seeping out of the cut on his forehead. What's more, we were in the middle of Central Park far from home … and it was quickly getting dark and colder by the minute!

My thoughts turned to terror as I recalled what Mommy

once told us, "You should never go into Central Park at night because that is when the big, vicious animals are released from their cages in the zoo so they can roam around freely in the park until dawn! If any of those beasts catch someone, they eat the person alive!"

That is why no one is allowed in Central Park at night, I reasoned.

Since it was twilight time, everyone would soon be leaving the park for their safety. I was terrified at the thought that fierce, man-eating, wild lions or tigers, polar bears and panthers would soon be out free, roaming in the dark through the park … looking for people to eat! I knew we would never be able to outrun them or hide from them once the animals were released from their cages in the zoo!

I silently prayed to God and begged Him to please send someone to help Paddy and me … now … before it gets completely dark and the wild animals come out!

Just then, someone called out, "Here comes a cop!"

Off to our right appeared a tall, kind-looking policeman. He ordered everyone to step back away. When he looked at Paddy's injury, he pulled a white handkerchief out of his right pocket and placed it directly over Paddy's wound.

"Keep that against the cut … that'll help stop the bleeding," he said confidently, "until we get you to the hospital. You'll need a few stitches, kid, to close that up!"

"How'd this happen anyway?" he asked matter-of-factly.

Paddy explained how he lost control of his sled after going over a large bump on Pilgrim Hill … and then crashed into the wooden barricade at the bottom.

"That sure wasn't too smart of the 'park people' to put a big wooden barricade like that at the bottom of a hill where they know you kids go sledding," the officer said shaking his head.

The officer asked Paddy a few questions. "Are his

parents here, did anything else hurt, what's his age, what's his name and where does he live? Paddy answered his questions and told him that his little brother, Bobby, was here as he gestured toward me.

Soon a black and white police car arrived to our left and stopped right on the path near us. Paddy and I got into the back of the police car while the officer put our sleds in the trunk. The officer turned on the siren and flashing red light on top as he drove us to Roosevelt Hospital on 59th Street and Columbus Avenue on the west side of Manhattan.

Paddy told the doctor in the emergency room that our parents were not with us, and since we didn't have a telephone at home, there was no way she could contact our parents to give them permission to treat him. The doctor said that under the circumstances, a few stitches were needed to treat Paddy's cut so if Paddy agreed, he would do it.

"Your parents would agree, I am sure," he explained.

Paddy agreed so the doctor proceeded with a nurse's help to stitch up Paddy's wound. When the doctor finished, Paddy's forehead was completely covered from one side to the other in white bandaging. We left the hospital and then realized that the only way we could get to where we lived on the eastside of Manhattan was to walk through Central Park. The buses were no longer running and there was absolutely no one around who could help us.

As we began the long, dangerous journey home, we dragged our sleds behind us as we were hit with brutal, bone-chilling cold air accompanied by a strong wind blowing so hard we had to push against it. Paddy said that we had to cut across the park to the eastside where we lived.

Alarmed, I told him, "Mommy said they let the wild animals out from the zoo at night into Central Park. Remember, she said they roam the park looking for people to eat!"

"I know, Bobby, but we don't have any choice. If we stay out here, we will freeze to death! Besides … maybe Mommy was just saying that to scare us so we wouldn't go into the park at night. I don't think they really let the wild animals out at night … maybe they just let them out **inside** the zoo area.

"We don't have a choice, Bobby. We have to get home or we're going to freeze to death out here. Let's start walking as fast as we can."

The park off to our right was cast in ominous darkness as it gave off frightening sounds from thousands of tree branches whipping around in the strong winds. The streets were completely deserted … no cars … no people … no buses … nothing but howling cold wind and the scraping sounds of our sleds behind us.

Just ahead there is an entrance to the park on our right. With the wind incessantly howling around us, Paddy shouts, "Bobby, I don't know if we can make it all the way up to 79th Street in this cold. We have to go into the park here and take our chances with the animals. We can walk quietly and use those big sticks over there to beat them off if they come after us!"

"I'm afraid of the wild animals, Paddy. I don't think we should go in the park. They can be anywhere in there, hiding in the bushes waiting to pounce out on us."

"We don't have a choice, Bobby; we are going to freeze to death trying to walk all the way uptown to 79th Street. Cutting across the park here is a shorter way home. We have to do it. Don't be afraid, I'll beat off any animals that attack us. Stay close to me. Let's go!"

Paddy's confident words were reassuring. Thank God he was with me! I was so scared as we entered the darkened park and followed the path which we prayed would bring us to the eastside ... without being attacked by wild animals!

The few lamp posts off in the distance along the pathway

shed light on the area surrounding them. We pushed against the strong, brutally cold wind for quite a while but then we saw the faint outlines of buildings on the other side of the park, the eastside! We apparently had gone halfway across the park already!

Our joyful moment was pierced by the fearsome sound of a lion roaring off in the distance! As this scary sound cut through the silence of the night, it sounded like it was far away but I knew that lions can cover a long distance very quickly … especially if it means a tasty meal like Paddy and me!

We stopped dead in our tracks and clung to each other in terror. Our worst fears were realized … man-eating lions must be out loose somewhere in the park! If lions are out, then other wild animals must also be out in the park!

"Dear God, please help us," I prayed out loud.

"Please protect us from the wild animals," Paddy whispered so the lions wouldn't hear him. "Bobby, walk as softly and quietly as you can on the snow. We'll have to carry our sleds now so they don't make scraping noises on the ground. If a lion or some other wild animal comes, hit it as hard as you can on its nose! Daddy once said that is how you stop a charging animal."

Walking gingerly on the snow-covered path, our steps still made loud, crunching sounds.

I cried out to God from the inner recesses of my heart, "Please God, protect us from wild animals … and help us find our way home. Please send someone to help us. You were once hunted when King Herod sent his soldiers to kill all the baby boys in his efforts to get You. Please send an angel to protect us from the wild animals, and help us get home safely."

"What's that?" Paddy suddenly whispered as he stopped and grabbed my arm. Looking frantic, he added, "It sounds like hooves coming up the path behind us. Quick, Bobby, let's run!"

We started running as fast as we could along the slippery

path. Now I could hear the distinct sound of an animal's hooves behind us as they pounded on the ground. A lamp post up ahead on the right side of the path is going to cast light on us for the animal to see us! The ground is so slippery, we cannot run any faster!

"My God, help us! Don't let the animal get us," I prayed out loud as the beast behind us quickly gained on us.

As we approached the lamp post, Paddy shouted, "Get your stick ready, Bobby; we're going to have to turn and fight for our lives! Stop by the lamp post so we can see what kind of animal it is."

At the lamp post, I turned around ready to swing my stick as hard as I could at the beast. The ground shook mightily as the beast slowed down in its final approach to us. I could hear it breathing heavily. Coming into the light, I could see that the beast was a huge white horse … with a smiling police officer in a white uniform sitting on top!

A voice called out, "It's good you called for help in this terrible weather, boys!"

I was so relieved to see a policeman … and his large, beautiful white horse! Now he can protect us from any wild animals, I thought … and can help us get safely out of the park!

Thank you, God, for hearing our prayers, I thought.

Paddy told him, "I got hurt sled-riding and had to go to the hospital to get stitches. Now we're trying to get to our home on the eastside in Yorkville. We thought you were a wild animal from the zoo!"

The policeman laughs, "We've been called a lot of things over the years, but never a wild animal from the zoo!"

I asked if he had seen any wild animals from the zoo running loose in the park.

He assured us, "There are **NO** wild animals from the zoo out in the park; they are locked up in their cages **at all times**. The only dangerous creatures running loose in the park at night are the human type that feed on innocent people. They're the worst kind of all but you won't find any of them out here tonight because of this terrible weather."

Paddy and I were greatly relieved to hear there are no wild zoo animals out loose in the park … and that the "human-animals" are not out here either!

Aren't you cold with only a thin jacket on," Paddy asked.

"We don't get cold," the officer smiled.

"You can follow me, boys; I will lead you to the exit that will take you out of the park and leave you on the eastside at Fifth Avenue. From there, you can walk north to 79th Street, then go east toward the East River until you get to St. Monica's Church."

Smiling, he added, "From the church, I know you'll know your way home. Now, as the wisest man of all once said, ***'Follow me!'***"

I was so happy to hear this! We thanked him and followed behind him and his big, beautiful, pure white horse. The freezing ice-cold air around us was now mysteriously warmer as Paddy and I walked directly behind the officer and his horse.

Soon the policeman said, "You can go the rest of the way by following this path, boys; it will lead you right out of the park."

We thanked him again as he slowly turned to ride off. A short distance away, he paused to wave. There was a brilliant white light shining all around him and his horse. That was so strange because there were no lamp posts near him!

"Don't' forget to thank **HIM** also," he called out. "And remember … follow all the right roads in life to lead you home. I hope to see you there."

"What did he mean, to thank Him also?" Paddy asked. "And what about seeing us at home?"

"I think he meant that we should also thank God for

sending him! He must be an angel, Paddy. I think God sent him to help us."

We turned to take another look at the policeman and his beautiful white horse … but they had vanished.

Paddy said, "Hey, where'd he go?"

"Didn't you notice, Paddy," I replied, "there was no steam coming from him or his horse breathing in the cold air? And he said that **THEY** don't get cold!

"I'll bet he was an angel!"

"Well … whether or not he was an angel, Bobby … we'd better get going. It's starting to feel deathly cold again."

Walking quickly along the path, it soon led us out of the park onto Fifth Avenue on the eastside.

I told Paddy, "It looks like we've survived getting eaten by all the wild animals from the zoo!"

Just then, the roar of a lion split the silence of the night igniting our pace into a run across Fifth Avenue! The cold night air didn't feel quite as bitter and painful now that we were on the familiar, though deserted, streets of Yorkville. When we reached the apartment building where we lived, we paused on the front stoop … very happy and greatly relieved.

Paddy rang the bell in the vestibule and as soon as Mommy "buzzed" the bell back, the inner door opened for us to quickly rush in. Looking up as we climbed the winding stairs leading up to our second floor apartment, we saw Mommy standing there with her hands on her hips … looking quite upset with us. That was until she saw the large white bandaging covering Paddy's forehead.

Staggering, she cried, "Oh, my God, Paddy, what happened?"

Speaking as dramatically as he could, Paddy said, "Mommy, while we were sledding on Pilgrim Hill in Central Park, some 'night raiders' came out and we had to fight them.

You know … the night raiders … all the wild animals they let out into the park from the zoo at night time! Well, Bobby and I took good care of them all!"

Mommy laughed, "Okay, okay, I'm proud you boys were able to fight off all those wild animals … now tell me, what else happened!"

Paddy told her how he crashed into a wooden barricade at the bottom of Pilgrim Hill and a cop took us to Roosevelt Hospital where a doctor stitched him up.

"How did you get home?" Mommy asked.

"There were no buses running so we had to walk home all the way through Central Park. We were freezing to death and lost in Central Park when a nice policeman dressed in an all-white uniform came riding up on a big white horse! He showed us the way out of the park. Otherwise, we would have been lost all night and froze to death from the cold."

Tears glistened in Mommy's eyes, "I am happy that God sent someone to help you find your way safely out of the park, boys. By the way, there are **NO** policemen in white uniforms riding on huge white horses in Central Park at night!"

Exactly.

Chapter 13

DON'T YOU JUST HATE IT!

"Happy birthday, Robert," Father Kelly says enthusiastically. "Thank you for taking time on your special day to visit me. How old are you now?"

"I am ten years old today," I tell him proudly.

"Ten, that is a wonderful age, Robert, if I remember correctly. But that was a long time ago for me."

"You have a good memory, Father," I tease.

"Ah, you have developed a sense of humor, I see. Very good! You need to have a good sense of humor to make it through life."

"I bet Jesus had a good sense of humor," I surmise.

Father smiles, "Yes, I'm sure He did."

Over the last few years, Father George Kelly of my parish, St. Monica's, has served as my spiritual advisor. The Archdiocese of New York decided this was highly-advisable given the remarkable stories circulating about me as a "blessed child of God" where countless miracles - and attacks by the Devil - were said to be happening.

Father eased back and said, "The school Sisters have done a good job keeping me informed of your … 'doings.' Some of the things they tell me are pretty amazing. I don't know if you realize it, Robert, but we priests and nuns at St. Monica's are greatly moved by some of the remarkable things we see God doing in your life."

I am surprised to hear this because that is how I feel about the work of the nuns and priests. They do so much in serving so many in so many ways.

"The nuns tell me you're relatively quiet and humble despite the extraordinary nature of what God does through you,"

Father discloses.

"That's because it's all so natural to me, Father. All the good things come from God; I'm only the **delivery boy."**

Father laughs, "That's a wonderful way to put it, Robert, God's delivery boy! It's good that you realize that on your own, you can't do anything. **All** healing comes from God."

"I sometimes forget that other people don't have the same experiences I do. That's why I get teased by kids who don't understand. I wish no one knew. People can be so mean."

"I know, and I'm sorry that happens, Robert. But you have to understand that for most people, not just kids, hearing about your experiences is really difficult to believe. There is a silver lining though. Having people doubt you, keeps you humble.

"Remember this, Robert … God knows every hair on your head and He knows what you're going through and will always give you what you need to use the gifts He's entrusted to you. Your challenge is to be faithful in using those gifts despite whatever hardships and sacrifices may come.

"In **this** life, no one knows better than your father what you're going through. While he's aware of the teasing by your peers, he told me his greatest concern is your exposure to the Devil. And I couldn't agree more. Your father said the reality of the Devil taunting you hit him like a 'ton of bricks' when he read what Jesus says in Mark 9:19-20.

"Let me read it to you. 'And they brought him to Jesus; and the spirit, when it saw Jesus, immediately threw the boy into convulsions, and he fell down on the ground, and rolled about foaming at the mouth. So Jesus asked his father, 'How long is it since this has come upon him?' And he said ... **from his infancy!'**

"Understanding that such things can actually happen to little children, your father doesn't want to risk that happening to you. You're at greater risk than most children because God has blessed you with extraordinary spiritual gifts.

"While that's your father's greatest concern, he also wants to make sure you properly use the gifts God has blessed you with. He tells me when you pray, God does miraculous things."

"Yes, Father, that's true."

"And so, your father has asked me to join him in doing whatever we can to be helpful to you. For starters, we put together a few suggestions we think may be helpful.

"First, we have asked the priests and nuns at St. Monica's to avoid treating you differently than your peers. We think part of the 'teasing problem' may have to do with how the nuns, in particular, treat you. You see, children are quite perceptive; they can pick up right away when the nuns treat someone in a special way."

"But I don't feel like I'm treated differently than anyone else, Father."

"I'm not surprised to hear you feel that way. But the reality is that the nuns acknowledge they relate to you much differently than any other student. However, they've promised to be more sensitive to the way they relate to you in front of others.

"Secondly, your father requested that you and I get together on a regular basis to discuss spiritual things. As such, I will be your 'spiritual advisor.' That's someone who understands what you're going through spiritually, and can assist and encourage you as needed.

"Does that sound like something you would like, Robert?"

"Yes, Father, I would like that."

"Very good. So why don't we meet every few weeks. Okay?"

"Yes, Father."

"During these visits, we can discuss anything you'd like including spiritual things that may have happened … good or bad … since the prior visit."

"That sounds very good, Father."

"Good. The last suggestion we came up with is aimed at fostering your spiritual development and understanding of the faith. We'd like you to complete a reading assignment from the Bible, which you and I can discuss at the next meeting. Would you like to do that?"

"Yes, Father, I'd like that very much."

"Good! Now before we discuss some of those details, has anything unusual, that is, spiritually speaking, happened recently?"

"Yes, Father, there are a few things, but there's one thing in particular that stands out."

"Do you mind telling me about it?"

"Sure, Father. A really scary, evil-looking woman began appearing at the corner near my block."

"Why do you say 'evil-looking?' What was there about her that appeared evil?"

"There was a dark black outline around her head. That's what I see around people who are bad. I also sensed the evil that was boiling inside her."

"I see. Please tell me what happened."

"Every time I passed her, she stopped me and asked me to go with her to her apartment. She said she and her friends knew about me … and what she said were my 'spiritual powers.'

"I told her I don't have any special powers; I only pray to God and He is the One Who heals people. But she ignored what I said and insisted that I go with her. She said that she and her friends could show me how to do magic … through an even greater power."

"I hope you didn't go with her," Father worries.

"No, of course not, Father. Each time she stopped me, I told her no thanks, I'm fine just praying to God. This always angered her especially when I added that I'd pray for her. Whenever I said this, she sneered and said she didn't need … or want … any of my prayers."

Raising his eyebrows, Father asks, "What did you say to that?"

"I told her I would pray for her anyway."

Father laughs and asks me to continue.

"The last time I saw her, she stood in my way and told me that I **must** go with her.

"When I told her I would **never** go with her, she twisted her face in a real scary way then she wickedly shoved her right hand at my mouth and shrieked, **'Don't you just hate it when someone reaches in and rips the very soul out of your body!'**

"I was so frightened I backed away and begged God to protect me as the image of a demon appeared right behind her!"

Father looks deeply disturbed hearing this.

"But then, her face returned to normal, and she grabbed onto my shoulders and pleaded for me to help her!"

Father asks, "So what did you do?"

"I prayed out loud to Jesus and asked Him to send St. Michael the Archangel to drive the demon out of her."

"What did she do when you prayed for her?"

"She just stood there staring at me with a blank expression , as if she was in a trance. When I told her that she should to go see a priest, she stepped back away and spit filth out of her mouth onto the ground in front of my feet.

"That is what I think of your f_ _ _ ing, useless priests," she wickedly hissed.

Without turning her face away from me, she turned her body around and slinked away all hunched over!

Father was understandably, terribly shocked hearing this.

After a moment, he composed himself to say, "Robert, what you describe is very, very serious. Have you seen this woman again?

"No, Father, I have not seen her since then."

"Thank God! You need to avoid her at all costs! Do you understand me?"

"Yes, Father."

"Did you tell your parents about this?"

"Yes, Father, I did. In fact, my father told me I must stay away from her - even if I have to walk blocks to avoid her."

"Your father is right, Robert. Under no circumstances should you ever talk to this woman again."

"After that time, I haven't seen her since. My father tried to find her but she stopped hanging out on the corner … and no one knows who she is … or where she lives."

"I see.

"Robert, listen carefully to me. There are times when the Devil does more than just taunt people as happened to you. The Devil is capable of doing far worse things to you to cause you to live in ways that are not of God. In the worst cases, the Devil has been known to even take control over how a person lives.

"From what you describe, it sounds like this woman is such a victim. Do you understand what I'm saying, Robert?"

"Yes, I understand, Father. Mommy explained what the Devil does and how it can hurt people. Daddy told me what to do if I ever come in contact with a person like that again."

"What did he tell you to do?" Father asks.

"He said I should walk away and just keep saying, 'In the name of Jesus Christ, I command you to leave me alone and not return!"

Father nods in agreement, "Only God understands why such things happen, Robert. Hearing that such disturbed people have approached you greatly concerns me. I am going to talk to your father about this.

"Robert, if you ever again find yourself confronted by people who appear to be disturbed by the Devil, refer them to me or to their parish priest … and keep your distance! This is an area of ministry that is as dangerous as it gets. Only specially-trained priests with the approval and authority of their bishop may intercede. Do you understand?"

"Yes, Father, I understand."

"In the meantime," he says drawing a deep breath, "I have written down three Gospel readings which I'd like you to read and reflect on what you think Christ is telling us. These three are among my favorites, Luke 10:25, Mark 9:38 and Matthew 15:21.

"It's interesting that I selected these readings before we had this discussion today. When you read them you will understand. Please read them over, reflect on their meaning, take some notes, and let's discuss your thoughts at our next visit.

"In the meantime, if you need to talk, you can call me at the rectory at any time … day or night. I will make time for you. Otherwise, I'll see you at our next meeting. Now bow your head for God's blessing, 'May God continue to bless and protect you, Robert, in the Name of the Father, and of the Son, and of the Holy Ghost. Amen."

"Don't forget to tell your father I need to speak with him … as soon as possible."

Chapter 14

MODERN-DAY LAZARUS

I recall quite painfully what happened when my mother and father decided to send my brother, Paddy, and me off to summer camp for the first time in our lives.

St. Vincent DePaul Summer Camp, a camp for poor children, was located in Spring Valley, New York, was where Paddy and I were to stay for an entire week. Even though my older brother would be with me, I was still quite afraid because I had never been away from home before … and … I had a very strong sense of danger waiting for me at the camp.

In front of St. Monica's Church on 79th Street in Manhattan, Paddy and I boarded the bus along with all the other poor kids from our neighborhood who were going to camp. The roar of the bus engine filled the back of the bus where my brother and I sat close together. Within moments, the view of St. Monica's Church and our parents standing in front waving to us disappeared as the bus sped quickly past one street after another.

Two young men sitting up front came along as chaperones for our group. Walking up and down the aisle, they did their best to keep everyone calm.

"Sit down! Stop yelling out that window!" they often shouted.

All the yelling and commotion made me feel even more insecure as my brother and I sat quietly in the back of the bus. Soon we went over the George Washington Bridge high in the air over the Hudson River then continued on some major highway. After a while, most of the kids calmed down except for an occasional outburst set off by something they saw outside.

The driver announced that we would soon be arriving at Spring Valley Camp so our chaperones told us to gather up all our belongings. My brother and I still had our bags of clothing tightly clutched on our laps. The bus soon turned off the highway and drove through a thickly wooded area with old, small houses off to the side here and there.

Finally, we pulled into a wide, open field as the chaperones announced that we had finally arrived at Spring Valley Camp. Everyone started cheering and hurried to get off the bus. Paddy and I sat quietly until we could get off the bus without being separated.

Outside, my worst fears were realized when we were told to line up according to age! I complained to a camp worker that I wanted to stay with my brother but he just told me it was all right. He said that I must go over to my age group.

"Seven and eight-year-olds to the right; nine and ten-year-olds to the left!" He shouted out to all the boys.

I looked over into Paddy's eyes and I was surprised to see that he, too, looked scared. We had no choice but to obey the orders of the camp workers but I kept my eyes on my brother every moment to make sure I did not lose sight of him. Our lines were only ten feet apart, but it seemed like a mile to me.

"All right, everyone stay in a straight line and follow me to our dormitory where we will be staying." The camp worker shouted to those on my line, "Move it out, get the lead out of your pants, guys! Let's go!"

I looked quickly over to Paddy who just shrugged his shoulders and called out, "It's okay, Bobby. I'll meet you later when we all eat together."

That provided little consolation. I was heart-broken and scared at the thought of being alone in a strange place, so far from everyone and everything I have ever known, and now being separated from my big brother.

I obediently followed the boys in front of me as we walked about one hundred feet across an open field to a large, two-story, stark-white, clapboard building. Outside the building was a high staircase, which we climbed, leading up into a damp, darkened second floor.

There were long, narrow cots neatly arranged filling all the available floor space from one side of the floor to the other. Off to the side was the large bathroom and a shower room. A strange, musty smell filled the air adding to my uncomfortable feelings.

"Okay, guys," the camp worker's voice boomed out loudly throughout the hollow area, "grab a bed and put your things underneath it. That is where you are going to sleep while you're here at camp. Come on, don't just stand there looking at me. Get a move-on!"

There was an instant scramble for the beds as all the boys ran for the beds they wanted. Running feet on the bare, wood-planked floor made loud thunderous "thumping" noises. I turned to the bed on my immediate left, placed my bag under it then sat on it.

Once everyone was settled, the counselor went over the ground rules stressing no cursing, fighting, stealing or disobeying. He then ordered us to call out our names and where we came from.

When it was my turn, I yelled out loud and clear, "My name is Bobby Walsh and I come from Yorkville in Manhattan!"

I yelled out loudly because the counselor criticized some boys saying they sounded like "church mice." We then hurried off to the main hall to eat. Down the stairs and across the middle of the camp's center we walked in single file. The building directly across from mine was where my brother, Paddy, was located.

I saw him come out of the building with all the other older boys! We greeted each other with a big smile and quickly came together and entered the large, noisy main hall. Sitting at the first table, the smell of delicious food filled our nostrils.

"You've got to get on line over there to get your food," one of the older boys told us.

Paddy and I followed everyone over to the line by the left wall. We got hot dogs, French fries and ice cold milk. What a treat this was! I was beginning to think I might like it here after all especially after I heard someone behind us say that we could eat all we want, all we have to do is go up and get more of whatever we wanted!

"It is not so bad here, eh, Bobby," Paddy said encouragingly. "You really like those hot dogs, don't you?"

He was referring to the two hot dogs I quickly gulped down in record time.

Paddy then told me, "Listen, Bobby, tomorrow they're going to force you to go in the big swimming pool … and you don't know how to swim yet. You've got to let them know so they don't force you into the deep part of the pool!"

After dinner, a counselor announced that we must go to our own building for the night. This was the moment Paddy and I feared … we are going to be separated for the very first time in our lives!

Fighting back tears, Paddy said, "I'll see you in the morning, Bobby. Don't worry; everything's going to be all right."

I was so sad my throat ached. I could only nod my head okay and tried to be brave as we walked our separate ways for the first time since we were born.

The counselors directed everyone to go with their individual groups out by the U.S. flag pole in the open field. I could see where Paddy was located. I was very, very scared and sad. As we stood saluting the flag, someone blew 'taps' on a horn as two counselors took the flag down. I then followed my group to our dorm, climbed the long outside staircase, and went directly to my bed where I nestled under my blanket.

Lying there in the darkened dorm, I could hear the sounds of the night. Hundreds of crickets outside calling to each other; what a nice sound. Inside, I heard the sounds of muffled cries from some of the boys. Other boys were homesick like me … but I was trying to be brave like my parents told me to be.

I remember them saying that, "Big boys don't cry!"

I was more fortunate than the other boys because I had my big brother with me in camp to watch over and protect me. These thoughts combined with the stress, worries and physical rigors of the day to take me swirling into the welcome abyss of sleep.

The next morning, the loud sound of reverie being played on a horn outside in the open field abruptly awakened me. Sitting bolt upright, I looked over in the bright sunlight filling our dorm and saw a puddle of yellow urine under the bed next to mine.

Sadly, the boy sitting on the bed had his face buried in his hands as he cried in shame. Our counselor hovered over him and called him a big baby! That was so mean! I felt so sorry for him.

The counselor threatened him, "If you don't stop wetting the bed, you're going to have to wear a diaper at night!"

I asked God to help the boy stop wetting the bed so he wouldn't be embarrassed in front of all the boys in the dorm. My prayer was rudely interrupted by the counselor yelling at me to get up and get going! I hurried downstairs to the flag pole where everyone stood silently saluting the U.S. flag as it was raised. Afterward, we all ran to the main hall for breakfast.

As I ran, I saw Paddy standing off to my right waiting for me! I was so happy to see him. Together, we went to the main hall and enjoyed a breakfast of cornflakes, milk and a buttered roll. As we ate, I told him about the bed-wetter and how mean the counselor was to him.

To my surprise, Paddy said, "Don't worry about the boy wetting the bed, Bobby. You'd better worry about what you're going to do today when they force **you** to go swimming! Your group is the first one to go down to the big swimming pool where everyone must to go in the water!"

Instant panic and fear! This was terrible … I had never been in a pool before, and I did not know how to swim! I was afraid that I was going to drown!

Seeing the fear on my face, Paddy advised me, "Your only hope, Bobby, is to tell your counselor that you can't swim, and make sure they don't force you to go into the deep part of the pool. I'm not going to be there today; they're taking my group over to the gym so I won't see you until dinner time tonight. Please take care of yourself, Bobby, and remember what I told you."

I felt instantly sick to my stomach as I watched Paddy walk away with his group. Before I had time to panic any further, my counselor announced that today was going to be our group's "pool day." As everyone cheered, he ordered us to put on our swim trunks and bring a towel down to the pool. It was completely fenced in and was located between our dorm and the baseball field off in the distance.

I reluctantly complied but explained to the counselor at the pool entrance that I was terribly afraid because I didn't know how to swim and had never been in a pool before… especially one that had a deep water area. He listened to what I said then told me not to worry about it,

"Everything will be all right," he said as he brought me over to the pool's edge and pointed to an area where he said the water was only a few feet deep so it would not be over my head. Feeling safe enough about the level of the water, I slowly eased myself into the ice cold water at this end of the pool. The other boys from my group called this area of the pool the **"sissy's end"** but I did not care.

While the boys swam around and enjoyed the water, I was

perfectly content to just relax in the water holding onto the side wall of the pool.

After playing for a while, all the boys left the pool, one by one, to go play softball or basketball. Since I was the last boy in the pool, I decided to walk around a little in the waist high water. Feeling a little braver, I inched closer to the center of the pool where the water was up to my neck. There was a thick blue and white striped rope stretching across the entire width of the pool here in the middle. Wondering what this was for, I ducked down under the water to see what was underneath.

Just then, someone violently shoved me from behind pushing me forward. As I tried to put my feet on the bottom, I found that the floor of the pool here was incredibly slippery … and it was slanted downward!

Frantically, I tried to scurry backward away from what I realized must be the deep end of the pool! However, both my feet kept sliding off the floor as if the floor was moving away from under me! With nothing to support me, I slipped down under the water with my eyes and mouth wide open!

Hideous laughter from a demon filled my mind conveying a message of doom as I wildly flailed about! I then knew who it was that shoved me into the deep end of the pool! I also immediately realized that I was instantly in a life and death struggle as I thrashed about trying to grab the thick blue and white rope … but it was nowhere near me!

Torrents of water rushed into my mouth and throat completely cutting off my air supply as fear and panic surged within me. Looking upward at the top of the water, I could see that it was about two feet above me.

Remembering that Mommy once said if you go down three times, you will drown, I wildly thrashed about in an attempt to reach the surface … and air.

Nothing worked.

The demon was screaming in my mind.

All I could hear was its alarming, gleeful words, "There is no one here to save you! Ha, ha … you're going to drown! You're going to drown!"

My lungs, throat, and head felt like they were going to explode. They hurt so very badly. The harder I struggled, the louder the demon laughed and taunted me! As I tried desperately to scream out for help, even more water rushed into my mouth and throat further choking me.

I felt myself sinking back down a second time. One more time and I am dead!

The demon gleefully cheered, "You're going down for the last time … then you'll be ours … you'll be ours!"

Hearing this threat, I struggled ever more wildly as I desperately tried to reach the surface. I could only keep my head above water for a second at a time then back down I went as if something was pulling me down!

No matter how furiously I flailed my arms on the surface and constantly kicked my legs, I could not get any air! My chest, throat, and head were bursting for air; they felt like they were going to explode! I was crying inside, terrified by the fact that I could not breathe or cry out for help.

I realized that there was no one here to help me.

Suddenly, my arms felt like they weighed a ton as fatigue set in so badly that I could not move my arms or legs any more. The surface looked like it was rising upward away from me as my body sank down a third time into the profoundly silent world under the water.

My arms were positioned straight up toward the surface as if I was reaching out to God. Amazingly, all the events of my life to date flashed by my mind's eye as I recalled my mother once telling me that this is what happens when you are dying.

The demon screamed out once again, "There's nothing

you can do … even **He** can't save you!"

Realizing that I was dying and had only a second or two of consciousness left, I instinctively cried out to God from the inner recesses of my being to save me.

I was suffering absolutely excruciating pain as I cried, "Jesus, I am too young to die. I haven't completed what I am supposed to achieve in life. Please, God, save me! I promise to use the gifts You gave me to help others! Please give me more time, God. Please save me!"

As I prayed, something grabbed the lower half of my legs and pulled me down further. I wasn't able to do anything now as my motionless body sank down into the depths of the water.

My eyesight faded to utter darkness as my mind slipped into unconsciousness … like going into a deep, deep sleep. I felt the mental, physical and spiritual parts of my being blend together in one harmonious union. This final moment is devoid of all else.

I realized that despite my prayers, I was dying. I felt my spirit flow up and out of my body. My spirit quickly rose and was suspended in the air above the water. Looking down, I saw my lifeless body submerged beneath the water! Looking down upon my still, lifeless body, motionless in the water, I realized that I had died … but I also realized that even though I had physically died, I was still alive!

My spirit, my being, my soul, was still alive!

Realizing this, I cried out to God once again, "Please, God, send me back into my body so I may complete the spiritual ministry you have blessed me with. I promise to do whatever I can to fulfill my mission in helping others. **Please, God, send me back; give me more time."**

Everything then went completely black … life as I knew it had ended.

A powerful, blinding, electrifying energy exploded throughout my entire being causing me to gasp and thrust my eyes wide open only to be blinded by a glorious white light! I could not see anything other than this beautiful white light.

Was I in Heaven? I thought. Where was I?

My nose, throat, and lungs were now filled with wonderful, refreshing air! All the water was gone! I was still physically alive!

What happened? A moment ago, the demons were taunting me as I was drowning, unable to breathe or move. I was in absolute agony. I remembered that they pulled me down into the depths of the water as I was in the process of dying.

Then I remembered looking down on my lifeless body drifting face down underneath the water! I know that I drowned; I physically died. But now, I was completely relaxed breathing fresh air as I hung onto the side of the pool!

Rubbing my eyes, my sight returned allowing me to see my arms were draped over the side of the pool. I did not feel any pain, and I did not have any difficulty breathing. There was no one else in the pool but now I noticed the dry legs of a tall young man who stood right in front of me at the poolside.

Looking up at him, I assumed he was a counselor so I bitterly complained, “Why didn’t you help me sooner? I was drowning!”

He crouched down and said, “From what I saw, you did just fine gliding under the water all the way over to here!”

I protested further, “I couldn’t do that! I don’t know how to swim! Why did you let me suffer like that before helping me. You’re supposed to help me!”

He answered, “As soon as you called for help, I was sent to help you, and so I did!”

“But I couldn’t yell; the water kept going in my mouth. How could you have heard me?”

Smiling, he said, “I was told.”

Looking at his legs, I noticed once again that they were completely, mysteriously dry!

"Hey, your legs are completely dry," I told him. "You couldn't have been the one who saved me. If you were, your legs would be all wet!"

"**WE** don't get wet," he said mysteriously as he smiled.

I looked away from the brilliant sunlight shining off his face, and looked around the pool area to see who else could have saved me. There was no one else there except this bright, mysterious counselor and me.

Smiling, he appeared to understand my confusion.

Looking deeply into my eyes for emphasis, he said quite dramatically, "When you make a promise … you must keep it!"

Before I could ask why he said this, he asked, "Do you remember the story of the ten lepers?"

"The ten lepers? Yes, I do … why?"

Nodding his head, he said simply, "Well ... "

Before I could comment on this, he rose, turned and gently walked off toward the enclosed, fenced-off end of the pool. As I watched him, a brilliant flash of light momentarily blinded me. When my sight returned, he was gone … completely gone!

I looked around the entire pool area, but he was nowhere to be seen! Neither was anyone else.

He quite simply vanished in thin air!

Recalling what he said about being "being sent," and "being told," and that, "They don't get wet," I realized that he was no counselor … he was, in fact, an angel who was sent by God in answer to my prayers to save me in my dying moments.

I also understood then why he said that I must keep my promises. I remember promising God that if He would return my spirit to my body, if He would physically resurrect me, I would use the spiritual gifts He blessed me with to lead others to Him. Like the one leper who was healed by Jesus, and then went back to thank Him, I should do the same.

Now I had a pretty good idea how Lazarus must have felt when Jesus saved him from physical death. Thank you, Jesus, Abba and Holy Spirit.

Chapter 15

INTRUDER FROM THE ABYSS

The Devil is the unseen contributor to much of the discord and turmoil in families throughout society today. The worst of all intruders. Many people today are unaware … or just don't believe … that the Devil may be behind many of the sufferings they are experiencing.

In keeping with the saying, "knowing the enemy is half the battle," I share this personal recollection how far the Devil can and does go in its attempts to achieve its evil purposes. Among the many things Satan does to turn people away from God, one of its most effective methods is to cause discord and unhappiness among family members.

The Devil uses its knowledge of our weaknesses against us especially when it comes to matters of pride and forgiveness. This is quite daunting considering how cunning the Devil is, the father of all lies, and second in intelligence only to God.

My own parents were not spared such attacks as they once unknowingly fell victim to the Devil's evil influence. There came a time when, despite greatly loving and respecting one another, my parents found themselves constantly bickering. Every day seemed worse than the last.

What follows is my personal childhood remembrance as these events unfolded.

Late one night, all the lights in our railroad-styled apartment were off leaving us in total darkness. This added to my sense of dread and a strong sense of impending danger. It didn't take long to find out why.

My father arrived home a little after one in the morning. I could hear him shouting in the hallway downstairs then mumbling something to himself as he stumbles up the winding stairs leading to our first floor apartment. He obviously has had too much to drink … once again.

Daddy settles in the living room where I hear him lie down on the couch on the right side of the living room. That is where he usually winds up when he comes home after drinking too much. Judging by the sounds of him tossing and turning, he is trying to go to sleep.

My thoughts are disturbed by a breeze that suddenly whips through all the rooms of our apartment. The air feels noticeably different. An extraordinary spiritual activity has begun … an activity that is definitely **not good!**

An unholy disturbance fills the air by something that is outside the natural boundary between physical life and the spiritual plane. All of us are exposed. I wait in dreaded anticipation for what is about to happen.

I don't have to wait long to find out.

From a distance far beyond the kitchen window, I sense the approach of an evil spirit heading directly toward our home … directly toward us! It is coming after Daddy … and for him alone.

Soon the demon is near. I go to where my mother is awake … and obviously also aware that something quiet unholy is approaching. As we both look out toward the kitchen we see a diabolical creature gliding slowly in our direction! Its outline is a dark shade of charcoal that stands out crystal clear in the darkness of our apartment. It is about four feet tall with a rounded head, no neck, and sloping shoulders. It has no eyes, no ears, and no hair is distinguishable. It appears to have a heavy cloth draped over its head and entire body.

It slowly approaches the entrance to my room as I lean back on my right forearm. Apparently my two sisters and one younger brother in our room also sense the presence of this demon. The baby sits up in her crib as my mother looks in the direction of the evil spirit. My brother and other sister sit up and look at this evil spirit as it drifts slowly into our room through the open doorway.

We watch in horrified silence as the demon glides slowly and methodically straight ahead toward the living room where Daddy is lying on the couch unaware that some unholy entity is coming his way. This evil spirit audaciously wants us to see it and to observe what it is doing.

Slowly gliding without any movement whatsoever up or down, or side to side, it proceeds perfectly straight ahead in a determined, very slow, unstoppable march toward the last room where Daddy is resting. As it passes us, the air about us becomes very, very cold.

The demonic spirit passes one foot in front of Mommy and me without pausing as it steadily glides straight ahead for the living room. Mommy makes the Sign of the Cross and I follow her example. As we do, we watch the spirit enter the living room by passing right through the closed right French door as if the door was made of air!

Now the demon is in the room with my unsuspecting, drunken father.

"Mommy, did you see that?" I whisper, wondering if she also saw the spirit and how it just glided through the rooms and then literally passed through the right French door.

"Yes, Bobby," Mommy whispers in return. "It's a ghost. Say a prayer!"

I call out to God for protection from this demonic creature.

My father shouts from what now sounds like a hollow cave, "What's all the God-damned commotion in there? What the hell is going on?"

Mommy answers, "Patsy, I know you're not going to believe this, but a ghost just floated right through the French door into the room there with you! I am not kidding. You'd better get out of there … right now!"

"You're sick," he snarls.

"I'm not kidding," she assures him. "Some black thing, a ghost, just went in there a minute ago. You'd better be careful because whatever it is, it is **NOT** human, it's a ghost, something very bad, I swear!" she warns.

"For Christ's sake, cut out the bullshit. Do you think I was born yesterday? You're pissed off at me, so now all of a sudden there's a God-damn ghost floating through doors. Very cute, very cute."

Once again a deadly silence falls upon our home as I sense something else unnatural is about to happen. My attention is drawn to the right French door and I watch it slowly open by itself! That is, it appears to be moving by itself. For sure, the spirit is moving the door. After a momentary pause, the door now swings back closed in the same slow, eerie way it had opened. The latch of the door clicks into place sending a loud metallic sound reverberating through the rooms.

"Did you see that," my mother asks my father.

"Yeah, real scary," he fumes angrily. "Grow up, will you … and leave the goddamn door alone!"

"I didn't touch the door, honest to God."

"Sure, sure you didn't. It was the ghost right?" he taunts.

The evil entity again causes the door to swing open ever so slowly. After a brief pause, it again slowly closes with another resounding "click."

"For the love of God, leave the God-damned door alone," my father shouts. "Stop playing games, I want to sleep; I am tired."

"I swear to God that I am not touching the door," Mommy answers sounding more alarmed. "It is moving by itself; the ghost is moving it. You can ask Bobby; he can see my hands right here in front of him. Tell Daddy, Bobby, have I been touching the door?"

"No, Daddy," I yell out, "Mommy didn't touch the door! And I also saw the ghost go through the door!"

"That's nice," Daddy snaps, "now you've got the kids lying for you."

I watch Mommy's hands and look beyond them to see the right French door once again slowly open ... then close. The curtains on the door sway gently back and forth as the door is moved by the evil spirit. Why is the demon doing this? What is it trying to accomplish?

"That's it, that's it; I've had it!" Daddy bellows angrily, "This horse shit is going to stop right now!"

Daddy gets up, turns on a light, then storms over to the French doors where he stations himself in front of the left French door and stares at us through the translucent curtains hanging down the full length of the doors. This is all so disturbing.

I can make out the ugly look on Daddy's face projecting anger as he sneers at Mommy … and wickedly bites his tongue.

"All right, now let's see the freaking door open," my father snarls. "Now that I am standing here watching you, let's see it open."

As soon as these words leave his mouth, the right French door once again opens in a slow, purposeful way. Through the now open doorway, I can see the expression on Daddy's face instantly change to one of shock and confusion. His mouth drops open as he stumbles backward and falls awkwardly into the armchair directly behind him. The spirit violently slams the door closed with a thunderous noise accompanied by an air of defiance and finality.

"Jesus, Mary and Joseph," Daddy cries as he repeatedly makes the Sign of the Cross in rapid succession, rolls out of the chair, then frantically crawls away on his hands and knees away from the French doors.

"Oh, my God," Mommy cries as she also makes the Sign of the Cross, "God, help us and protect us!"

The right French door again flies violently open but this time Daddy comes running madly through the opening and runs out to the kitchen where he grabs the straw broom from the right corner between the refrigerator and the wall.

In a flash, he comes thundering back through the rooms with a fierce, combative expression on his face as he continues to bite down on his tongue. Thrusting himself headlong past the French doors into the living room, he is swinging the broom wildly in the air from one side of the room to the other!

"Come out and show yourself, you God-damn coward!" he shouts at the invisible spirit!

"Come out and fight me like a man, you God-damn no good son-of-a-bitch!" he curses not realizing the nonsense of what he is saying.

I can't believe Daddy is fearlessly confronting the spirit … and surprisingly it is not responding!

My father continues to use the broom to wickedly pound the chair by the left window. Shouting one curse after another, he actually challenges the spirit to fight him!

The rest of us huddle closely together and peer through the glass French doors as we watch Daddy repeatedly swing the broom through the air in futile attempts to hit the spirit that is somewhere in the room with him!

Moving in our direction, Daddy beats the armchair in front of the left French door. Dust goes flying in the air after each powerful whack from the broom. Daddy now focuses his anger on the open space between the two doors and violently punishes the air there. This final effort leaves him gasping for air as he staggers backward, totally exhausted, and collapses into the left armchair by the left window. As he sits there perfectly still, the only noise in the house now is his labored breathing.

He says, "I don't know what's going on here, but I can tell you one thing for sure, a door does **not** open and close by itself. It must be a ghost!"

Mommy assures him, "Bobby and I saw that ghost glide into the room before it started playing around with the French door. This is very bad. None of us are safe now with a ghost thing in our home. You've got to call St. Monica's and get a priest to come right away to bless our home."

Daddy nods in agreement as he sits slumped in the armchair. He has instantly sobered up. It is amazing to see what a visit by a ghost can do.

Mommy adds, "Meanwhile, what are we going to do tonight?"

"Don't worry," Daddy says calmly, "I'll sit up tonight with the lights on and keep watch. I have a feeling there won't be any more trouble tonight. Perhaps that thing accomplished what it intended and left. You can go back to sleep now; I'll keep watch. Everything will be all right."

Feeling secure knowing that Daddy is going to keep watch to protect us from the Devil if it returns, I climb back onto the bed and snuggle as closely as I can to everyone else.

The demon was to come again.

Chapter 16

THE BASEBALL MIRACLE

When I was 12 years old, I tagged after my older brother, Paddy, and a large group of his friends. We went over to Central Park in Manhattan to play "self-hitting" baseball with the two hardballs they had.

They decided to play at an enormous open field where there were baseball diamonds facing each other. The two oldest guys in the group chose players for their team. Ultimately, everyone was picked for either team … except me. No one wanted me because I was much younger than everyone else … and I was rather chubby

Paddy complained that someone should take me.

"Come on, guys, this is not fair. Somebody should take Bobby."

When neither team wanted me, Paddy said, "Okay, Bobby, is going to play on OUR team. You guys shouldn't be so cruel to Bobby; he's a good kid. Besides, God does miracles through him all the time!"

This brought even more laughter by the players surrounding us.

The captain of the other team was especially cruel in his insults, "Well, Paddy, it's going to take a miracle for your … ***LITTLE*** *brother* … to hit the ball!"

The demeaning comments continued; I felt humiliated and embarrassed.

Paddy put his arm around my shoulder to comfort me and said, "Don't listen to them, Bobby; they're just a bunch of stupid jerks. You know you can do anything you put your mind to … especially if you ask God to help you!"

Paddy's words were so comforting and true. I felt that I

could, in fact, do almost anything through God Who helps me … as long as what I ask for is something good.

As luck would have it, our team was up first. I, of course, was going to bat dead last after everyone else on our team. Each player on our team got a hit so before I knew it, I was the next one to go up and hit. The other team immediately started laughing and teasing. They were so sure that I would not be able to hit the ball, they all layed down on the field laughing.

I stood there for a moment holding the ball in one hand and the bat in the other. I closed my eyes as I lifted my entire being to God and asked for a miracle.

"Please dear God, help me hit the ball," I prayed. "If I hit it really well, they'll know that's a miracle from You, and then ... they will believe in you."

I threw the hardball up in the air and as it came down, I swung the bat at it with all the might I could muster.

To everyone's amazement, I did hit the ball ... and did I!

From where the other team's players were laying on the field, they watched incredulously as the hardball I hit soared up higher and higher and higher until it was barely visible! It was as if the ball was being carried upward and outward into the sky by some unseen, powerful wind!

The ball travelled farther and farther in the air ... crossing the entire ballfield we were playing on ... and then the next ballfield facing us ... and then the ball finally soared over the trees on the other farside of this vast open area! The height and distance the ball had travelled was hard to believe! It had to have travelled well over 500 feet!

Even I was amazed!

No one on either team could believe what they just saw! No one, that is, except Paddy who jumped up and down and cheered loudly.

"Who's laughing now?" he shouted. "Look at that! I told

you guys that God does miracles through Bobby!"

The other team couldn't find where the ball I hit had landed so far away. After awhile, they were forced to bring out the only other hardball they had so the game could continue. Later in the game, when I got up to bat a second time, everyone on the other team not only stood up on the field, they went far back in the outfield.

The other team's captain taunted me saying, "You were lucky before when you hit the ball, **CHUBBY**. The ball had to be carried out by a strong wind. No one can hit a ball that far, not even professional ballplayers ... and especially NOT chubby little kids like you! You'll never do that again!"

Another player called out, "I dare you to do it again! If you do, that'll prove God really exists and miracles really do happen."

Yet another player shouts to the others, "Hey, guys, don't make the kid mad! If you make him angry, he may hit the ball like he did the first one that got lost."

Then directing his comments to me, he pleaded, "PLEASE, kid, don't lose that ball on us; it's the last hardball we have! You lose it, and the game is over."

Once again, I stepped up with the ball in one hand and the bat in the other. Closing my eyes and mind to everything except God and myself, I realized that if I could hit the ball like I did last time, everyone would recognize that it is a miracle! And therefore, they'll realize God really does exist and can do miralces if we have enough faith ... and ask for is something that is good.

So I prayed, "Please, God, help me hit the ball again. Only this time, even farther!"

With everyone watching, I threw the hardball up in the air then swung the bat as mightily as I could. The ball soared high up into the air again as if it was being carried up into the sky by some powerful wind! The ball continued to travel farther and farther in the air crossing the entire ballfield we were playing on ... and the next ballfield ... and finally over the trees on the other farside of this vast open area!

Once again, no one could find the ball I hit. Since that was the last hardball they had, the game was over. Strangely, no one seemed to mind. Instead, everyone who played with us that day in Central Park left with a memory they would never forget ... they had all witnessed a remarkable miracle ... twice!

Chapter 17

ABDUCTED BY THE DEMONS

After the last visit with my spiritual advisor at St. Monica's, Father George Kelly, I found it very difficult to sleep at night as thoughts of God, angels, miracles … and devils filled my mind. As usual, the voice of the demon tried to cast doubt upon my thoughts of God, His teachings and how it all applied to me. I resisted listening to the demon's provocative statements and its numbing questions.

At two in the morning, I still could not sleep with such thoughts flooding my mind. One of the reasons I could not sleep was because I was so uncomfortable lying on the sofa in the darkened living room.

In the next room, there is a small lamp shedding light throughout that room. It sits on the right side of a large corner bureau that has a rather large attached mirror facing me. The light in the next room cast against the utter darkness of the room I am reflects life - so much good intermingled with the incessant tauntings and threats of the Devil.

Thinking back over past experiences, a voice I do not recognize suggests that the events involving demons perhaps never really happened!

To prove it, the voice argued, "You should challenge a demon to come **right now** if it really exists! That would settle the matter for once and for all!"

Without reflecting on the enormity of the dangers involved, I foolishly give in to this suggestion and challenge the Devil to come and show itself to me if it really exists. Instantly, I realize that I have made a horrendous, catastrophic mistake … one that may well end my life as I know it. Without appropriate forethought about what I was doing, I have foolishly called the

Devil to come and show itself!

Instant fear, panic and terror grip me as I realize that the Devil is wasting no time in accepting my invitation. It is coming and I feel that there is nothing I can do to stop it.

I stare into the next room at the mirror on the corner bureau facing me at a diagonal angle. As I do, a black shrouded figure of the demon enters that room and moves directly in front of the corner bureau! It is four feet tall and is composed of pure evil. Its right shoulder is pointed in my direction as it slowly glides in front of the bureau from left to right.

To my horror, I can see that the demon has no reflection in the mirror, and as it passes in front of the lamp, it doesn't block the light of the lamp! When it reaches the end of the bureau, it stops moving and stands perfectly still. Then this hideous creature slowly turns to face me, and in a flash, rushes upon me and envelops me within itself. In that instant, I am cast into utter darkness, evil, despair and hopelessness.

I feel myself, the essence of my being, my soul, being carried away by not one, but several demons. At a herculean speed, I am carried away in a tunnel of total, utter darkness. There is no light anywhere, only pitch-black nothingness as I am carried away deeper and deeper into the black endless abyss.

I am not dreaming; I realize this is really happening to me. What's more, there is no one here who can help me, and I am powerless to save myself. But then … I remember that God exists and that wherever He is, He must know what is being done to me. So I cry out to Him from the inner recesses of my being and beg Him to please forgive me for my foolish mistake.

"Please save me, God, from the demons carrying me off into the abyss of eternal horror where they will torture me forever, and keep me from ever seeing You or my loved ones again."

Nothing happens as the demons continue to carry me farther away in the utter darkness.

"Please, God," I cry even louder, "Please, God, have mercy on me! Please spare me, please save me from the demons. I am so sorry for what I did. Please have mercy on me. I am too young to die; I have too much yet to do in leading others to You. Please give me another chance, God. Please don't abandon me to these demons!"

My soul, my spirit, suddenly pops out of the path rushing to desolation. I am moved off to the right suspended perfectly still in the middle of nothingness.

There is only stillness, no light, no sound, no scents, absolutely nothing other than the demons hovering in the utter darkness around me. They surround me and direct indescribable hatred at me. It appears that they are being commanded by God, the superior being, to stand off, but they remain, seething, apparently waiting for permission to seize me once again and carry me off with them into the hellish abyss.

As I hang suspended in nothingness, I wonder if this is where and how I will spend all eternity for my foolish mistake inviting the demon to show itself to me. Maybe they were forced to stop by God because I called out to Him. With no hope other than God, I continue to cry out and beg Him for mercy.

"Forgive me, God," I cry, "spare me, protect me from the demons.

Give me another chance at physical life where I can complete my spiritual mission."

I feel the demons loosen their hold on my being as they slowly withdraw backwards and angrily fade off into the darkness. My spirit is slowly turned so that I am now facing downward, perpendicular to whatever is below. I feel myself slowly drift downward. I can now see my body frozen still as it lays on the couch in the darkened living room. My eyes and mouth are open and I am completely motionless. It looks like I am physically dead.

Gradually, my spirit floats down to inches above my body, parallel to my body to a point where my spirit faces my body.

Then I feel the remarkable sensation of my spirit pouring into my physical body as if my spirit is made of liquid. Once my spirit has fully re-entered my body, I again can feel temperature, hear silence, and I can breathe. God heard my cries for mercy and rescued me out of the clutches of the demons in the darkness of the abyss!

Now I have an idea of how the blind man, Bartimaeus, must have felt when Christ heard his cries … and rescued him out of the darkness.

Chapter 18

THE HEAVENLY TAXI

When I was 16 years old, my eight month old baby sister, Diana, was seriously injured in a terrible fall at home on the day before Christmas Eve. Since Daddy was not home at the time (he was at work), I accompanied Mommy in taking the baby to the New York Hospital Emergency Room. My older brother, Paddy, and my sister, Kitty, stayed home and watched over the seven younger siblings.

Tests taken at the hospital indicated that baby Diana suffered a badly fractured skull and a concussion. The doctor said the baby had to be admitted to the hospital for treatment and further observation.

Baby Diana cried pathetically and clung to us as we stood by the crib and tried to comfort her in the hospital room. She wanted Mommy and me to take her home but we had to leave her there. Leaving baby Diana in the hospital was one of the most difficult, saddest things I have ever had to do.

With the baby of our family injured and hospitalized, our small apartment in snow-covered Yorkville that night before Christmas Eve was filled with tears and sadness.

I begged God to please heal my baby sister so she could come home and be with us during Christmas. Later that evening, I called upon Saint Anne and the Blessed Mother Mary and asked them to go to Jesus and ask Him to heal my little sitter, Diana. Knowing how greatly Jesus loves His mother and grandmother, I believed they might be able to encourage Jesus to heal the baby.

The next day, Christmas Eve, I continued begging Saint Anne and the Blessed Mother to ask Jesus to miraculously heal my baby sister. While I was deep in prayer later that afternoon, I envisioned baby Diana lying quietly in her crib in New York

Hospital. There was a beautiful white light shining down upon her. In that moment, I sensed that God had healed my baby sister!

I excitedly told my parents about the vision just as the telephone rang. Daddy answered the phone; it was a doctor calling from the hospital. He told my father that the baby appeared to have been miraculously healed! An X-ray that had been taken showed that the fractured skull was healed … and the baby no longer showed any signs of the concussion! In fact, the doctor said the baby was doing so well she could go home!

Once Daddy hung up the telephone and told us the good news, our home erupted with loud cheering. We immediately made plans to go get baby Diana and bring her home for Christmas.

I went into the living room and said a heartfelt prayer of thanksgiving to God ... and to Saint Anne and the Blessed Mother Mary for their help. Standing by the front window facing the street, I looked out and saw that there was a wicked ice storm blanketing the city!

Mommy, Daddy and I bundled up as best we could and quickly headed out for New York Hospital on 70th Street and York Avenue. At the hospital, the doctors excitedly told us about baby Diana's miraculous recovery.

Happy and jubilant, we walked out the front doors of New York University Hospital with Diana bundled up and into the darkness of the winter night … and one of the fiercest ice storms to hit the city in years!

The one block we had to walk to York Avenue was slanted upward and was completely covered with ice. As we very carefully walked, howling winds savagely whipped frozen sleet against our faces. While I snuggled the baby securely in my arms, Mommy and Daddy walked on either side of me and tightly held onto my arms to help me avoid slipping on the ice.

The brutally cold air, strong wind and icy street made it

almost impossible for us to walk up that one sloped street. At that time, we were the only people out walking in the brutal storm. There were absolutely no cars and no people anywhere to be seen.

As we struggled against the wind and icy ground to maneuver up the slanted street, I prayed to Saint Anne and asked her to please ask her Grandson, Jesus, to send us a taxi cab.

When we reached the corner of York Avenue, there was a taxi cab waiting for us! It had a soft, golden light shining inside … and a smiling driver waiting for us!

As soon as we got settled inside the warm, cozy cab, Daddy said to the driver, "You must be an angel sent by God to help us! Nobody else is out tonight in this terrible storm!"

"We are happy to serve," the driver said as the cab slowly made its way 12 blocks along York Avenue to the apartment building where we lived in Yorkville.

When we arrived, I carefully got out of the taxi cab still closely snuggling the baby bundled in my arms. Looking up, I could see all of my siblings sitting at our second floor window watching us with great anticipation.

Their cheers were so loud, they could be heard well above the howling winds! Once inside our warm apartment, we all huddled together in the living room in front of the Christmas tree. With baby Diana sitting happily in the center of us all, Daddy told everyone how a taxi cab was miraculously waiting for us at the corner of the hospital … 12 blocks away!

Nodding with tears in her eyes, Mommy added, "You know, we never told the taxi driver where we live; we never told him where to take us! **He knew exactly where to go!**"

"I guess he really was an angel sent by God," Daddy says.

Mommy then led us all in a prayer of great joy in thanksgiving to God for the wonderful Christmas gift He gave our family that extraordinary Christmas Eve.

Chapter 19

THE DEVIL'S CHAIR

The demon had lately become more audacious in its efforts to consume my spirit, my soul. I was now afraid to sleep at night because I had been awakened several times from a sound sleep to discover the demon lurking in the shadows of my room seething, leering at me, casting its intense hatred and disdain upon me.

It appeared to be waiting for my weakest moment to seize me, carry me off again into the darkness. As soon as I remembered to pray in the name of Jesus, it would leave. Several times during the day, I saw things fall over or be violently thrown about in whatever room I happened to be in. Wherever I went, I sensed its presence nearby … except when I was in St. Monica's Church or in our Catholic grade school.

My younger brother, Larry, and I lay down opposite each other in what had become our shared bed … two thickly cushioned arm chairs pushed together in the living room. No lights were on in our small apartment. At the time, the rest of our family was trying to sleep in their beds located in the other rooms of our apartment.

Suddenly, Larry and I both sensed the approach of a demon. It was heading toward the living room where we then sat bolt upright facing each other.

Larry quickly moved next to me, and whispered, "Bobby, I sense the Devil is coming toward us! Do you sense it too?"

I acknowledged his words as the closed French doors slowly swung open as the demon entered our room and positioned itself to the left of the left French door facing us.

It was a frightening demon that presented itself in an enormous size. Even in the darkness of our room, its jet-black figure could clearly be seen. The top of its featureless head nearly touched the ceiling. Strangely, slight puffs of dark, charcoal-colored smoke slowly came out of the middle of its shrouded figure.

Larry screamed out, “Mommy, please come help us! There is a devil in the room with us!”

Mommy didn’t respond so Larry cried out even louder, “Mommy, **PLEASE** come help us! There is a devil in the living room by the French door! **PLEASE help us!”**

With the monstrous demon glaring down upon us, the left French door slowly moved away from the wall and closed … squeaking eerily all the way!

As Larry cried out again for help, the French door started moving again as it opened and rested against the wall … squeaking once again as it did.

The French door remained still for the moment as I finally heard that Mommy was awake! Thank God! She woke up Daddy, and told him that there was a devil in the living room where Larry and I were trapped.

“You’ve got to go help them, Patsy,” Mommy cried.

“Oh, for God’s sake,” Daddy complained, “what now? Can’t a man get a decent night’s sleep around here?”

“Stop complaining, and go help them!” Mommy shouted at him.

While Daddy went out to put on the kitchen light, Mommy came boldly right into the living room. Being eight months pregnant, she moved slowly and cautiously.

Without realizing it, she walked right in front of the demon and then said, “Oh, my God! It is so cold in here!”

Mommy apparently could not see the demon as Larry and I could.

As soon as Mommy turned on the lamps to the right and left of the sofa, I could no longer see the demon … but I could sense it was still stationed there to the left of the French door.

Stepping over to the open door, Mommy watched as the door began to move away from the wall toward her. Protecting the baby in her tummy, Mommy quickly backed away. When the French door was halfway closed, she abruptly raised her right hand in front of the door. Surprisingly, the door flashed back away from Mommy's hand so fast that it was suddenly back against the wall!

It moved so fast, I almost did not see it happen!

Daddy now arrived and immediately said, "Holy God, this room is freezing!"

The mention of God obviously angered the demon. The left French door slowly moved away from the wall and began closing again all by itself as it continued that eerie squeaking sound.

Seeing this, Mommy stepped away but Daddy stepped over to the door and ripped off the curtain that was hanging on it. As he did, the door slowly opened once again right in front of him!

Mommy, Larry, and I quickly went into the next room, and watched as Daddy stepped over to the door and firmly grasped the doorknob with both hands and leaned all his weight against the door holding it securely against the wall.

I could sense that this only further infuriated the demon.

Shockingly, the French door slowly began to open despite Daddy's mighty efforts to prevent it from moving!

"God damn it!" Daddy cried as he finally had to let go of the doorknob and step back out of the way of the squeaking door.

As the French door slowly closed, Mommy began to pray out loud. Daddy stomped out toward the kitchen saying that he knew exactly how to "stop all this nonsense."

He returned dragging along the very, very, heavy wooden "captain's chair" from the kitchen.

"Be careful, Patsy," Mommy cautioned him. "There's a

devil in there doing that to the door!"

Without hesitating, Daddy went right over to the French door, and wickedly jammed the heavy captain's chair at a forty-five degree angle under the doorknob of the door virtually locking the door into place against the wall.

Stepping away, Daddy said, "There, that should keep the God-damn door in place! Now let's see something move it!"

Daddy stepped back to stand between Larry and me in the next room. Mommy, afraid of what might now happen, stood directly behind Daddy to protect her and the baby in her tummy.

We stood together in silence and watched to see what, if anything, would now happen. I sensed the intense anger of the demon; it was absolutely furious to be so challenged by Daddy… especially with me and the others watching.

A powerful atmosphere of evil enveloped us as the captain's chair shockingly began to slowly scrape a few inches against the living room floor while the French door slowly moved away from the wall! It stopped moving as if the demon wanted to make sure we were all watching.

Mommy prayed even louder; Daddy began to shake.

In the flash of a moment, the captain's chair was violently turned to the left even though it was still jammed up against and under the doorknob of the French door! After a few seconds, the heavy captain's chair violently flew high up into the air to our left and lodged itself in the area between the ceiling and the adjoining wall. The French door remained perfectly still.

The sturdy captain's chair just hung up there in the air lodged against the wall and ceiling. Then in a flash, the captain's chair was slammed down at lightning speed onto the floor where it was broken up into countless little pieces! Now, the French door slowly closed and cast off that terrible, eerie squeaking sound.

Larry and I held onto each other as Daddy collapsed,

falling hard to his knees onto the floor next to Larry and me. He was sobbing as he repeatedly made the Sign of the Cross.

Mommy stumbled backward and nearly fell as she also made the Sign of the Cross and prayed for God's help.

As suddenly as this diabolical attack had begun, it ended. Our home was no longer filled with an air of a demonic, onerous presence. This latest event made it abundantly clear that the demon was more audacious than ever. It clearly wanted to impress upon us who was the "captain" in our humble home.

It was time to call the exorcist once again.

Chapter 20

THE BABY IS CHOKING!

This is an extraordinary true story about an encounter I had with the greatest of all spirits … the Holy Spirit.

This story actually begins when my wife, Margie, and I were 22, a young married couple already blessed with two children - our daughter, Peggie, and our first son, Rob. At the time, we were living in a very small, three-room apartment we rented in Flatbush, Brooklyn.

We had saved nearly enough money for a down payment on an old vacant, two-story house we were interested in buying on Lefferts Boulevard in Richmond Hill, Queens. It was owned by a local real estate company located only a block away from the house. It was the lowest priced house in the neighborhood and had more than enough space for our needs. However, it required a down payment that was more than we had at the time.

Margie and I sat with our two little babies and prayed for God's guidance on how to proceed. An inspiration came to mind almost right away! We believed it was the Holy Spirit's answer to our prayers so we decided to act upon it. I made an appointment to speak with the owner of the real estate company, a lady named Irene.

At our meeting, I repeated the inspiration that came after praying, "Margie and I want to buy your house but we don't have enough money for the down payment so we prayed for God's advice. He suggested that we ask you to loan us the balance of the down payment needed which I can pay off by working for you as one of your real estate salesmen!"

Irene sat back and looked shocked to hear this suggestion.

I quickly added, "That way, you'll get to sell the house at the price you want … and you'll have one of the top salesmen in all of Queens."

Irene laughed, "I can't believe you just suggested that I loan you my money … to buy my house! In all my years, no one has ever done that!"

After she stopped laughing, she said, "Well … anyone with that much gall to make a sale is going to make a great salesman in this business! I agree."

I thanked her and explained that I could only sell homes during the day because at the time I was a junior clerk on the night shift at the New York Stock Exchange on Wall Street.

She shook her head again and laughed, "Of course."

After we signed the necessary papers, we rented a small truck and with the help of my brother, Larry, we moved ourselves from our tiny apartment on East 9th Street in Flatbush, Brooklyn to our first home on Lefferts Boulevard in Richmond Hill, Queens.

And so, Margie and I joyfully moved into our first home with our one year-old little girl, Peggie, our new baby, Rob, a few pieces of furniture … and lots of faith. The first thing we did after moving in was to sit together on the floor of the empty living room and say a prayer of thanksgiving for our good fortune.

We had virtually no money left after we made the down payment so the only furniture we had were the few pieces of furniture we had in from our small Flatbush apartment. But we were happy, very happy.

We located the local Catholic church, Our Lady of Perpetual Help, on 115th Street in South Ozone Park where we began to attend services and prayed for God's continued blessings on our young family.

Every morning I walked one block to the real estate office where I worked as a salesman after passing the licensing test. In late afternoon, I would walk to the "A" train at the corner of Lefferts Boulevard and Liberty Avenue and ride the subway all the way to the Wall Street area where I walked to the New York

Stock Exchange and worked until midnight.

That trip to and from Queens and Manhattan every day gave me special time to pray and reflect. My long day and hectic schedule also gave me a good appreciation for the long hours, hard work and personal sacrifices mothers give every day in caring for their families.

When not working, I spent whatever time I could with Margie, the kids … and fixing things in the old house that had become our humble but happy home. With such a hectic schedule, I went on only a few hours sleep a night but was happy to do this for my family. I realized, however, that this meant I could not always be there to help Margie or to watch over our little ones.

That is when I turned to God and begged Him to look over and protect Margie and our children in my absence. I trusted with every fiber of my being that God was listening and would help.

It wasn't too long before my faith was rewarded.

On a hot summer day, six months after I started working at the real estate office, I was at the office working with a couple who were looking for a home in Richmond Hill. As we looked through the book of listings for available homes, a frightening vision suddenly filled my mind. I envisioned my eight-month old son, Rob, sitting in his baby carriage in the backyard of our home … choking to death on leaves that were stuck in his throat!

I told the couple sitting at my desk to continue looking over the listings while I went "to take care of something!" With that, I literally ran out of the office as fast as I could and sped directly to my home a block away.

Never doubting the reality of the vision I saw, I knew that every second could mean the difference between life and death for my son. I prayed as I ran across moving traffic at the corner of Lefferts Boulevard and Liberty Avenue, and continued running as fast as possible to my home now half a block away.

When I got there, I ran along the walkway on the left side of our home and entered the backyard. There to my horror, I saw baby Rob gagging on green leaves! He was already turning blue from the lack of oxygen. He was sitting in his gray carriage right next to the privet hedge where he apparently had been pulling the leaves off and eating them … exactly as I had seen in my vision.

Margie was right inside the back door at the time washing dishes at the kitchen sink. When she saw me running past the side window, she came rushing out to join me.

I carefully pinched the leaves I could see lodged in the back of Rob's throat, removed them, then repeated the process until I could see no more left. Holding him upside down, I then pressed the back of his tongue downward causing him to throw up. Still more leaves that were lodged in his throat came out!

A quick look in his mouth confirmed that his air passageway was now clear. With a loud gasp, baby Rob began to breathe normally. Rather than crying after such a terrible ordeal, baby Rob smiled at us!

Margie and I did the crying as we stood there in bright sunlight hugging our little baby, and thanking God. Little did we know at the time that this would not be the last time that God would reward our faith in an extraordinary way with our son.

There are several morals to this story – and this book - but high among them is the great value of praying in faith to God for what you and loved ones need. And for parents, in particular, trust your instincts! Can you imagine if I had not!

Stay close to God through prayer and the sacraments – Confession, Mass and Communion, and remember what Jesus tells us in Matthew 19:26, "With God, ALL things are possible!"

Chapter 21

"CAN YOU HEAL ME TOO?"

While attending a little league baseball game with my son, Jimmy, a loud, disturbing sound of a crash filled the air from the street next to the ballfield.

A terrible, heart-rendering scream followed.

I ran to see what happened and discovered a 12 year old boy sprawled in the street bleeding and badly injured. The bones in his left leg were protruding grotesquely through his pants by his thigh and lower leg! He had been run down by a motorcycle that was speeding up the street. The motorcycle was on its side 20 feet farther up in the street with the dazed-looking driver standing next to it.

I knew the boy who was badly injured. He was Vinny, one of the students I had in my Confirmation class at Ss. Cyril and Methodius Church in Deer Park where I was a religious education catechist at the time. I asked one of the bystanders to call 911, and knelt down next to Vinny who was conscious and terrified.

I tried to reassure him, "Hi, Vinny. You're okay but you should stay as still as you can. We're going to take you for a ride in an ambulance so the doctors at the hospital can check you out."

"My leg burns and hurts pretty bad, Mr. Walsh. Is it okay?"

Thank God … Vinny couldn't see how very badly his leg was injured.

"Yeah, it's okay, Vinny; it's just a little scraped up, that's all. Does anything else hurt?"

"I kinda hurt all over."

"That's okay. Don't worry, Vinny, you'll be okay. Just lie still for me. Okay?"

"Thanks, Mr. Walsh. Please stay with me … I'm scared."

"Sure, Vinny. I'll stay with you."

I silently prayed that God would spare Vinny from suffering … and heal his terrible injuries.

When the ambulance arrived, I stayed where Vinny could see me at all times as the medics examined him before carefully securing his leg for the trip to Good Samaritan Hospital nearby. I explained to the medics that I was Vinny's catechist from St. Cyril's Church and that Vinny wanted me to stay with him since his family wasn't here.

"Yes," Vinny called out, "Please let Mr. Walsh stay with me. Please!"

Worried that Vinny might slip into shock, the medics allowed me to ride in the back of the ambulance with Vinny. My wife, Margie, stayed at the ball field with our son, Jimmy, while I rode in the ambulance with Vinny. On the way to the hospital, I sat right next to him and held his hand … and kept smiling. He never took his eyes off me … not for a second … as the ambulance sped along. I continued praying silently for God's help and mercy on Vinny.

When we arrived at the hospital, I assured Vinny that I would stay nearby as he was rushed into the emergency room, "I'll be right outside, Vinny."

While the doctors were conducting their preliminary examination, Vinny's frantic parents arrived and spoke with the doctors. They came out of the meeting crying.

Vinny's father explained, "The doctors tell us his leg is broken so badly in several places, they are not sure what they can do! They say they're not sure if they can save his leg!"

Vinny's mother grabbed me by the shoulders, "God listens to you, Mr. Walsh. Please go in there right now and pray over Vinny before they take him to the operating room. Ask God to heal him, please!"

"We told the doctors we want you to pray over Vinny

before they operate on him so they're waiting for you," Vinny's father added, "You better go in there now."

I quickly entered the private emergency room where Vinny and the doctors were waiting. As soon as I entered, I was greeted by a big smile and greeting from Vinny. I assumed the IV hooked up to him was administering pain medication because he didn't appear to be suffering from his horrific injuries.

"Mom and Dad said you were going to pray for me," he said eagerly.

"Yes, I am, Vinny. I'd like you to pray with me. Okay?"

As Vinny nodded, I closed my eyes and eased down into the inner recesses of my being where all I can sense is the presence of God. I asked Him to please heal Vinny … completely … and spare him any suffering. When I opened my eyes, I discovered Vinny had gone off to sleep.

Turning to the medical staff, I said, "God bless you for all the healing you do with the gifts God has given you."

A saturating peace come over me as I watched the medical people hurriedly transport Vinny off to the operating room.

I joined Vinny's parents outside in the waiting room, I told them, "Vinny joined me in praying for God's graces to heal him and keep him from suffering. He's sleeping now and is on his way to the operating room. Let's pray for his healing."

Standing together in the waiting room, we held hands and prayed for God's mercy and healing. Before leaving, I asked them to let me know how things progress. Throughout that evening and the following day, I kept my promise to continue praying earnestly for Vinny's healing. Late one day, Vinny's mother called with an extraordinary update.

"The doctors said the surgery went quite well; they were able to save his leg but weren't too sure about how well he might be able to walk. However, they're now saying that something miraculous is happening! I want you to go to the hospital and find out for yourself. Besides, Vinny has been asking for you, Mr. Walsh. Please go visit him."

That afternoon, I went directly to Good Samaritan Hospital and went up to the floor where Vinny's room was located. I stopped at the nurse's station to confirm which room Vinny was in.

"Oh, you're here to see the 'miracle boy,' Vinny," the head nurse said mysteriously.

When I asked what she meant, she explained, "Vinny's leg was virtually shattered when he came in to the emergency room yesterday but now … it is miraculously healing itself … all on its own! And amazingly, the boy feels no pain even though he's not getting any pain meds!"

Over hearing this, another nurse came over and added, "Oh, you must be talking about Vinny. You should have heard his mother taking about some man, a 'healer,' who came from St. Cyril's Church and prayed over the boy in the emergency room before the doctors operated. I have to tell you … I am not someone who has ever believed in miracles … but looking at what has happened with Vinny now I know that miracles are for real!"

I smiled and said, "Well, Jesus did say that with God all things are possible! That is … when we turn to Him in faith."

The nurse then smiled, "You're the healer, aren't you?"

"No … Jesus is the healer … I am just the witness."

I left them and made my way to Vinny's room where I discovered there were three other boys sharing the room with him. Vinny greeted me with a big smile and told me how the doctors and nurses were calling him the "miracle boy."

When I asked why, Vinny in his youthful innocence matter-of-factly replied, "Because my bones are healing all by themselves … and I have no pain at all!"

Then without hesitation, Vinny called out to the other

three boys in the room with him, "This is the man, Mr. Walsh, I told you about. He's the one who asked God to heal me … and God did!"

The little boy directly across from Vinny asked, "Hello, mister. Do you think you can ask God to heal me too?" Before I could answer, the other two boys called out and also asked me to pray for them as well. So I stood by each boy's bedside – one at a time - and extending my hands above each, I asked God to pour out healing graces from His Sacred Heart and send them showering down upon each of the children.

Standing in the center of the room, I invited them all to pray together with me to Jesus to ask Him to heal all the other people who are in the hospital. This was such a special, holy moment to be joined by young innocent children - and their guardian angels - praying together.

As I was leaving the room, one of the boys said, "Hey mister … I feel better already!"

"Me, too," another boy said.

As I looked to the third boy, he said, "I don't feel better … but my pain is gone!"

Chapter 22

FATHER JOHN LAZANSKI

One of the most moving spiritual events of my life occurred unexpectedly on a bright Sunday afternoon in Boston, Massachusetts in late 1980.

In Boston on business over the weekend, I walked over to St. Anthony's Shrine on Arch Street to attend the one o'clock Sunday Mass. This was to be the first of many extraordinary visits to this holy site.

Upon entering, I was immediately impressed by the powerful presence of God in the Blessed Sacrament in this relatively small church. I was also struck by the size of the congregation present awaiting Mass. The church was jamb-packed with people quietly praying before Mass. There was little to no room to stand anywhere in the back of the church or on either of the two sides.

Curiously, however, I noticed there was one seat available in the fourth pew up in the front right section. After quickly making my way up there, I politely squeezed into the second seat from the aisle.

After saying my initial prayers before Mass, I noticed that I happened to be the only man sitting in this pew … and all the ladies were staring at me and whispering to one another! Each one greeted me with a warm smile and an enthusiastic nod as if they somehow expected me. I had the very distinct feeling they were aware of something I wasn't … but I also sensed that I would soon find out what was behind their curious behavior.

As the music started for Mass to begin, I was surprised to see a tall, elderly priest in brilliantly colored liturgical garb come out from the sacristy on the right side literally jumping up and down as he entered the sanctuary banging on a tambourine!

As he danced around the sanctuary, I studied his appearance. Well over six feet tall, he was quite thin with gray, wiry hair, and a face that was so deeply wrinkled it was a little scary-looking! Despite his daunting appearance, I immediately sensed there was something quite holy and extraordinary about the priest. I would soon learn why I had this feeling.

After the singing ended, the priest reverently genuflected in front of the altar and began to pray. I would later learn that this highly-charismatic priest was quite famous throughout the Boston area … and well beyond. His name was Father John Lazanski, a Franciscan priest who was stationed at the small St. Anthony's Shrine since 1965. He was 71 at the time I first met him that fateful day.

A native of Pottsville, Pennsylvania, Father John entered the Franciscan order in 1942, was ordained in 1948 and served as a missionary in Sri Lanka from 1952 to 1961. At St. Anthony's Shrine in 1975, he helped form a remarkable ministry of healing while playing a prominent part in the charismatic movement in the Boston area. At the heart of his healing ministry were healing prayer services he conducted at the Shrine on Sundays after the p.m. Mass. Over the years, reports spread far and wide describing the many miracles that occurred when he prayed over people.

After this Mass I attended, Father John announced to the congregation that the usual healing prayer service would then begin. He said, "As we usually do, I and my brother priests will go around the church and stop at each pew to pray over whoever is located in the first or second aisle seat in each pew."

These words set off a resounding wave of cries, singing, prayers and supplications rising from every corner of the small church. As Father John made his way around the far left side of the church, I sensed the glorious presence of God in the Blessed Sacrament along with the Blessed Mother, the angels and saints. Joyful cries filled the air announcing that some healing that had taken place over in that area of the church unseen from where I was standing.

Before long, Father John made his way up the center aisle praying over people in each pew as he did. Just when he arrived at the pew I was in, a distraught mother came rushing up the center aisle with her little daughter in tow. The little girl looked terrified as she limped up alongside her mother and clung to her. Sadly, her right leg was badly deformed. It appeared to be several inches shorter than the other leg … and her right foot was locked up in a position where the heel was stuck up a few inches off the ground.

The mother sobbed loudly with a strong Irish accent as she beseeched Father John to heal her poor daughter.

Father John surprised me by shouting at her, "Mother! Mother! Be still! For the love of God, stop babbling at me! I want you to use that same emotion to beg God to heal your daughter … NOT ME! It is God and God alone who heals!"

"What is your daughter's name?"

"Maggie. Her name is Maggie, a nick name for Margaret."

"Ah … of course," Father said softly, "little Maggie … God's little pearl!"

I looked at little Maggie; she appeared to be no more than seven years old. And she still looked terrified by what was happening around her. I felt so sad for her, this innocent little child of God. At that moment, I loved her as if she were my own little daughter.

As soon as little Maggie looked up into Father John's eyes, something quite amazing happened. Her appearance of fear and anxiety completely vanished - replaced by an expression of utter joy and peace! It was as if a shade in a darkened room was gradually lifted up allowing bright, glorious sunshine to rush in and fill the room!

Given Father John's rather intimidating facial appearance, I found little Maggie's instant reaction to Father John so impressive. This was especially impressive given that she was such a small, frail child standing before such a tall, rather scary-looking priest in the midst of the large, noisy gathering of highly-charged, emotional strangers in the crowded church.

Father had two other priests bring out a wooden chair for little Maggie to sit on right there in the center of the aisle. Neither one of her little thin legs could reach the floor. Father John then knelt down on the hard ceramic floor directly in front of little Maggie. Her eyes never lost sight of his.

Turning to me and the others standing in the pew to his immediate left, Father said, "Your group will be the immediate prayer group joining me to ask Our Lord to heal this little child of His."

As I prayed fervently from the inner recesses of my heart and soul, I watched Father John place his left hand under little Maggie's badly deformed right knee, and his right hand under her locked right foot. Father John then raised his head toward the heavens and prayed fervently in words that were barely-audible.

Then, amazingly, Father John gently, matter-of-factly stretched little Maggie's right leg and foot to a normal size! Just like that – without thunder or lightening – little Maggie's short leg and locked foot were miraculously healed by God at the hands of Father John!

Rising and holding little Maggie's right hand, Father John walked around the center aisle with her so that everyone could plainly see that both her legs were now the same length … and her right foot was no longer locked in an upward position!

Little Maggie's mother was so shocked, she stumbled backward with her eyes bulging as she collapsed in a heap onto the ceramic floor. While some people were attending to her, something else utterly remarkable happened.

One of the priests brought out a large, portable microphone and handed it to Father John who immediately used it to shout out a question to little Maggie.

His words reverberated roundly throughout the public access system, "Do you know what just happened?"

Then he thrust the large microphone directly in front of little Maggie's face so she could answer.

Without hesitation, she joyfully replied in her delicate voice, "Yes … Jesus healed me!"

Before I could reflect on the profound significance of her words, Father John surprised me by quickly following up with yet another question for this innocent child.

"Why?" he asked.

He again thrust the large microphone in front of her little face.

From the inner beauty and innocence of her youth, little Maggie simply explained, "Because He loves me!"

Father John roundly smiled and nodded in agreement.

Poetically, little Maggie then held her mother's hand and led her back down the center aisle … walking perfectly normally!

While I was still processing what had just happened, Father John turned to the pew I was in and immediately clasped the right hand of the lady in the first seat next to me. Both his hands caressed her hand as he asked what she would like Jesus to do for her.

The lady's entire body was visibly quivering as she looked up into the face of the much taller priest and explained, "My hand is so deformed from arthritis that it's been locked in a closed fist for many years."

Surprisingly, Father sternly asked, "Do you harbor any unforgiveness toward anyone?"

Hesitantly, she replied, "No, Father. No. I have no unforgiveness against anyone in my heart."

With his eyes closed, Father John now appeared to be deep in prayer.

Then he, asked, “Do you truly believe that Jesus can heal your hand?”

“Yes, Father, I do.”

Nodding, Father John abruptly pulled away both his hands and shouted, “Then what are you waiting for? Open your hand, woman!”

Trembling, she slowly and dramatically raised her badly deformed hand high into the air where everyone could see it. Then amazingly … she slowly, fully opened it for the first time in many years!

“Now you must be like the one leper who went back to thank Jesus,” Father told her. “Make sure you thank Him!”

Leaning forward, Father then placed his right hand firmly on top of my head and began to pray for me! As he did, a powerful stream of graces poured down upon me from above! When I looked into his eyes, it was like looking into two mystical pools of spiritual goodness and holiness.

“There’s a special aura of light around you,” he said. “Come to see me afterward.”

In the next instant, he moved on to pray over someone else further up the aisle.

The lady to my right nudged me and said, “You think that was amazing, eh? I want you to look closely at the lady next to me.”

When I did, I was confused because I didn’t see anything that struck me as unusual about her.

“I am sorry but all I see before me is a lovely, very Irish-looking lady,” I said.

Smiling, the lady said, “You see me looking at you, don’t you?”

I nodded yes.

Then the lady took a copy of the Boston Globe Newspaper out of her pocketbook and held it up for me to read. On the front page was a large photo of the lady with one word printed in large letters at the top, **"MIRACLE!"**

The caption underneath stated that she had been blind from birth but after Father John Lazanski prayed over her at St. Anthony's Shrine on Arch Street, she was able to see!

I looked back and forth from the lady's eyes and the front page of the newspaper and realized what had happened.

The lady added, "Weeks ago, I was standing right where you are right now when Father John came by and prayed over me. When he removed his hands from my eyes, I could see for the very first time in my life!"

The other lady added, "When you came in here earlier, we sensed that there was a special reason you decided to sit right here with us. You had no way of knowing that the seat you took in this pew was reserved for us prayer-warriors who pray with Father John in his healing ministry!"

The lady who was healed of blindness, added, "We heard what Father John said to you about having a special aura. You have to follow up with him."

A third lady said, "Knowing Father John, you're being here today was no coincidence, no coincidence at all!"

When I finally got to visit Father John weeks later, he said that he remembered me quite well from the day little Maggie was healed.

"You were right there praying with me when God healed that precious child. Her mother tells me the doctors were amazed. They said it was a remarkable miracle … something they had never seen before!

"Then, I remember seeing you with a beautiful light, an aura, surrounding you that day. Clearly, that signified for me that you are one of those people whom God blesses in every age with the gift of healing. Having said that, there are some important things for you to understand.

"First of all, the gift of healing comes with a great responsibility; as Jesus says, 'To those whom much is given, much is expected!' That means you are accountable to almighty God to use the gift He has entrusted into your care! You must freely use this gift, and NEVER withhold it from anyone whom God sends your way. Therein lies my greatest fear … that I may not properly use the gift of healing! Please pray, Bob, that I never fail to use the gifts God has given me.

"In terms of healing ministry, there are some important things I want to make sure you are aware of. When you pray over someone, do not allow yourself to doubt - for even a second - whether or not God can heal them … no matter how impossible it may seem to you. Remember Christ's words, 'With God, ALL THINGS ARE POSSIBLE!'

"At times, you may become doubtful about the gift of healing. When this happens, I want you to remember that ***God is not an Indian giver!*** Once God gives a gift, He doesn't take it back … whether or not you believe you have such a gift … and whether or not you use it!

"There's one more thing … something that could be a matter of spiritual life and death. When the Devil comes after you as surely it will, it is critical that you strictly follow the teachings of the Church in terms of the deliverance prayers you say when battling the demons. You must never use the prayers that are reserved only for priests. In the heat of the battle, you must always have more faith in God than you have fear of the Devil. Do you understand what I am saying, Bob?"

"Yes, father, I fully understand. I only use prayers of deliverance that are allowed for members of the laity like me. And, I have already been subjected to fierce attacks by the devil many times while I was ministering to people tormented by the demons."

At his request, I shared many of the experiences I had in deliverance ministry. Father John listened intently and a number of times appeared greatly concerned.

"You must always be prepared, Bob, for such encounters by going to Confession, Mass, Communion, fasting and praying! To do so otherwise, can be spiritually fatal for you and the victim. Do you understand?"

"Yes, Father, I understand. Thank you for your advice."

Father appeared to relax as he said, "Now tell me about some of the times you witnessed the miraculous Hand of God healing people."

As I shared some of the breath-taking miracles I had witnessed in my lifetime, Father John was so elated he acted as if he were watching his favorite baseball team scoring the winning runs in the World Series! He explained that some of these miracles reminded him of similar events in his ministry.

Apparently reminiscing, Father shared, "I have seen the Lord's mystery of love expressed in healing for all forms of suffering for the mind, body … and the spirit! Truly … nothing is beyond His capacity to heal our deepest wounds."

Father John then conducted an hour-long prayer service in which he anointed me in healing ministry which he said included deliverance. Afterward, he asked me to pray over him before we shared a prayer of thanksgiving to God.

Over succeeding years, I visited Father John a number of times and together, we prayed for people who had requested healing prayer. In many of these cases, I later learned that God had answered their prayers in remarkable, if not miraculous, ways.

One time when I stopped at the rectory for a visit, I was surprised to see the lobby of the rectory was completely filled with priests from one end to the other! I made my way up to the front desk where I asked if a call could be made to let Father John know that his "friend from New York," as he called me, was there for a visit.

The priest shook his head and said, "I am sorry, Father John cannot have visitors; he is gravely ill. We don't expect him to be with us very long."

I was surprised and deeply saddened to hear this; I had no idea he was that sick.

"I am so sorry to hear that," I said, "but Father John made me promise that whenever I came by to visit that I would let him know. So, please call up and let him know that his "friend from New York" is here to say hello.

"It was HIS request," I stressed. "Please call up and leave that message for him. Thank you."

The young priest looked annoyed but did as I asked. After giving the message, he listened to something in return that appeared to surprise him.

After hanging up the phone, he turned and directed his remarks to the room full of priests, Father John said he's coming down to see his friend from New York!"

Every priest in the lobby looked at me and wondered who I was that Father John would come down off his death bed to see me!

I laughed and told them, "Look, fathers, I'm no one special, Father John is your saint! Nothing he does should surprise you."

That did little to stop the priests from staring at me while we all waited for Father John to come down from his room on the second floor. And come down he did with the assistance of another priest. Father John was crouched over holding onto an IV pole while the assistant priest carried a small oxygen tank for him!

Smiling, he paused at the foot of the stairs and said, "My friend, I've been waiting for you. Come … God sent you to tell me what I need to know!"

With all the room of priests looking on, Father John and I made our way slowly off to a small room in the back where we usually met. After I helped Father John get settled, he immediately explained, "I have been so sick that I cannot get out of bed to celebrate Mass and pray over people as I have done my entire priesthood. Every time I have asked God to heal me so I can get up and do so once again, I see a vision of your face! That tells me that God has sent you here today to tell me what it is that I need to know. So please tell me!"

Surprised by this, I blurted out, "Father, I am sorry, I have no idea what it is that God wants you to know!"

Annoyed, Father gathered up enough energy to snap at me, "Don't you understand? What you have to say is not important; it is what God wishes to tell me. So close your eyes and empty your mind so God can let you know what it is that He wants me to know! Tell me whatever comes into your mind!"

After sitting in complete peace and quiet, I was surprised that a wonderful, remarkable memory did come to mind!

I recalled a Friday night Mass I had attended years earlier at the Church of the Miraculous Medal in Wyandanch, Long Island. At the Consecration of the Mass, the pastor, Father Basil, invited me and two homeless people who were there to come up and stand around the altar.

As he raised the Eucharistic Host, I distinctly heard the voice of God clearly say to me, **"Here I am!"**

I immediately understood what God's words meant. God was telling me that through the Mystical Body of Christ, God was miraculously present in the consecrated Host, in Father Basil, in me ... and in the two homeless people present! And so, I told Father John that this was the only thing that came to mind.

Father John immediately began to cry out and praise God so loudly that several priests came rushing in to see what the stranger from New York was doing to their saintly Father John!

He gruffly ordered them to leave, "Get out! Let us be! I got my answer! God let me know what I need to know through my friend here from New York!"

Once the priests left, Father John explained, "50 years ago, right out of the seminary, my very first assignment was to the parish of the Miraculous Medal in Wyandanch, Long Island! At that time, I wasn't yet aware that I was blessed with the gift of healing. My greatest spiritual gift was prayer … deep, abiding, faith-filled prayer!

"And so, God is reminding me that even if I cannot get up out of bed, I can still pray for people!"

"I am so happy you got your answer, Father."

"Thank you, Bob. But now that I understand … I still want to get up, say Mass and pray over people as I have done my whole priesthood! So … please pray that God will heal me!"

As I did, I felt the familiar ecstatic shower of graces pour down upon Father John. I left without speaking with any of the priests outside.

About one year later, my wife, Margie, and I stopped at St. Anthony's rectory and asked to see Father John.

The young priest at the desk said, "I am awfully sorry to tell you but Father John recently went to God on December 22, 1991 following a long, painful illness. As you may know, Father John was blessed with a remarkable, miraculous healing ministry"

"Did anything unusual happen before he died?" I wanted to know.

"Well, yes, it was actually about a year ago that he was on his death bed when someone he called his 'friend from New York' came to visit. Father John later told us that his friend told him what God wanted him to know … and then he prayed over Father John.

"The very next day, Father John got off his death bed and

celebrated Mass and prayed over people 'till the day he died! Our 'miracle worker' was himself miraculously healed through the intercession of some layperson, a healer unknown to all of us who lived with Father John.

"Unfortunately, before he died, Father John didn't tell anyone who this 'friend from New York' was … or what it was that he told Father John God wanted him to know. And none of us have any idea who this 'friend from New York' is!"

"I know who he is," Margie said mischievously.

The young priest laughed but seeing that Margie was serious, he begged, "We priests would love to know so we can find out what it was that this 'friend from New York' told Father John about what God wanted him to know."

Margie looked to me and said, "You are looking at him! My husband, Bob, is Father John's 'friend from New York!' He can tell you exactly what he told Father John that day."

I explained what happened that fateful day a year earlier - how God reminded Father John that his greatest gift was not the gift of healing … it was, in fact, the power of prayer … and that the greatest healing prayer, of course, is the Eucharist.

Thank you, God, for the gift of the Eucharist … and for my beloved friend and spiritual advisor, Father John Lazanski.

Chapter 23

MIRACLE OF THE EUCHARIST

Soon after being anointed in the healing ministry by Father John Lazanski, I was serving as an Eucharistic Minister in my parish, Ss. Cyril and Methodius, in Deer Park, Long Island, New York. It was then that I was blessed to witness a glorious, utterly remarkable miracle of the Eucharist.

I was the last Eucharistic Minister to leave the altar area with the presiding priest, Father Thaddeus Rooney, our pastor. The ciborium he handed me contained very few consecrated Hosts in it … barely enough to cover the bottom. Waiting there for him to give me additional Hosts from an extra ciborium, I was stunned to watch him put all the extra Hosts into his ciborium! He then gruffly motioned for me to go to my station to begin distributing the few Hosts I had!

To say I was annoyed is an understatement - especially since he and I would be distributing Holy Communion next to each other in the center aisle. That is the most populated one in our large church … and all I had were a few Hosts in my ciborium! Thank God I quickly realized how inappropriate my reaction was while serving Holy Communion. Feeling ashamed, I cried out to God to forgive my worldliness.

Still worried that I was going to run out of consecrated Hosts, I stood next to Father Rooney at the front of the center aisle and began distributing Holy Communion to each person who came up on my line. That is when I noticed that something incredible was happening … something utterly miraculous.

Each time I looked down into the ciborium to retrieve another Host, I could clearly see there were many more Hosts in the ciborium! At first, I thought I might be imaging what was happening but every time I looked back down into my ciborium, I clearly saw the group of Hosts actually moving quickly about as more and more Hosts miraculously appeared and filled the ciborium … higher and higher! Now I worried that the consecrated Hosts might actually spill over the top of my ciborium!

As the realization of what was happening more fully set in, a stream of warm, brilliant, golden light came cascading down upon Father Rooney and me through the stained glass windows high above us. I was immersed in the exhilarating, ecstatic graces of God in those holy moments until the last of the people on my line had received Holy Communion.

A feeling of indescribable joy filled me as I turned and dramatically held my ciborium out with both hands toward Father Rooney to show him that my ciborium was now miraculously full with consecrated Hosts up to the very brim! Father Rooney gave me a puzzled look and then simply emptied the remaining Hosts from his ciborium into mine and walked away!

It was obvious that Father Rooney was not aware of the remarkable miracle of multiplication of Eucharistic Hosts had just happened right next to where he was standing! I realized then that no one, in fact, in the entire Church knew what just happened! That is when is dawned on me that God had performed this miraculous multiplication of sacred Hosts just for me to witness and enjoy!

Lord, I am not worthy … but I thank you for allowing me to witness Your remarkable miracle of the Eucharist.

Chapter 24

"JUST ONE MORE CHRISTMAS!"

One day, my brother, Larry, asked if I would go pray over one of his best friends, Gary Wolcott, who was fighting inoperable brain cancer at the time.

The doctors at Sloan Kettering Memorial Cancer Hospital estimated that Gary had less than a few weeks to live. The cluster of brain tumors were the size of a golf ball leaving Gary paralyzed on the entire left side of his body. He was otherwise able to function and think normally.

Gary and his wife, Annette, were good, faith-filled Catholics who lived with their three children in a modest home in New Dorp, Staten Island, New York. On the day scheduled for healing prayer, I walked up the steep, inclined block where they lived. It was exceedingly hot and humid that Saturday afternoon in July.

As I struggled up the street, I couldn't help but notice the countless neighbors sitting on their stoops. It seemed that each and every one of them stopped what they were doing and stared at me as I walked by. When I got inside Gary's home and greeted the family and the local parish priest who joined us, I foolishly said that I couldn't believe how "nosey the neighbors are on this street!"

Gary smiled and gently explained, "All our neighbors are out there because they knew you were coming to lead us in a healing prayer service! They are planning to join us in prayer!"

I don't ever remember feeling more foolish and embarrassed!

As we prayed in the living room, Gary sat in a chair in the center so we could sit in a circle around him. While we were praying, Gary's children were running around the circle of chairs giggling and having fun. How beautiful this is, I thought. I imagined that this must have been what Jesus encountered so many times when He prayed over people.

I was impressed how Gary repeatedly said, "If this is my time to die, please Lord, let me live to enjoy one more Christmas with my family!"

Days following the healing prayer service, I was told that a miracle was happening! The doctors at Sloan Kettering Cancer Hospital said that Gary's cluster of brain tumors was shrinking ... and his paralysis was gradually easing! By Christmas, the tumors and paralysis were completely gone, so the oncologists declared it was an "**Act of God!**"

On January 1st, however, I received a phone call telling me that Gary died from a burst appendix! His wife, Annette, asked me to explain how God could get their hopes up by curing Gary of brain cancer, and then take him anyway from something as curable as appendicitis!

I reminded Annette how Gary had prayed during our healing prayer service that past July.

"Gary said if it was his time to die, he wanted God to allow him to enjoy one more Christmas with the family. Quite apparently, God granted Gary's wish but He wanted to make sure we realized it ... so He first miraculously healed Gary of the cancer."

When Annette remembered this, she realized that God had, in fact, miraculously blessed Gary and the family with one more Christmas together.

Chapter 25

THE "SPECIAL" AMBULANCE

When my son, Rob, was 17, both his lungs were collapsing one at a time. The thoracic pulmonary specialists at Stony Brook University Hospital on Long Island said the only way Rob could survive was to have the top 15% of both lungs removed since that area of each lung had "blebs" - a congenital condition in which there are no air sacs in that part of the lung. As Rob grew, pockets of air formed and burst causing the lung to collapse.

The only way this could be remedied at the time was for the surgeons to do a radical bilateral thoracotomy/blebectomy. This procedure involved cutting Rob open from the front of his body to the back to allow the surgeons to access the lungs to remove the apical section of the lungs – one lung at a time.

The doctors decided to operate on the right lung first since that one appeared to be weaker than the other. The surgery on the right lung went well except that the anesthesia and pain medications dangerously suppressed Rob's respiratory system!

Despite this, the surgeons said as soon as Rob recovered from the first surgery, they would have to operate as soon as possible on the left lung … before it collapsed again!

After Rob recovered from the first surgery, he was resting at home five days after we brought him home when at two o'clock in the morning, my wife, Margie, and I heard Rob moaning badly.

He could barely say, "Mom, Dad, my other lung went down! I can barely breathe … we have to go back to the hospital!"

The best hospital to take Rob to was, of course, the one where he was just operated on; they were completely familiar with his delicate condition. The only problem was that Stony Brook Hospital was a 45 minute car drive away from where we lived in Deer Park! Everything considered, we decided that was the best thing to do so I called ahead to Stony Brook's emergency room and told them about Rob's condition and asked them to alert Rob's surgeons to get ready because we were coming!

We placed Rob in the back of our station wagon where he could lay down. Margie was lying down next to him to comfort him while she quietly prayed. Realizing time may be the difference between life and death of our son, I drove as safely but quickly as I could along the empty highways.

Along the way, a police officer in an unmarked car pulled up alongside us … and looking in the back of our car, he could to see Rob and Margie lying there. He nodded to me and sped ahead with his police lights flashing as he led the way for us all the way to Stony Brook Hospital.

As soon as we arrived at Stony Brook's emergency room, several medical staff rushed Rob inside where he was quickly placed onto life support equipment. After his doctors examined him, they huddled a few feet away from where Margie and I were standing. They appeared quite concerned so I went over to them and asked what was wrong.

The lead surgeon, Doctor Alan Butler, said, "Mr. Walsh, we have a serious problem … his other lung has collapsed and is now pushing against his heart as it tries to fill the vacuum in his chest! He is hooked up to life support equipment in the ER but we need to get him to the operating room down that hallway to our right! We can't detach him from the life support equipment and we can't bring the operating room equipment we need here.

"And we are running out of time … his vital signs are dropping. I am afraid we are losing him!"

I told him, "Well, you doctors do your job and my wife and I will do ours … we are going to pray for a miracle that God will let us know what to do!"

I went over to Margie and told her the bad news. She

immediately began to cry.

I told her, "Margie, let's pray that God will tell us what to do right now."

Standing there in the hallway across from the doctors, we held hands, closed our eyes and prayed. I asked all the angels and saints, and all my relatives who are already with God to please ask God to tell us what to do. In the next instant, I got the answer.

My mind was filled with a vision of an ambulance parked in the Stony Brook Hospital's ER parking lot! I understood immediately what this meant.

I ran over to the doctors and excitedly told them, "Don't you have an ambulance that has life support equipment on it for accidents that happen out on the highway? Just unhook all that equipment and bring it all here to the ER so you can hook my son up to it and take him down the hall to the operating room!"

The doctors looked at one another and without saying a word, Dr. Butler turned and quickly used the phone to call someone.

After speaking with someone on the phone, he hung the phone up and turning to the other doctors, he dramatically said, "It's here!"

He quickly barked out several orders then the doctors all ran in different directions.

Turning to Margie and me, he said, "You may have just saved your son's life! There is only one ambulance on all of Suffolk County that has life support equipment … and it is here in our bay right now!"

Margie and I hugged the doctor.

He told us, "Keep praying! Please pray that we have enough time …your son is in very bad condition."

They were worried that the first lung was not healed and might also collapse causing death. In addition, he had a very bad reaction to the anesthesia from the surgery only a week before.

Soon, loud bells were going off as a group of doctors came literally running down the hallway pushing a gurney that had all kinds of tubes, wires and other equipment piled up on top of it. That was the life support equipment they had just disconnected from the one unique ambulance they just happened to have in the hospital's ER parking lot!

After they hooked Rob up to the equipment, Margie and I were allowed one minute to go in and see him. We didn't know if this would be the last time we would see our son. Given his dire circumstances, it was very difficult for us to be positive and uplifting but it was our job then to encourage him, to pick up his spirits going into yet another painful operation. Rob had been so tired, so worn out, in constant pain, so depressed from all his suffering.

We tried to appear as optimistic as possible as we encouraged him. I told him, "Rob, this is the final stage of healing for you! This is the last surgery you will need!"

He replied in barely audible words, "But what about the pain meds, Dad? They don't work for me!"

I smiled and told him, "Oh, they're going to work just fine this time; you'll see, son! Let's hold hands now and thank God for arranging this healing for you!"

Margie and I gave Rob a kiss then waited with him to be taken to the operating room. He was still in poor spirits after our prayer so I silently asked God to please help me do something to cheer him up. Just then, I remembered what a great sense of humor Rob had so I decided to try something silly.

I said, "Rob, we heard there is a **highly-flamboyant** gay fellow by the name of Jeffrey who works somewhere here in the hospital. Now, if he comes here to take you to the operating room, don't be surprised if he takes a liking to you because you're so good looking!"

Just as I finished saying this, a tall, very effeminate aide came sauntering in with his hands on his hips! Standing in front of Rob, he said, "Hi, I'm ***JEFFREY*** … I'm here to take you to the operating room! We're going to take very good care of you!"

Although it was painful for Rob to laugh, he smiled broadly and nodded his head. Margie and I stood there in the hallway watching Jeffrey happily singing as he rolled our greatly amused son on the gurney to the operating room! Afterward, Margie and I asked where we might find that wonderful aide, Jeffrey, so we could thank him and express our great appreciation for how he picked up Rob's spirits on the way to surgery.

The hospital staff told us that there was no aide on staff by the name of Jeffrey! Thank you once again God for hearing our prayers and answering them in so many wonderful ways.

Now came the hard part … waiting to hear if our son was going to make it … and what kind of condition he would be in after another painful surgery. Margie and I spent many hours praying in the waiting room of the hospital until Doctor Butler finally came out. He said the surgery went remarkably well but cautioned us that we needed to pray that Rob could endure post-surgical pain given the difficulties he has with anesthetics.

It was mid-morning when we were finally allowed to see Rob after he was released from recovery and placed in a room. Going up in the elevator, Margie cried that she didn't know if she could bear to see the condition Rob would be in given the terrible effects a second, radical, front-to-back surgery.

I told her, "Margie, where is your faith? Look at what God has already done for our son. Don't you think He can now shield Rob from terrible pain? Let's pray right here, right now, that God will spare Rob excruciating pain!"

As we prayed, I felt the familiar, comforting, tingling of God's graces descend upon us as we hugged and prayed in the elevator.

When we walked into Rob's room we were amazed to see

him sitting up perfectly straight drinking a glass of orange juice! He greeted us with a big smile and said with full voice, "Hi, guys!"

He had good color in his face and looked very good! Margie asked how bad the pain was.

"Not bad, Mom. Not bad at all!" he said.

"Rob, what pain medication were they able to give you?" I asked.

"Nothing. They said they couldn't give me anything so I guess it's the anesthesia from the surgery that's covering up the pain."

Doctor Butler walked in shaking his head, "We couldn't give Rob anything. The fact that he's not feeling the pain of surgery is nothing short of a miracle!"

Rob continued to heal well and is now, many years later, living proof of the reality of Christ's words that with God … all things are possible. Thank you, God, for answering our prayers.

Chapter 26

THE MAN IN THE NEXT HOSPITAL BED

The Fortini-Mongelli family on Long Island are among the nicest people we know in Ss. Cyril and Methodius parish on Long Island. One day, my wife, Margie, and I were asked by them if we would go to Good Samaritan Hospital to pray over the family's grandpa who was seriously ill.

When Margie and I arrived at the hospital we were impressed to see a great many of the Fortini-Mongelli family were already there waiting for us to join them in healing prayer. There were so many, they could not all fit into their grandpa's hospital room! What faith … what Christian witness … what love!

After greeting one another, we prayed earnestly together for their grandpa's return to good health. It was so uplifting to see all the family members crowd around the grandpa's bed when it came to the part of healing prayer where everyone is encouraged to lay hands on the person being prayed over.

As soon as we finished praying, the man in the next bed, Charlie, who had been quietly crying, anxiously called out, "Can you all pray for me? I am so sick but my wife here … and I … we don't know how to pray the way all of you just prayed … and we don't have any other family."

Hearing this, I quickly stepped over to stand next to his wife at the bedside and gladly said, "Of course you have other family! You have all the Fortini's here along with my wife, Margie, and me! WE ARE YOUR FAMILY!"

Turning to the large group of Mongelli family members gathered in the small room, I called out, "What do you say, shall we adopt Charlie and his wife as part of the family?"

A loud, resounding cheer rose up from all those gathered in the small room and adjacent hall, "YES … YOU ARE PART

OF OUR FAMILY!"

Charlie and his wife were overwhelmed with the goodness and kindness expressed by this loving family. After they finished expressing their heartfelt appreciation, I asked all the Fortini-Mongelli family to come crowd around Charlie's bed so we could all pray for Charlie … and his wife.

Following our customary healing prayer format, we soon reached the point where I reminded Charlie and his wife that Jesus calls us all to forgive everyone … everything … and that includes forgiving ourselves. And in terms of God forgiving us, remember that St. Dismas, 'the good thief on the cross,' asked Jesus to forgive him and remember him when Jesus came into His kingdom. Jesus then told him, 'this day you will be with me in Paradise!' All we have to do is ask God for forgiveness and do our best not to sin anymore."

Charlie surprised us all by praying loudly, "Dear God, I'm truly sorry for anything I ever did wrong in life; please forgive me … please remember me, too, when I stand before you!"

Very early the very next morning, Charlie, unexpectedly got to meet St. Dismas as he, too, found himself standing before our loving, forgiving, merciful God. No one really knew that it was even possible that God might call Charlie home that very next morning! Just think of what might have been missed if the Fortini-Mongelli family did not take time to be so kind and loving … to someone they had only then adopted.

You never know how very important it may be to take time – no matter how tired or busy you may be - to be patient, kind and caring … and to do whatever you can to encourage others to turn to almighty God.

As Jesus says in Matthew 5:7, "Blessed are they who are merciful."

Chapter 27

THE BREAD THAT HEALS

While distributing Holy Communion as a Eucharistic Minister at Mass at Ss. Cyril and Methodius, I strongly sensed there was someone approaching on my line who was greatly distressed. I soon discovered who it was.

Maryanna, an acquaintance at our church, stepped forward and stood before me waiting to receive Our Lord in Holy Communion. I was overwhelmed with a wave of deep sorrow and compassion for her as I sensed that she had malignant cancer. In the next moment, I experienced the exhilarating awareness that Jesus Christ was really and truly there with Maryanna and me … right there, right then … miraculously in the Eucharist.

Looking down into the ciborium filled with consecrated Hosts, I cried out to Jesus from the inner recesses of my being to heal Maryanna of the cancer. Such soul-filled prayers are expressed without the use of words … just pure love and faith.

As I raised the Eucharist up in front of Maryanna, and looked into her eyes, I realized that she somehow understood that I was aware of the cancer … and that we were both aware of the true presence of Jesus in the Eucharist between us.

Filled with great hope and faith that God had heard my unspoken prayer in that moment, I confidently said the blessed words, "This is the Body of Christ."

Maryanna replied, "Amen."

At that very moment, I felt the familiar, ecstatic shower of healing graces pour over her and me as she received Holy Communion.

Years later, Maryanna came over after Mass and said there was something she just had to tell me. She asked me if I knew what it was that she was going to tell me. I told her, yes, I remembered quite clearly what happened many years before when she was on my Communion line at Mass.

Maryanna excitedly explained, “Years ago, I was terribly upset when I was on your Communion line because I had just learned I had malignant cancer. When you were about to give me Holy Communion, I sensed that you somehow knew I had cancer and were praying for me as you gave me Communion! When I received the Host from you, I felt a wave of tingling healing graces pour all over me. I was almost ‘slain in the spirit.’

“A few days later, oncologists at Sloan Kettering Cancer Hospital in Manhattan did more tests, and were amazed to tell me the cancer had disappeared!”

I thanked Maryanna for sharing with me how wonderfully God had rewarded her faith. Then I told her, “Now you must be a leper and go thank Jesus for healing you!”

Chapter 28

MIRACLE OF THE STONE FLOWERS

So here I was, "Jimmy's Boy," on my way to visit for the very first time the hallowed place where my Grandpa Sheridan was healed and later personally witnessed so many miracles at Saint Anne's Shrine in St. Jean the Baptiste Church in New York.

Grandpa spent so many years there attending Mass, meditating in the presence of the Blessed Sacrament on exhibition

and praying at Saint Anne's Shrine for the healing of countless people.

As I climbed the front steps leading up to the entrance of St. Jean's Church, my mind was flooded with flashbacks of the countless times that I, too, had personally witnessed God's miraculous healing of people who cried out to Him in faith.

As I entered the church, I was filled with a sense of spiritual anticipation and awe. Stepping through the inner doors, I entered this utterly magnificent church and I was immediately immersed in a warm, powerful life-force that filled the entire the church! My first reaction was that this feeling must be from the presence of Saint Anne's relic … but my heart told me otherwise. I sensed that this remarkable presence was something far, far greater … something infinitely sacramental and indescribably beautiful … an all-loving, all-consuming life force.

What I sensed was the personal presence of God. However, my attention was drawn to the right rear of the church where I saw an alcove that had the appearance of a grotto. Positioned at its center was a simple, all-white, marble statue of

Saint Anne standing with her young daughter, the Blessed Virgin Mary who appeared to be around eight years old. An extraordinarily bright white light filled the entire grotto but oddly … it did not cast its light out on the area outside the grotto.

I realized that it was the holy Shrine of Saint Anne that I had heard so much about my whole life. As I walked over to the shrine, I sensed the presence of my Grandpa Sheridan nearby. Such a wonderful, joyful feeling swelled within me that I said "I love you, Grandpa!"

When I reached the now retired Communion rail stationed in front of the grotto containing the statue, I positioned myself at the rail to the left of the statue and studied the statue of Saint Anne and her daughter, Mary.

The figure of Saint Anne was holding what appeared to be a scroll of paper in her left hand. Her right hand was resting just above the right shoulder of Mary standing at her right side. There was a crown on Mary's head, and she appeared to have a slight smile. Her right hand was holding what appeared to be an Easter lily, and the forefinger of her left hand was pointing upward in the direction of a large, stained-glass window immediately above the grotto.

Standing there, I wondered what was the full significance of the statue. Before I could reach some conclusions, I sensed someone was behind me but when I turned around there was no one there. A wave of spiritual electricity surged through me as I noticed a glass reliquary hanging on the wall immediately to the right of the grotto.

Stepping over in front of it, I discovered that it contained the relic of Saint Anne! The relic was about two inches long, half-inch wide, and was light-brownish in color with a thin strip of paper wrapped around it with the name, "Anne," printed on it! Literature on a table nearby explained that the statue represented Saint Anne and her daughter, the Blessed Virgin Mary, and that the relic was, indeed, from Saint Anne.

I placed my hand over the glass cover that was only an inch away from the relic of Blessed Saint Anne within the reliquary case. Closing my eyes, I prayed fervently as I asked her to tell her Grandson, Jesus, how much I love Him and appreciate all He has done for me and my loved ones. I felt quite at home, familiar, being in such close proximity to Saint Anne's relic. I truly felt her presence right there with me at that very moment.

After a while, I stepped back over to my left and knelt down in front of the statue of Saint Anne and the Blessed Mother. Rather than praying for other people as I have done my whole life, I asked both of them to intercede on my behalf with Jesus for a special gift!

I asked if God would allow me to witness a remarkable, physical miracle … something that I could not possibly mistake. The reason I asked for this was due, in part, to the unrelenting assaults by the Devil in its attempts to cast doubt upon my calling to a life of healing and evangelization. I apologized for being so weak in faith to make such a request but I nevertheless persisted in my request.

After a few moments, I opened my eyes, and saw a large, gray, eerie-looking, statue of stone flowers stationed right at the foot of the statue of Saint Anne and Mary! I clearly did not see this unique-appearing statue of gray flowers before.

The entire statue was gray in color and appeared to be made of the same type of marble as the statue of Saint Anne and the Blessed Mother. It appeared to me there were 144 of these stone flowers. They looked like roses fanned out in all directions from the center of a small vase at the bottom. The entire floral statue stood about three feet tall and about three feet wide. As I studied it, I felt immersed in a powerful, benevolent aura surrounding me and the entire area.

One flower in particular caught my attention. It was a

very small, helpless-looking little flower located at the very bottom back area of the statue of flowers. Its little head was poignantly drooped over the edge of the flower pot, slumped toward the floor as if it were overwhelmed with profound grief and sadness.

This filled me with intense sorrow as I studied it and thought how extraordinary it was that the sculptor thought to include this frail, little image among the other large, beautiful, powerful-looking flowers. I realized how hard the sculptor must have worked to create this specific part of his creation, and that he, himself, must have cared for this little, imperfect flower as much as he did for all the other beautiful ones he created.

For me, the imagery of that little flower symbolized all those among us who are vulnerable in any way … and the sculptor symbolized our God who loves all of us … including those who are less-fortunate.

I turned back toward the statue of Saint Anne and reiterated my request for a physical miracle that I could clearly see to confirm for me that I am called to a life of healing and evangelization. For me, my request was like asking God for a spiritual vitamin pill.

After a short time, I was distracted once again by the stone flowers. To my utter amazement, as I watched, a pink-colored oval area began to appear on the sides of all the flowers! Then pencil-thin lines suddenly began to appear within the oval areas on the flowers; it was as if they were being drawn by an unseen hand! These lines had the appearance of capillaries that circulate blood throughout our bodies.

My guardian angel told me to look closely and watch what was happening right before my eyes, and to study how this extraordinary bouquet of stone flowers was changing. My angel knows me well. He knows that the time would likely come when I might doubt the miracle that I was witnessing … unless the miracle was especially clear and breath-taking.

Now the flowers began to develop streaks of maroon color … the color of human blood. One of the large bell-shaped flowers closest to me had a maroon-colored line around the very top of the bulb about one-eighth of an inch wide, and about one eight of an inch from the top … and it was expanding downward. Then I noticed that this was also happening to all the other stone flowers!

I was amazed to see this as I realized that I was witnessing an incredible physical miracle clearly, slowly unfolding before me. As I watched in wonder, the transformation of the stone flowers steadily continued.

My angel advised me once again to watch closely and to realize what was happening so that I would never forget. I did as my angel suggested and remained kneeling and watched in utter amazement as more maroon streaks and pink areas with capillary-looking lines slowly developed on all the flowers spread throughout the stone statue. Meanwhile, the blood-colored line encircling the tops of all the flowers' heads had spread further downward … as if blood was somehow being slowly poured into the flowers!

In the next instant, a vision of my guardian angel appeared to my left. As I looked to him, he strongly encouraged me - without speaking words - to get up and immediately go to the front of the church! I wondered why he would suggest that I leave at that moment when I was in the midst of witnessing such a remarkable physical miracle. He also had to see the miraculous event that was unfolding.

Why would he urge me to get up and leave at this moment? What could possibly be so important at the front of the church to compare with what was happening back at Saint Anne's Shrine?

Hesitant to leave, I looked over once again at the

miraculous stone flowers still in the process of filling with the color of human blood. I really did not want to get up and leave … however, I felt compelled … not obligated … to do as my angel suggested.

And so, I reluctantly rose, turned my back on the unfolding miracle, and walked toward the front of the church. As I did, I wondered what could possibly be so important that my angel would ask me to leave such amazing, ongoing miracle.

When I got to the front of the church, I immediately understood. There, present on the main altar in the midst of a very large, magnificent monstrance was Jesus in the Blessed Sacrament! That was what was more important than the miracle taking place at the statue of Saint Anne and the Blessed Mother!

I dropped to my knees at the altar steps and adored Him. I could feel the love of His presence, His personage, alive, right there! He was there in an unmistakable, personal, intimate presence. I closed my eyes and bowed my head in reverence and thanked Him for my life, for my loved ones - past, present and future - and I prayed for their needs and well-being and ultimately for their salvation.

Then I asked Jesus to forgive me for asking for the miracle … but I told Him that I was so happy that I did ask … and that He did grant my request. As I knelt before Jesus in the Blessed Sacrament, I realized that God clearly satisfied my need for reassurance. Part of me felt like the doubting apostle, St. Thomas. How appropriate that my middle name is Thomas since St. Thomas was the apostle who found it difficult to believe that Jesus had risen from the dead. It wasn't until Jesus appeared to him and told him to place his finger into His wounds that Thomas finally believed.

Jesus then said, "Blessed are they who have not seen, and yet believe!"

After basking in that Son-light of Jesus, I rose and walked

toward the rear of the church intending to leave. When I reached the back of the church, however, my angel encouraged me to look over at the grotto now. The extraordinary, bright white light still filled the entire Shrine.

When I went over to the statue of Saint Anne and the Blessed Mother, I was amazed to see that the statue of stone flowers had been transformed into real, living flowers! Now there was a strikingly-beautiful, full bouquet of maroon-colored flowers, roses, exactly where the stone flowers had been!

Momentarily frozen, I stared at the flowers realizing that they were precisely where I had seen the stone flowers. I felt a shower of spiritual electricity surge over my entire being; the same feeling I experience when God intervenes in miraculous healings. I walked over to the grotto remembering how the gray, stone flowers were miraculously changing color earlier.

As I stood in front of the grotto, Jesus' words reverberated in my mind, "Blessed are they who have not seen, and yet believe!"

I dropped to my knees and stared in utter amazement upon the beautiful spectacle ... a full bouquet of vibrant, maroon-colored, living roses. Even the stems were the color of human blood! They were in the precise same place and disposition where the stone flowers were located.

Earlier, the stone flowers were dead, but now, they were miraculously brought to life. There was no question but that these uniquely-colored, living roses before me were alive. I closely studied the flowers to determine if there were any differences. There weren't. They were exactly the same size and shape as before. It was then that I noticed the little flower located at the bottom rear area of the flower-pot. It was still there, still drooped over the side toward the floor.

Only now, this delicate, little flower was clearly alive and filled with the color of blood. Reflecting on this little flower, I realized that when this flower was made of stone earlier, it was steeped in grief, sorrow and despair. Now it was filled with life through the loving intervention of Jesus. The little flower now appeared to be bowed over in joyful reverence to God!

I wondered at the full meaning, the symbolism and significance of the miracle that had taken place there at the grotto. My angel suggested to better understand, I should back up away from the Shrine and look up at the stained-glass window located directly above the grotto. When I did, I fully understood the significance of what the miracle of the stone flowers conveyed.

There, directly above the Shrine where the miracle of the stone flowers occurred, was a stained-glass window showing a priest distributing Holy Communion to children! The symbolism of the transformation of the stone flowers into living, vibrant flowers was now obvious to me. We are like the dead, stone flowers until Jesus pours His Precious Blood upon us in Holy Communion thereby transforming us into beautiful, living children of God. What a remarkable way this miracle reflects the infinite significance of the Eucharist.

Deeply moved by the reverence reflected in this small, delicate flower, I, too, bowed my head and adored God as I thanked Him for the gift of eternal life made possible through the supreme sacrifice of His Son, Jesus Christ.

Chapter 29

"THE STATUES ARE TURNING PINK!"

I took time during lunch one day to attend Mass at St. Jean the Baptiste Church. Afterward, I prayed before the Blessed Sacrament and then I went to Saint Anne's Shrine in the back of the Church.

The miraculous flowers I saw there at the Shrine days before were gone. All that was left now was a deep indentation in the commercial carpeting where the vase holding the stone flowers had been. I realized that only something of enormous weight could leave such a deep, distinct indentation in the carpeting … like the weight of the miraculous stone flowers.

I went around the corner to St. Jean's rectory and spoke with the pastor, Father John Kamas, a deeply-spiritual, faith-filled priest. He appeared surprised and impressed to hear of the miraculous event involving the transformation of stone flowers.

After some thought, he said, "If what you say truly happened, then you should realize what a special blessing God provided for you. Ask God to help you fully understand its meaning and significance."

Before giving me his blessing, he added, "By the way … if something else occurs that strikes you as miraculous, please come and let me know."

Little did he or I know at the time … there would be many, many more miraculous experiences there at the Shrine.

The first occurred the following Monday when I stopped in at the nearby Lenox Hill Hospital Blood Center where I had donated blood for over fifteen years. While donating blood, I recognized the color of my blood in the collection bag was exactly the same color as that of the miraculous flowers at Saint Anne's Shrine. I told the nurse there about the miracle of the transformation of the flowers and its powerful meaning. Respecting her privacy, we will call her Madeline.

She said she was quite familiar with Saint Anne's Shrine since she made countless visits there over the years. I encouraged her to go see the dent made by the flower pot in the commercial carpeting. The dent was still there several days after the miracle happened.

"Thank you; I think I will," she said. "There's been something troubling me for some time. Maybe this is God's way of sending me some encouragement."

At my suggestion, we met the next day at the Shrine and we knelt together at the rail and prayed for Saint Anne and the Blessed Mother's assistance. After a few moments, Madeline said she did notice a circular-shaped dent in the commercial carpeting right where I said the flower pot had been located when the miracle of the stone flowers occurred. To my surprise, Madeline got up and actually climbed over the railing in front of Saint Anne's Shrine!

Getting down on her hands and knees, Madeline put her face down just inches above the circular, dented area, and explained, "I want to closely examine this area."

Madeline began to vigorously and repeatedly rub the dented area to see if the commercial carpet there would return to its normal shape. However, nothing she did changed the deep impression in the carpeting; it retained its distinctive shape showing that something of great weight left its image in the commercial carpet. Thoroughly exhausted, Madeline eventually stopped and remained motionless for some time as she knelt there staring at the area.

Then looking up at the statue of Saint Anne and the Blessed Mother hovering above her, she froze perfectly still as her eyes widened and her mouth hung open. When I looked at the statue to see what she was staring at, I, too, was amazed.

The hand on the statue of the Blessed Virgin Mary was actually glowing a distinctive pink color!

"It looks like God has answered your prayers, Madeline," I told her. "Look how the Blessed Mother is pointing upward toward Saint Anne … and toward the image in the stained-glass window above where Holy Communion is being distributed. That is where you will find the answer to your prayers."

Madeline nodded in agreement and thanked Saint Anne and the Blessed Mother for answering her prayers in such a clear, dramatic way.

Chapter 30

"HE DESERVES TO SEE THE FLOWERS!"

A week after the miracle of the gray, stone flowers, I was at work as a vice president of a major bank on Wall Street. Unplanned, a fellow officer barged into my office, sat down and dramatically stated that there was something she just had to tell me! Respecting her privacy, we will call her Alison.

Her demeanor was usually quite formal and business-like; however, this time, she appeared confused and unsettled. Before I could say anything, Alison told me that there was a 47 year-old co-worker at our bank who had just learned from the cancer hospital that he had 40 malignant tumors throughout his heart and lungs … and that it was too late to do anything for him! They said he had only a few weeks left to live!

Respecting his privacy, we will call him Harold.

Adding to Harold's grief, the bank told him that under the circumstances he must retire from the job - immediately - on disability. He had worked at the bank for many years, and had to leave due to his prognosis.

Alison quickly added, "The reason why I am telling you this is … well … many people here at the bank know you have a healing ministry … so we are hoping that you will try to help Harold. Will you?"

"Yes, of course, I will," I answered.

Before I could say anything else, Alison blurted out, "What happened is a miracle; he deserves to see the flowers!"

She appeared as stunned as I was to hear her say this!

"Why did you say that, Alison," I asked. "What do you mean? WHAT happened that was a miracle?"

Alison just stared at me, unable to say anything.

So I asked, "And what do you mean that he deserves to

see the flowers?"

Looking even more exasperated, Alison practically shouted, "I don't know! Those words just kept coming into my mind all morning … and I knew I HAD to say them to you. Somehow I knew that you would understand!"

Looking embarrassed now, Alison abruptly rose and hurried out of my office without saying another word. Although I was surprised by her words, I realized that this had something to do with the recent miraculous events I had experienced at Saint Anne's Shrine. For one thing, what happened at the shrine certainly was a miracle and that did appear to be what Harold needed right now. The miraculous transformation of the gray, stone flowers into living flowers in the color of human blood also appeared to apply in some way to Harold's situation.

I strongly sensed that what Harold desperately needed was not only a physical healing, but a spiritual transformation as well. And so, I decided to encourage Harold to go to St. Jean the Baptiste Church to venerate Saint Anne's relic and ask her to intercede on his behalf with her Grandson, Jesus.

Saint Anne would help Harold find his way back to God. My job was simply to get him there.

Later that same day when I met with Harold, he confirmed the terrible news that he had cancer.

"The doctors told me there is little they could do. They said … it's too late." He said solemnly. "It is terminal."

Sadly, Harold added that no one in his family or group of friends was interested in praying for him! He said this was because of the life he led in which he had greatly offended those who were closest to him. Now, although he was contrite, and in great need of their prayers and compassion, no one was interested … even though they knew he now had terminal cancer.

"I am so afraid," he confided. "I don't want to die; I am so afraid to meet God after the terrible life I have lived."

Immediately, the story of the "good thief," St. Dismas, came to mind, so I shared it with him.

"Harold, listen to this. In the Bible, we hear about Dismas; he was the 'good thief' who was being crucified on the cross next to Jesus. Dismas told Jesus that he had lived such a terrible life that he deserved to be crucified! Here he was at the end of his life in his dying moments and he realized how badly he had lived … but he was sorry. So he asked Jesus to remember him when he came into His kingdom. Jesus told him that he would be with Jesus that day in Paradise!

"Harold, Jesus made sure that story is in the Bible to let us know that when we are sorry for our sins, there is nothing that God will not forgive!"

Harold sat there deep in thought with his head slumped down, then he pleaded, "Please tell me more about God's forgiveness for sinners like me."

"Okay … how about the story God tells us in the Bible about the 'prodigal son'? In Luke 15:11, Jesus tells us how a son went off and dishonored his father by living poorly and wasting his inheritance. But when the son was desperate and sorry, he came back home. When the father saw him approaching, the father ran out into the field to forgive him and welcome him back home! The father in that story is like God who is always ready to forgive us, and to joyfully welcome us back home.

"That includes you, Harold! To be forgiven, you have to acknowledge what you did wrong, be truly sorry and serious about changing your sinful ways. This means that you must also forgive yourself. Sometimes, that is the most difficult thing to do … to forgive ourselves."

Harold nodded affirmatively, "Please tell me how, Bob. Please tell me how."

I asked Saint Anne to help me find the right words. Then I remembered that I had a paper in my pocket with notes I had gathered on the subject of forgiveness.

"Harold, I have some notes here on God's advice about forgiveness in the Bible. Let me share with you what God says about forgiveness.

"In Ephesians 4:32, God tells us to forgive as He forgives, 'Be kind to one another, forgiving each other, just as in Christ God forgave you.'

"To make sure we get the point, God tells us three times in the Bible HOW He forgives. He tells us that when He forgives, He also FORGETS what we did wrong!

"In Paul's Letter to the Hebrews 10:17, God tells us, 'Their sins and iniquities **I will remember no more.'** In Isaiah 43:25, He tells us, 'I wipe out your offenses; **your sins I remember no more!'** And in Jeremiah 31:34, God tells us, 'I will forgive their iniquity **and remember their sins no more!'**

"Then in Paul's Letter to the Corinthians 3:20, God says, **'You must forgive as the Lord forgives you!'**

"And how many times should we forgive … and be forgiven? Well, in Matthew 18:22, Jesus says that we should forgive '77 times!' That is the Hebrew way of saying … **without end!**

"Then hanging on the cross, Jesus gave us yet another example of forgiveness, Harold, when He said, **'Father, forgive them for they know not what they do!'**

"You know, when Jesus said that, Harold, He included you and me!

"Finally, in the prayer Jesus taught us, the Our Father, Jesus tells us that we are to forgive **as we will be forgiven!"**

With tears streaming down his face, Harold nodded repeatedly so I guided him, "Hearing God's guidance on forgiveness, Harold, let's take a moment now to think of anyone who needs our forgiveness and forgive them … including forgiving ourselves ... and do so as God forgives.

"For anyone we may find especially difficult to forgive, we place them down at the foot of your cross, Jesus, and we ask you to look down upon them with Your love, mercy and forgiveness.

"Thank you, God, for the gift of forgiveness."

Hearing God's encouraging words clearly brought comfort to Harold.

Sitting there rocking back and forth like a little boy with tears streaming down his face, he prayed aloud, "Thank you, God, for forgiving me. Thank you."

"Go to Confession, Harold, as soon as you are able."

Looking puzzled, he asked, "Bob, how can a priest … who is only a man … forgive my sins?"

I explained how Jesus personally created the ability for priests to represent Him in the Sacrament of Reconciliation. He did this when He told the apostles in John 20:23, "If you forgive the sins of any, they are forgiven!"

Harold understood; all he needed to hear were Christ's words.

"I will go to Confession as soon as I can," he said.

I then explained how God's healing often works and suggested that we arrange a healing prayer service at St. Jean the Baptiste Church. He agreed and was eager to do so before starting chemotherapy and radiation the following week at Beth Israel Hospital in Manhattan to try to extend his life.

Harold called the next day with the sad news that he was unable to get any family members or friends to come pray with him at the church.

Despite this disappointment, I told him that all we need are the two of us as Jesus assures us in Matthew 18:20, "When two or more of you are gathered in My Name, I will be there."

I suggested that he and I attend a Sunday morning Mass at St. Jean's so we could pray for healing during the Eucharistic celebration, especially during the prayer, "Lord, I am not worthy to have you come under my roof; but only say the word, and I shall be healed!" (Matthew 8:8)

"After Mass, we can pray by the relic of Saint Anne in the back of the church and ask her to please intercede," I added.

Harold agreed and was quite eager to do so.

Afterward, I called the pastor of St. Jean's and explained Harold's situation and that I would be bringing him to Mass the upcoming Sunday.

On Sunday, however, I had a nightmarish time trying to get to where Harold lived in Manhattan. A sudden, wicked snowstorm was bombarding our area resulting in numerous accidents on the roads. On the Long Island Expressway, I lost two hours when accidents caused the police to close two different exits resulting in monumental traffic jams.

I was not entirely surprised at this difficulty. Such unexpected, implausible events and obstacles often happen when I am on the way to pray over someone.

I was determined, however, to get to the city to pray for healing with Harold - no matter how long it would take or how difficult it might be. I was not going to allow the Devil to discourage me from persisting to fulfill what I felt strongly was God's calling. In no small way, this was a test of my own faith and commitment.

And so, I asked Saint Anne and the Angels of Dominion to help clear the roads before me … and prevent any further obstacles that the Devil might put in my way.

When I finally got to Manhattan, I was lost. I could not find the building where Harold lived so I called him and got further directions. After finally finding him, I drove him to St. Jean's where Mass was just beginning as we entered the church.

Soon, the lector was reading the names of the sick when we heard him clearly say, "And we are asked to pray in a special way today for our brother in Christ … Harold!"

The pastor obviously had Harold's name added to those being prayed for at that Sunday's Mass.

Harold was so surprised and touched, he cried.

I leaned over and whispered, "See how much God loves you, Harold. He knew that none of your family and friends would pray for you … so He arranged for all the people in church to pray for you!"

Following Mass, we went back by Saint Anne's Shrine where Harold and I each placed a hand on the glass reliquary containing the relic of Saint Anne. I placed my other hand over Harold's chest area where the cancer was rampant. Praying fervently, we asked Saint Anne to intercede with her Grandson, Jesus, for Harold's healing.

As we prayed, an electrifying feeling of healing graces poured over both of us as Harold loudly cried out, "Oh, my God … the statue is turning pink!"

We watched in amazement as the right hand on the statue of Mary that was pointing upward turned a pink color! Then the pink coloring gradually filled the entire statue of Saint Anne and the Blessed Virgin Mary! It was absolutely breath-taking to see the entire statue glowing brightly in beautiful hues of pink color!

An elderly lady who was kneeling at the railing in front of the shrine saw the miracle of pink coloring as it happened. Stunned, the lady made the Sign of the Cross … then fell straight backward onto the floor!

After assisting the lady, Harold and I stood there and prayed as the statue of Saint Anne and the Blessed Mother continued to glow in beautiful hues of pink coloring.

I told Harold that this was a miraculous sign

from God to encourage him in his faith.

Harold replied, “As this was happening, Bob, I felt a tingling sensation all over my body. I feel like God healed me of the cancer!”

I also sensed that God had, indeed, interceded in some miraculous way for Harold. After saying a prayer of thanksgiving, we reluctantly had to leave. As we did, the entire statue of Saint Anne and the Blessed Mother was still glowing that beautiful, vibrant pink color!

While I drove Harold home, he reiterated several times that he was sure God had cured him as we stood in front of the Statue of Saint Anne and the Blessed Mother. He also said that he was no longer afraid to die if that was God’s will for him.

A week later, Harold called to tell me that the latest whole-body PET scan of his heart and lungs showed that the 40 cancerous tumors had virtually disappeared! All that was left in the place of each tumor was a pin-dot where each tumor had been located! This was God’s way to make sure that everyone - including the oncologists - knew that He had intervened and rewarded the faith of those who cried out to him.

Harold said he had already begun to change his former sinful ways … and started the process of mending the many relationships he had broken.

Over the course of my life, I have witnessed many miracles; however, Harold’s miraculous cure was one of the most amazing in terms of how it transpired. By the way, the cancer doctors treating Harold said that his healing was not medically or physically possible. And so, the oncologists declared Harold’s healing to be “an act of God!”

The following day, I again visited Saint Anne’s Shrine on my lunch hour so I could take pictures of the statue that was still miraculously glowing in the beautiful pink color. Afterward, I walked up to the front of the church and knelt before the Eucharist on exposition in the monstrance on the main altar. I thanked God for allowing me to witness yet another magnificent miracle. As I prayed, I felt the presence of countless angels and holy souls surrounding me.

The following Sunday evening at the 7 p.m. Sunday Mass at my parish, Ss. Cyril and Methodius in Deer Park, Long Island, I assisted at the Mass as a Eucharistic Minister. After Mass, I told another Eucharistic Minister, a lady of great faith, Anna Pistone, about the miracle that happened at Saint Anne's Shrine. Anna was one of the holiest prayer-warriors I have ever known.

As I showed her one of the photos I had taken of the statue of Saint Anne and the Blessed Mother Mary, the photo became very warm … and literally began to glow even brighter, more vibrant a pink color as I held it!

Anna exclaimed, "Oh, my God, Bob, look! The picture of the Blessed Mother and Saint Anne is changing! It's glowing!"

The statue of Saint Anne and the Blessed Mother was glowing brighter … then softer … then brighter again! It was as if the photograph was a video-tape! This remarkable miracle continued for a few moments as Anna and I looked on in amazement.

Thank you, Saint Anne and Mary… and praise God!

Chapter 31

FRAGRANCE OF SAINT ANNE'S FLOWERS

One day I was on my way to an appointment when I got off at the 14th Street IRT Lexington Avenue subway station in New York City. As I stepped off the train, I sensed the presence of Saint Anne right there in the midst of the crowd, thunderous noise and hustling activities of the underground world of the subway.

Briskly walking along in the back of a group of 20 people heading toward the street exit, we were all suddenly immersed in a powerful scent of a sweet, magnificent fragrance of flowers!

Everyone in the crowd noticed the beautiful aroma. In particular, three teenage girls who were walking at the front of our group abruptly stopped, looked about the area and spoke loudly about the exotic fragrance saturating the air around us. All the people in our group also stopped and joined the girls in looking around to identify the source of the heavenly fragrance.

I looked around the surrounding area to see if there was a flower shop nearby in the subway. A quick scan of the area showed there was no flower shop anywhere to be seen. In fact, nothing was seen that might account for the beautiful fragrance hanging mysteriously in the air about us.

Then I noticed that the three girls at the head of our group were wearing St. Jean the Baptiste school jackets.

I immediately understood what was happening.

The heavenly fragrance was like that of the beautiful living flowers that were miraculously transformed from stone flowers at Saint Anne's Shrine in St. Jean the Baptiste Church.

I realized that Saint Anne wanted to make sure I did not doubt the remarkable, breath-taking miracle she had arranged for me earlier through her beloved Grandson, Jesus.

The crowd of people who were blessed to smell this

heavenly fragrance soon dispersed and hurried on their way. I wonder if any of them realize the significance of what happened. God reached out and immersed them … not just me … in the wonder of a miraculous event.

Thank you, Jesus, for the gift of a flower's fragrance.

Chapter 32

MY VISIT TO PURGATORY

During a visit to Washington D.C. in early April 1991, my wife, Margie, and I stopped at the Basilica of the National Shrine of the Immaculate Conception. I had no idea that this visit was to be one of the most remarkable spiritual experiences of my life.

As background, the Basilica is one of the ten largest Roman Catholic churches in the world! Designated by the United States Conference of Catholic Bishops as a national sanctuary of prayer and pilgrimage, it is America's preeminent Marian shrine dedicated to the patroness of the United States – the Blessed Virgin Mary under her title of the Immaculate Conception.

Open every day of the year, the Basilica is host to nearly one million visitors annually as it attracts pilgrims and tourists alike from across America and other countries. It has been visited by Pope Francis, Pope Saint John Paul II, Pope Benedict XVI and Mother Teresa of Calcutta and it rivals the great sanctuaries of Europe and the world.

The Basilica is Byzantine-Romanesque in style. Its massive, unique superstructure is home to over 70 chapels and oratories that related to the peoples, cultures and traditions that are fabric of the Catholic faith and the mosaic of America. The Basilica also houses the largest collection of contemporary ecclesiastical art in the world.

We decided to attend Mass in the lower church, the "Crypt Church," located beneath the Basilica's magnificent structure. As Mass progressed, I found myself reflecting on Purgatory and wondered if any of my relatives who died before me might be there.

As Catholics we believe Purgatory is a place where some souls may go to have the stains of sin removed before joining God in Paradise. This belief is based, in part, upon the words of God found in the Bible.

First of all, in Revelation 21:27, God tells us that "nothing unclean" can enter Heaven. These words of God are clear. However, listen further to what Jesus tells us in Matthew 12:32, "Whoever speaks a word against the Son of Man will be forgiven, but whoever speaks against the Holy Spirit will not be forgiven **either in this age … or the age to come."**

Christ's words infer that some offenses can be forgiven in the next stage of life **"in the age to come."** Purgatory is that place where some offenses can be forgiven.

This is confirmed for us in the Catechism of the Catholic Church in item number 1054: "Those who die in God's grace and friendship imperfectly purified, although they are assured of their eternal salvation, undergo purification after death, so as to achieve the holiness necessary to enter the joy of God."

We Catholics also believe that it is possible for those of us who are still physically alive to help souls who are in Purgatory satisfy - in whole or part - such purification on their behalf. God permits us to help through our prayers and sacrifices. The greatest way we can help souls in Purgatory is by joining our prayers to the Holy Sacrifice of the Mass - the consecration of bread and wine into the Body and Blood of Our Lord, Jesus Christ.

While attending the Mass at the Crypt Church, I was concerned about the spiritual well-being of my grandpa who died suddenly years before. Accordingly, I offered the Mass for him … in case he was in Purgatory.

After Mass, I had a startling vision of angels prostrating themselves on the floor with their arms extended outward toward a Tabernacle that was located at the far other end of the Crypt Church!

Margie and I hurried there but I no longer saw the angels

before the Tabernacle. A light nearby indicated that the Eucharist was present in that Tabernacle. We prayed there for a while before moving to the next small altar area to our right. Looking up, I was pleased to see the name of Jesus' grandmother, Saint Anne, noted high above the area.

In that instant, I felt my spirit taken straight up out of my body at a herculean speed in the spiritual plane of life. Hurtling upward, my breath was taken away but I found no need to breathe. I was immersed in saturating warmth that permeated the very essence of my being and the entire area. There was an incredibly refreshing fragrance that I instinctively recognized as purifying incense.

Suddenly, I came to a complete stop and remained motionless, suspended in the midst of a place I instinctively knew was Purgatory. My entire entity luxuriated in complete peace, happiness, security and contentment.

My being was suspended about 20 feet below a surface of absolutely beautiful, pure white light. I understood that the area above it was the full presence of God, the angels and gloried souls with Him in the Paradise part of Heaven.

The rest of Purgatory below the glorious, white surface was like an ocean of purifying, billowing incense colored in various shades of gray. Each shade of gray signified a separate level in Purgatory where varying degrees of purification were occurring. The farther down from the surface above, the darker the gray color but never black.

Immersed within the different levels of Purgatory were countless souls in the process of being purified. To my great surprise, alongside every soul, I could see their guardian angel still ministering to them!

Apparently, when we go to Purgatory our guardian angel doesn't leave us; our angel stays with us until we are purified and enter Paradise! God in His infinite love and mercy allows our spiritual advisors/companions to continue their work in Purgatory. Although I was allowed to see the guardian angels, I was not permitted to recognize any of the souls whom I saw in Purgatory.

I realized that all the souls in Purgatory could look up and see the glorious, white light above them where they were all heading. As they were being purified, they rose higher, closer and closer to their ultimate destination with God in Paradise.

My attention was then brought to the presence of the Blessed Mother Mary suspended high up in the middle of Purgatory where all the souls below could see her. Although she was far from where I was positioned, I could clearly see her … and hear her.

She looked upward and indicated that I should do the same. When I did, I saw two angels stationed about ten feet above where I was located. These angels were at the highest point of Purgatory … immediately below the glorious, white-lighted surface of Heaven.

They were looking downward past me and each had one arm extended downward in a welcoming gesture. Their other arms were extended upward toward God above in the brilliant light of Paradise.

At that moment, I realized that I was brought here to Purgatory to witness everything that was happening.

I looked down in the same direction at the angels and saw a young man being carried upward by two angels toward the light above. There was an indescribably ecstatic look of joy on his face as the light above reflected on him.

I was witnessing a young soul ascending up through Purgatory on his joyful rise to eternal peace and happiness in Paradise. After he rose directly up into the light above, my attention was brought back to the Blessed Mother.

She told me she was the "Patroness of Purgatory."

The Blessed Mother then told me, "The last purification

needed by that soul to be freed into the fullness of God's presence was the Holy Sacrifice of the Mass you just offered!"

This puzzled me. I didn't recognize the young man who the Blessed Mother said was freed from Purgatory as a result of the Mass I offered! I had offered that Mass for my grandpa Sheridan … not for someone I didn't know.

Apparently understanding what I was thinking, the Blessed Mother explained, "When the person you offer a Mass for does not need the benefit of that Mass, God in His infinite love and mercy allows that person to give it as a gift to someone else in Purgatory!"

Then the Blessed Mother told me the single most amazing thing I have ever heard.

She told me, "If you add up all the people who have ever lived, are living right now, and those who will live in the future, and add up all their prayers and sacrifices … **all that does not equal the benefit of just one Mass**! That is because you combine your prayers to the perfect, supernatural gift of my Son, Jesus, at the Holy Sacrifice of the Mass."

In the next instant, I was thrust back into my present state standing next to Margie before the Tabernacle in the Crypt Church. I could once again feel cool air and hear the sounds of physical life around me. It seemed to me that I had been gone a long time but Margie said I was staring at the Tabernacle for only a few moments. Realizing what happened, I thanked God for blessing me in so very many extraordinary ways:

- for allowing me to visit and witness the reality of Purgatory;
- for allowing me the great joy of seeing and hearing the Blessed Mother;
- for allowing me to discover that our guardian angels stay with us in Purgatory;
- for allowing me to better understand the immeasurable

value of the Mass and;

- for allowing me to witness the young man freed from Purgatory into the fullness of Paradise.

And I am most grateful that God allowed me the great comfort to realize that my grandpa Sheridan apparently was not in Purgatory!

Chapter 33

OUR LADY OF GARABANDAL

At eight-thirty on Sunday evening, June 18, 1961, the first of a remarkable series of events was about to occur that would transform the tiny, poor village of San Sebastian in Garabandal, Spain into one of the most famous religious sites in the world.

Nestled in the gorgeous Cantabrian Mountains in northwestern Spain, Garabandal is located 60 miles southwest of the provincial capital not far from the French border. At the time, there were only 70 rustic stone houses closely huddled together on a narrow strip of land overlooking the beautiful wooded valley. In many ways, this area looked like a remote area at the top of the world.

The 300 people who lived there enjoyed a simple, quiet, predictable life tilling their land with the use of oxen, carting their produce on the backs of donkeys, baking bread over wood fires, wearing strange pegged, wooded clogs to walk over narrow stony paths from one house to another and to farm plots. In the evenings when their day settled, townspeople paused to pray the rosary in the simple little church located in the village.

At the epicenter of the profound religious events to occur, were four innocent, pre-teen girls. Given how removed their village was from the rest of the modern world, these girls were relatively unsophisticated when compared to children their age in most other parts of the world.

On that first, fateful evening at the beginning of countless miraculous events that were to follow, the four girls were playing in what the townspeople called the "calleja," a rock-filled lane leading out from the village. Years later, the central visionary, Conchita (Maria Concepcion) Gonzalez, recalled exactly what happened. What follows are Conchita's exact words as she looked back to those extraordinary events in her early life.

"I was 12 years old then and I was with my three friends, Mari Cruz (age eleven), Mary Loli Cruz (also age twelve) and Jacinta Gonzalez Cruz (age twelve). We heard a loud noise like thunder. Because we had just finished taking apples from a tree that didn't belong to us, we felt we had made the Devil happy and our guardian angels sad. We began throwing small stones to our left side with all our strength for this side is where the Devil is said to be. After that, we began to play marbles.

"Suddenly, a very beautiful figure appeared to me, shining brilliantly without hurting my eyes. Then the other girls also saw him. We froze for a moment and when we got our thoughts back, we ran toward the church, very frightened.

"I can still see it in my mind. The figure was an angel, very strong in build, with a very young face, like a boy of nine years old or so, yet he looked so masculine. He had, you would say, brilliance about him that was too beautiful to explain, and a large, almost transparent pink-reddish set of wings. Actually, they were not exactly wings. They were not attached to his body. They were more like a halo would be, like a light gleaming from behind him. He wore a long, blue tunic. He had dark eyes and tan skin. Very beautiful.

"I was supposed to be home early the night it happened, but I did not get home until 9:30. My mother (Aniceta) was angry with me. When I told her that I had seen an angel, she said, 'Is that all? On top of coming home late, you come home saying all these things!'

"But it is true,' I said, 'I have seen an angel!'

"The next day, we did not see the angel but at night when I went to bed, I heard a voice say, 'Don't be troubled. You will see me again.'

"The angel appeared to us eight times during June 1961. On July 1, the town had put up safety barriers. I guess there were as many as 500 people. Many of them were praying along with us.

"When the angel appeared, he was smiling and then said, 'I have come to announce to you a visit by the Virgin, under the title of 'Our Lady of Mount Carmel,' who will appear to you tomorrow, Sunday.'

"The next day, Sunday, was very busy. Many people including religious were now in the village. Cars were parked everywhere. People we had never seen before were offering us gifts.

"Around six in the evening, we were near the spot in the Calleja when the Blessed Mother appeared with an angel on each side. One was St. Michael and the other was St. Gabriel. The angels were dressed exactly alike and looked like twins. Next to the angel who stood to the right of the Virgin, we saw an eye of great size. It appeared to be the eye of God.

"I felt as if the Virgin had been away on a long trip and returned. She was like a friend, a good, good friend, just like a mother. She was like no other woman. She wore a long white dress covering her feet, with a blue mantle and a crown of golden stars. Her hands were open. On the right wrist a brown scapular hung. Her hair was dark chestnut brown and wavy. Her face was oval-shaped with fine features, beautiful full lips and a delicate Roman-type nose. Her skin color was lighter than the angels' but yet darker - it was different. Her voice was too lovely to describe. She was like you or me, very natural, just extremely beautiful and graceful."

Conchita's above words set the stage for what was to be the first of 2,000 apparitions by the Blessed Mother to the four little girls in and around the village of Garabandal from 1961 until 1965. It is worth noting that this was remarkably similar in many ways to holy events that took place years before at Fatima and Lourdes. The Blessed Mother was again appearing to young children … in a humble location … this time, the village of San Sebastian de Garabandal in Spain.

Many of Our Lady's visits at Garabandal occurred at a site located about one-quarter mile to the north at a high ridge with nine beautiful pine trees overlooking the quaint little village of Garabandal. However, the Blessed Mother also appeared to the girls inside the local church, outside the door of the church, in the homes of different villagers, on various streets of the village and in the town's one cemetery.

And they occurred at all hours of the day and night.

The Blessed Mother's messages contained prophecies of profound, supernatural events that were to affect the entire world. These foretold four of the greatest supernatural events in the history of mankind according to the Blessed Mother as told to the visionaries. Here are the prophesies the young visionaries tell us were given by the Blessed Mother:

1. **A world-wide warning** will come from God. It will be experienced by everyone in the world;
2. **A great miracle** will be performed by God. This would be regarded as the greatest miracle of all times;
3. **A permanent sign** will appear after the great miracle. The sign will be something that has never been seen before, and will remain forever in "the nine pines" above the village of Garabandal. And finally,
4. **A chastisement** will occur, a punishment, but it will be conditional upon the response of mankind to the Blessed Mother's messages calling everyone to live in ways pleasing to God.

Of all the extraordinary events that occurred at Garabandal, there is one that stands out above all the others. It is an astonishing miracle that emphasized the importance of the Eucharist. As background, an angel bearing a golden chalice had appeared several times to the four girls and gave them Holy

Communion using consecrated Hosts the angel took from the tabernacle at the nearby church.

Then on June 22, 1962, the angel told Conchita that God would perform a "special miracle" in which the people would be allowed to see the Sacred Host appear on Conchita's tongue at the very moment she received the Communion Host. The angel said that people in attendance would be allowed to physically see this … "in order that they may believe."

Conchita wrote in her diary that this would take place on the 18th of July. The angel later told her that she should announce this message 15 days in advance of the miracle. Conchita did as instructed - she told everyone to prepare to see this miracle!

With hundreds of witnesses present, the miracle of the visible Host did occur but it did so at 1:40 in the morning of July 19, 1962. The event was actually recorded on movie film by Don Alejandro, a businessman visiting from Barcelona. The witnesses afterward stated how they watched Conchita kneel down at that time and stick out her tongue to receive the Host.

At first, absolutely nothing happened, nothing was visible. But after a few moments … a bright white Host, thicker than usual, shockingly appeared on Conchita's tongue and remained there for a few moments before Conchita consumed the sacred Host.

Conchita refers to this particular event as the "little miracle" which she said was intended to call our attention to the reality of the Real Presence of Our Lord in the Holy Eucharist.

Over the five years, when the Blessed Mother appeared to the girls, several miracles occurred. Among these, were the many times the girls held up countless religious articles for Mary to kiss … then they miraculously returned each of the religious articles to the rightful owners!

In addition, the girls often ran very fast up and down the rocky hill while their heads were pointed upward as they saw and listened to the Blessed Mother. People following the girls could barely keep up with them. Sometimes, the girls even ran backwards up and down the rocky hill without falling or getting hurt!

Every time the Blessed Mother appeared to them, the girls went into an ecstatic state in which they were totally oblivious to everything around them. Doctors and others studying what was happening, often stuck the girls with needles and suddenly flashed bright lights in their eyes … with no reaction from the girls.

Conchita added, "The people who witnessed us go into a state of what was referred to as ecstasy said our heads would instantly snap upward. At times, we would crash very hard to our knees. I knew or felt nothing of this. Some people would actually prick our skin with needles during these states. Although I did not realize it then, later I would see puncture and bruise marks on my skin."

A shocking event witnessed by many was when several big, strong men could not pick up one of the girls … and then … as everyone watched … one of the girls would effortlessly pick up another high into the air with ease! The girls explained they lifted one another so they could reach the Blessed Mother in order for her to kiss the religious objects they had been given by strangers to be kissed by Our Lady.

On June 18, 1965, more than 2,000 people gathered in Garabandal. Americans, English, Italian, French, Germans, and Polish were among the people who joined groups from different parts of Spain. The Spanish were in the minority since the apparitions had received virtually no publicity in Spain. The French constituted the largest group. There were journalists, television cameras from the Italian TV network, and cameramen from "NO-DO," the Spanish official documentary news program.

Late this evening around 11:30 p.m., Conchita left her house and walked to the road leading to the Nine Pines to the place called the "Cuadro." There, she was in ecstasy for 16 minutes during which time St. Michael the Archangel appeared to her and delivered a message from the Blessed Mother for the entire world.

This message from Our Lady was quite disturbing, "Since my message of October 18th has not been made known to the world and has not been fulfilled, I tell you this is my last message. Previously, the cup was being filled; now it is overflowing.

"**Many cardinals, bishops and priests are on the road to perdition, and with them, they are bringing many souls!**

"The Holy Eucharist is being given less importance (honor). We must avoid God's anger with us by our efforts at amendment. If we beg pardon with sincerity of soul, He will forgive us.

"I, your Mother, through the intercession of St. Michael the Archangel, want to tell you to amend your lives. You are already receiving one of the last warnings. I love you very much and do not want your condemnation. Ask sincerely and we will give to you. You should make more sacrifices. Think of the Passion of Jesus."

As she did with all the messages she received from the Blessed Mother, Conchita also conveyed this disturbing message … exactly as it had been given to her. The next morning, this message was made public to members of the clergy and to all others following the extraordinary events at Garabandal.

Unfortunately, such words about "cardinals, bishops and priests being on the road to perdition, and bringing with them many souls," brought adverse reaction from Catholic clergy.

However, it would be many years later that the world would learn the full meaning and sad reality of the Blessed Mother's disturbing message at Garabandal in 1965.

In the year 2000, law enforcement authorities announced shocking disclosures of decades of sinful, sexual misdeeds by

Catholic cardinals, bishops and priests involving the sexual abuse of children worldwide! These terrible sins against children and others were fully supported in countless court documents … and were admitted by the Catholic clergy involved!

A mountain of irrefutable evidence clearly showed how Catholic cardinals and bishops, in fact, did knowingly allow this terrible tragedy to continue. In part, victims were paid large sums of money to be silent, not press charges and thereby avoid media disclosures. Even more shocking, was the admission by cardinals and bishops involved that they transferred the perverted priests who were committing such heinous crimes to other parishes where these priests then victimized other innocent children!

Faced with a mountain of evidence in a historic number of criminal and civil cases, and with the unavoidable glare of media attention upon them, Catholic cardinals and bishops had no choice but to **FINALLY** take proper actions to end to the sexual abuse of children.

How incredibly sad and tragic.

When these terrible events came to light in the year 2000, they showed the authenticity of the events at Garabandal given the shocking comments made by the Blessed Mother in 1965 that "many cardinals, many bishops and many priests were on the road to perdition and were bringing many souls with them!"

The last time the Blessed Mother appeared to Conchita was on November 13, 1965. What follows are Conchita's own words describing this last visit by the Blessed Mother.

"When I reached the pines, I began to take out the religious objects that I had brought. As I was doing this, I heard a very sweet voice, clearly that of the Blessed Virgin calling me by name.

"I answered, 'What do you want?' Then I saw her with the infant Jesus in her arms. She was dressed as usual and smiling. I said that I had brought the rosaries (an enormous number) to be kissed and the Blessed Mother replied, 'So I see.'

"I said, 'How unworthy I am, dear mother, of the numerous graces I have received through you. And yet you come to me today to lighten the little cross that I now carry.

"Then the Virgin said, 'Conchita, I have not come for your sake alone. I have come for all my children, so that I may draw them closer to our hearts.

"Then she said, 'Give me everything you brought with you so that I may kiss them.' I gave her everything. I had a crucifix with me. She kissed that also and said, 'Place it in the hands of the Infant Jesus.

"After having kissed everything, she said to me, 'Through the kiss, I have bestowed on these objects, my Son will perform prodigies. Distribute them to others.'

"This is the last time you will see me here but I shall always be with you and with all my children. Conchita, why do you not go more often to visit my Son in the tabernacle? He waits for you there day and night.'

"I told the Virgin, 'I am so happy when I see the both of you. Why don't you take me now to heaven with you?"

"When you present yourself before God, your hands must be filled with good works done for your brothers and for His glory. But at the present time, your hands are empty!"

Over the following years, Conchita visited with Padre Pio, Mother Teresa, Pope Paul IV and many other notable people. In time, Conchita relocated to America, married in 1972, and was blessed with children and grandchildren.

In mid-September 1994, my wife, Margie, and I attended a day of recollection at the Marian Shrine of Our Lady of the Island located in Manorville on Long Island. Following an outdoor Mass celebrated there, we were standing in front the 18 foot tall statue of the Blessed Mother holding the Baby Jesus located immediately behind the open altar area.

It was then that a middle-aged man came over to us and standing in our way, dramatically said, "Excuse me, I don't know who you people are but I know that it is very important for me to introduce you to someone over here. Please come with me."

With beautiful sunshine shining brightly down upon us, Margie and I followed him a few steps over to the area directly in front of the statue of the Blessed Mother and Baby Jesus. Standing there with her back to us was a tall, slender woman. As the man spoke to her, she turned around to face us.

I couldn't believe who it was … it was the saintly visionary from Garabandal … Conchita!

Her eyes glistened as she smiled and politely greeted us as we introduced ourselves. Before anything could be said, a group of six people entered our circle.

A man serving as the spokesperson for the group said, "I don't know who you people are, but I know I must introduce you all to Sister Andrea from the Philippines. She is the nun who the Blessed Mother appears to!"

Before anyone could greet her or say anything else, a young woman rushed into our circle and eagerly said, "Hello, everyone. I'm sorry for interrupting you, but I must introduce myself. I am Barbara Gargulio … the Blessed Mother speaks to me through inner locutions!"

Before anyone in our circle could say anything, I told this holy group of people about the vision I had years earlier when I was in the lower Crypt Church in the National Shrine of the Immaculate Conception in Washington, D.C.

"After attending Mass there, I stood before a tabernacle located in the far back wall. Printed above it was the name of Jesus' grandmother, Saint Anne. She and the Blessed Mother have always been close to my heart – especially when I have prayed for the healing of people.

"In that moment standing in front of the tabernacle where

Jesus was present, I was spiritually carried away in a flash to Purgatory! Everywhere I looked, I saw billowing, gray-colored incense purifying countless people there! A unique fragrance filling the air was indescribably more beautiful than anything I had ever smelled before.

"There were so many people there in Purgatory, it was far beyond my ability to estimate. Looking down, I saw to my surprise and delight that each person in Purgatory still had their Guardian Angel alongside them!

"The farther down I looked, the darker the gray-colored incense looked … but it never became black. Above where I was situated was a solid surface of brilliant, glorious white light. It was indescribably more beautiful than any white light I had ever seen on earth. I understood that above that light was the part of Heaven where God, the angels and glorified souls reside.

"My attention was then brought to the incredibly beautiful lady stationed at a distance from me. I recognized immediately that it was the Blessed Mother suspended in the upper middle area of Purgatory where all the souls and Guardian Angels below could see her … just below the brilliant light of God above.

"The Blessed Mother was smiling as she looked at an area just below where I was suspended. Looking down, I saw a young man who was being escorted upward by two angels as they all looked up at the light above. The young man's face had a look of ecstasy as he was brought up by the angels into the light of God directly above!

"He and the two angels passed so close to me, I could have reached out and touched them! After they rose up into the light of God above, my attention turned back to the Blessed Mother. Although she was at a great distance from me, I could hear her as if she was standing right next to me.

"She said that she was the 'Patroness of Purgatory.'

"And then, she told me that the Holy Sacrifice of the

Mass which I had just offered for my grandpa was the last vestige of purification needed by the young man who was escorted by the angels up into Heaven!

"The Blessed Mother then told me the most profound thing I have ever heard. She told me that if I add up all the people who have ever lived, and add all the people who are living now, and add all the people who will ever live, and then add up all their combined prayers and sacrifices … **that does not equal the benefit of just one Mass that is offered for someone!**

"She explained this is because we unite our prayer in a Mass with the perfect sacrifice of her Son, Jesus, in the Eucharist! After the Blessed Mother said this, I found myself back in front of the tabernacle in the lower Crypt Church where I could feel temperature once again, and hear surrounding silence."

The moment I finished sharing this miraculous experience, Conchita slowly lowered her head, turned and without saying a word quietly walked away! Sister Andrea, too, lowered her head, turned and also walked away followed by everyone in her group! To my dismay, Barbara Gargulio then turned around and literally ran away sobbing!

I turned to Margie and said, "Oh, my God, Margie, look at what I have done! Here we are in the midst of these holy women of God from all over the world … and I tell THEM something miraculous that happened to me! I should have asked them to tell us about THEIR miraculous experiences!

"I couldn't help it, Margie, I had an irresistible urge to tell them about my visit to Purgatory. I just had to tell them!"

The spokesperson for Sister Andrea's group, heard what I said, so he came back and told me, "I heard what you said. You shouldn't feel badly. You see … earlier today here at the Shrine, the Blessed Mother appeared to Sister Andrea and told her that an 'age of tribulation' was beginning in which no one would be spared from suffering! She said that sinful people AND good, righteous people alike will suffer!

"The Blessed Mother then told Sister Andrea that the way she will know this message comes from God the Father and not from the Devil, is by telling Sister Andrea something that will happen in the future … later today! The Blessed Mother explained that only God knows the future … not the angels, the saints or the devils. Therefore, having a prophesy fulfilled will assure you that the message is from God the Father.

"The Blessed Mother then told Sister that later today – completely unplanned – visionaries will come together here at the Shrine and when they do … a man in their midst will speak about Purgatory!

"When he does, you will know that the message about an 'age of tribulation' truly comes from God the Father."

Margie and I were greatly moved by this. As we later walked along one of the paths with Sister Andrea and her group, I asked Sister, "Did the Blessed Mother have anything else to say that you could share with us?"

Sister smiled and said without looking at me, "Yes, as a matter of fact, the Blessed Mother had a message for you! She said to tell the man who speaks of Purgatory that he is not living as he is called! He is called to pray more often and fervently, to fast, to do penance … and to evangelize far more than he does."

Sister stopped walking and looking right at me for greater emphasis, she added, "And the Blessed Mother said to tell you that there is no time for you to delay. **You should begin right away!"**

I was completely surprised and taken back by these words. Although I have always tried to live a good, prayerful life, I knew that what the Blessed Mother said was absolutely true. I was not praying often or fervently; nor was I fasting, doing penance and or evangelizing as I knew I was called to do.

I thanked Sister Andrea for sharing this with me, and

assured her that I was going to follow the Blessed Mother's advice … starting right away! Later that day, I would get my very first opportunity to do so.

After my wife, Margie, and I said goodbye to Sister Andrea and her group, we inadvertently caught up with Conchita and her group of prayerful people gathered over in another area. Among her circle of friends and family was her dear friend, the famous "blind apostle," Joey Lomangino. He had been blinded in a terrible accident when he was only 17.

Joey first met Conchita in Garabandal after he visited with Padre Pio in San Giovanni, Italy. Padre Pio is the priest who was blessed by God with the gift of the Stigmata, the bleeding wounds of Christ on his hands, feet and side.

When Joey asked Padre Pio if he thought he should go visit Garabandal where the Blessed Mother was said to be appearing to four children, Padre Pio said, "Of course!"

Hearing this, Joey immediately travelled from Italy to Garabandal, Spain where he met Conchita and the other visionaries there. Joey and Conchita would go on to become lifelong friends. In fact, in keeping with the Blessed Mother's locution to Conchita one time, Joey later established a center on Long Island in New York dedicated to spreading the news of the many glorious events at Garabandal.

After briefly visiting with Joey and the other special people in their group, I had the opportunity to speak privately with Conchita off to the side. Standing there with her, I again had the unmistakable feeling that I was in the presence of a very holy, wonderful woman of God.

I thought, "No wonder, the Blessed Mother appeared to her so many times!"

At one point I asked her, "Why did you walk away from us earlier when I spoke of Purgatory? Was there something in what I said that was offensive in some way?"

She giggled obviously amused that I was worried about offending her.

Smiling, she softly assured me, "No, there was nothing you said that offended me."

In the next instant, her expression changed to a more serious appearance as she explained, "You see, earlier today at the Shrine, the Blessed Mother told me …"

Conchita's following words flowed much along the same lines as those of Sister Andrea about "an age of tribulation."

When Conchita finished speaking, I was strongly inspired by the Holy Spirit to offer words of admiration and encouragement.

"Conchita, I and so many other people around the world greatly admire you, and are inspired by you. I personally know how painful and difficult life can be when you try to lead others to God. The Devil does everything it can to interfere with God's plans. So you must continue to be strong in your faith, and know that the Blessed Mother and St. Michael the Archangel will protect you AND your loved ones."

After a pause, I was further inspired to offer her some important advice, "Forgive me for saying this, Conchita … but God blessed you with visits from the Blessed Mother – not just for you - but for all His children! You have a responsibility to continue sharing those blessings you received with everyone!"

(It wasn't until years later that I discovered the Blessed Mother told Conchita the very same thing back in 1965!)

"I will pray for you, Conchita, every day, I promise, especially at Masses I attend. Please do the same for me."

Her beautiful, gentle countenance radiated as she promised to do the same for me.

After wishing Conchita and her group well, Margie and I headed toward the parking lot off in the distance. When we arrived there, we saw Barbara Gargulio waiting for us! As soon as we reached her, she eagerly told us why she ran away from us after I spoke about my miraculous visit to Purgatory.

Barely able to contain herself, she eagerly explained, "In a locution earlier today at the Shrine, the Blessed Mother told me that an 'age of tribulation' was beginning …"

Barbara proceeded to tell us virtually the same thing Sister Andrea and Conchita separately told us about the Blessed Mother's message earlier including how only God the Father knows the future … and how a man will speak about Purgatory!

Since that day in mid-September 1994, Margie and I have not met one person who can honestly say that their life is without some form of tribulation. Some people believe, "that's just life." However, there is no mistake about the fact that people who follow the Blessed Mother's advice are far better able to handle life's many trials and tribulations than those who don't.

By the way … that advice is the very same she gave us through little children in Lourdes, Fatima, Medjugorje … and Garabandal.

Chapter 34

THE LADY CENTURION

I brought a small group of people to St. Jean the Baptiste Church to pray for God's healing at Mass and afterward by the statue of Saint Anne and the Blessed Mother.

Among them was a deeply-faithful Catholic lady, we will call her, Janice, to respect her privacy. She had a sister who was dying of intestinal cancer. We will call her sister, Angela.

Since Angela was an atheist, she did not want me or anyone else for that matter to come pray over her.

Her sad remarks were, "You guys are lucky. You have someone you can yell at and blame. But I feel sorry for you putting your hopes into something or someone who does not exist!"

Nothing Janice or I said made any difference. Angela was adamantly set in her views.

But then, she interestingly said, "The only way I will believe there is a God is if my malignant cancer miraculously disappears! If your God really exists … tell Him to cure me of my cancer. Then I will believe!"

"If that is what it takes, then that is what we will pray for," Janice promised.

Turning my attention to the faith-filled sister, Janice, I encouraged her to remember Christ's words in Matthew 8:13. Jesus tells us of the faith of the Roman Centurion who said that he was not worthy that Jesus should come under his roof, that Jesus needed only to say the word and his servant would be healed. Jesus said that He had not seen such faith in all of Israel!

Then Jesus said, "Go let it be done for you according to your faith."

The centurion's servant was healed in that hour!

I told Janice that Jesus was showing us that we could pray the same way for others; we can be "centurions" for others who do not believe! And so, Janice agreed to serve as a centurion for her non-believing sister.

As planned, we attended the 5:30PM Mass on a Tuesday, venerated the relic of Saint Anne afterward, and then we stood back by the statue of Saint Anne and the Blessed Mother Mary. I felt the familiar tingle of spiritual graces flow over me and Janice as we prayed.

The next day, Janice called to tell me that at the same time we were praying at Saint Anne's Shrine the night before, her sister, Angela, collapsed in terrible pain and was rushed to the hospital. Amazingly, several tests showed that Angela's late-stage, intestinal cancer had miraculously disappeared.

Angela now believes in God.

Chapter 35

"SHE IS BRAIN-DEAD!"

To respect the privacy of the 12 year-old girl in this story, we will call her, Jennifer.

One Saturday afternoon, Jennifer and a group of her young friends raced across a four-lane road near a major shopping center in Huntington, Long Island. As they did, a car sped toward them with the driver sure he would not hit any of the youngsters. He was dead wrong.

The car violently slammed into Jennifer, the last girl running across the road. The impact thrust her body high up into the air and as she landed, her head slammed against the concrete curb causing her skull to crack open. Some of her brains spilled out onto the road as she slipped into unconsciousness.

As quickly as that, Jennifer was at death's doorstep.

She appeared to be lifeless but a faint pulse was still detected by the medical people who soon arrived. A medical helicopter was called to the scene so Jennifer could be quickly airlifted to a hospital that had special "head trauma" facilities for such injuries.

Soon after arriving at the hospital, the doctors thoroughly examined Jennifer, and although she was still alive, the EEG machine that monitors brain activity indicated that Jennifer was now hopelessly brain-dead.

When the family arrived, the parents had the doctors connect Jennifer to life-support equipment in the hopes that the medical team might have time to discover something they could do to save her life.

After a while, the doctors told the parents that Jennifer was irreversibly brain-dead with injuries that were so severe, parts of her brain were missing! They said that recovery simply was not possible. The medical team gave the parents some papers and said that they should consider taking Jennifer off the life-support … and donating her organs to save the lives of others.

Outside in the waiting room, a large group of family members and friends had gathered. When the parents came out and told them what the doctors had said, everyone wept.

Everyone, that is, except the grandfather.

"Don't sign those papers yet," he said.

"I know someone who knows a man who has a remarkable healing ministry. I want to get that man here before you sign anything!"

The parents agreed. That is when I was called to the hospital.

When I arrived at the ward for critically-ill people, I walked into a large waiting room filled with about thirty of Jennifer's family and friends.

The prominent, silver cross I was wearing immediately alerted the grandfather that I was the "healer" they were waiting for. He warmly welcomed me and explained the dire circumstances.

"The doctors say Jennifer is brain-dead from the injury and that there is nothing they can do now to save her. They want her parents to sign the papers to take Jennifer off the life-support so that her organs can be donated. But we don't want Jennifer to die so her parents are waiting in there for you … to see if your prayers can heal her!"

I told him, "God is the one who does the healing, not me … but there is much you and the family can do by praying out here while I am in there praying over Jennifer.

"First of all, you must forgive everyone, everything, including forgiving yourselves. Then you must tell Jesus exactly what you want Him to do for Jennifer … and make sure you have faith that God can heal her as Jesus says, 'With God, all things are possible!'"

With his promise to lead the others to pray that way in the waiting room, I walked through the doors into the ward where Jennifer lay brain-dead. Standing around her bed were her father and mother and another woman. A surgical team stood at the far end of the ward; they were waiting to take Jennifer to the operating room to remove her organs.

Before I could reach Jennifer's bedside, I was confronted by a very angry, tough-looking nurse who stood in my way and snarled, "What you are doing is sinful … giving the parents false hope! That child is already with God. She's brain-dead! You are delaying the donation of her organs to give life to others!"

"Are you a Christian?" I asked.

"Yes. I am a Baptist."

"Well then, we share a common Christian faith since I am Catholic, and I believe in Christ's words that all things are possible with God. Therefore, you should pray with us!"

"I'll tell you what," she said menacingly, "if you take too long with your … 'prayers,' … I am going to have the security guards haul you right out of here real fast!"

With that, I stepped over to the right side of Jennifer's bed and greeted those standing around her bed.

"My name is Bob Walsh; I am here to lead you in healing prayer. We begin in the name of the Father, and of the Son, and of the Holy Spirit. Amen.

"Let's take a moment to acknowledge Christ's presence among us as He said, 'When two or more of us gather in His name, He will be with us.' Surely, He is with us right now since we are gathered in His holy name … for Jennifer."

During that moment, I observed how badly Jennifer had been injured in the car accident. The top of her head was encased in a large, cone-shaped bandaging through which a dreadful-looking, two-inch transparent shunt extended directly up and out of her heavily bandaged head. Her eyes were fixed, half-closed with a lifeless, motionless stare. She was intubated with tubes in her mouth, a NG tube in her nose, and her arms and legs were tied down because her body occasionally convulsed.

Across from me above the bed was the brain-monitoring device, an EEG machine, on which there was a constant straight line indicating there was no brain activity. By all accounts, Jennifer was, in fact, brain-dead. I knew from many prior experiences to ignore such discouraging signs and focus instead on the limitless love and power of God. As I had seen countless times before, truly all things are possible with God as Jesus says.

On the other side of the bed from me stood the girl's father, then a lady next to him, a lady at the foot of the bed, and the smirking nurse stationed about ten feet away. Off in the distance, I could see the surgical team waiting to take Jennifer to the operating room to remove her organs.

To begin our prayer, I explained that Jesus calls us to first forgive everyone … everything … without exception. And that includes forgiving ourselves – sometimes that is the most difficult forgiveness to give. I then encouraged the father, mother and other woman to forgive everyone as Jesus calls us all to do. I asked everyone to indicate when they had, in fact, forgiven everyone, everything by nodding.

After a long while, no one had nodded, and so I repeated that it was Jesus who said that we should first forgive. To help them to forgive, I reminded them that Jesus hanging on the cross asked God the Father to forgive everyone "for they know not what they are doing."

"If Christ can forgive all of us including those who crucified Him, we are called to follow His example. How can we ask God to heal Jennifer if we have unforgiveness in our hearts?"

Finally, each person nodded indicating that they had forgiven everyone, I then encouraged them to tell God exactly what it was that they wanted Him to do for Jennifer.

As I prayed, I invited Jesus' grandmother, Saint Anne, and His mother, the Blessed Mother Mary, to join us at Jennifer's bedside as we prayed to Jesus for Jennifer's healing. We said the Our Father, and then I encouraged everyone at the bedside to lay their hands on Jennifer as we called upon the Holy Spirit to pour His healing graces down upon her.

I led them, "Come, Holy Spirit, pour Your breath of life and healing into Jennifer. May every breath she takes be Your Holy Spirit coming in to absorb all that needs healing. Restore her to the fullness of life and good health. We ask this in Christ's name. Amen."

While I prayed these words, I was immersed in the familiar, ecstatic, tingling sensation filling every fiber of my being.

Suddenly, the EEG machine began to beep loudly … and the straight line began moving up and down indicating brain activity!

Jennifer's father cried out, "She has brain activity!"

At that moment, Jennifer fully opened her eyes, turned her head in my direction and looked straight up into my eyes! At that moment, it was like I was looking right into the eyes of an angel!

Seeing this unfold, the combatant nurse was so shocked that she was "slain in the spirit." (fainted as she fell heavily backward) onto a push-cart filled with various medicines. What loud, alarming noise it created!

The Holy Spirit then gave me the words to say to Jennifer who was obviously fully awake … still staring up into my eyes, "Jennifer, you've been in a car accident; you're okay. You're in a hospital; Mommy and Daddy are here. Squeeze my hand once for yes, and two for no. Okay?"

Her little hand squeezed my hand once … and as she did

… an exhilarating, tingling sensation shot straight up my arm! Her little hand was now holding mine!

Through all those tubes, there was a smile on her face! This beautiful, little child of God was smiling up at me! As her eyes looked deeply into mine, I realized that Jennifer understood the wonder of what just happened! She somehow understood that God had just miraculously healed her.

As it seemed so appropriate for me to say, I leaned over and whispered to her, “Jennifer … now don’t forget to thank God for helping you. Okay?”

Smiling even more so, she squeezed my hand one more time.

As I made my way out of this critically-ill, intensive care unit, the surgical team that was waiting only moments before to take Jennifer to the operating room to remove her organs now came running over.

“Everyone out, everyone out,” one of the doctors shouted.

I left this incredible scene and went outside into the waiting room where the grandfather asked me if Jennifer’s parents had signed the papers to donate her organs.

“No, they haven’t,” I told him. “That is because Jennifer has just come out of the coma! Now it is time to pray that she stays out of the coma … and that she has no permanent injuries.”

After a moment’s pause, cries of joy and happiness erupted in the waiting room as many of Jennifer’s family and friends cried. Several literally got down on their knees and shouted praises to God! How I wish everyone could witness such a remarkable, breath-taking encounter.

By the way, the last time I saw Jennifer several years after I prayed at her bedside, she was still functioning quite well … even though some of her brain-matter was lost.

Thank you, God, and thank you, Saint Anne and the Blessed Mother, for once again interceding on our behalf.

Chapter 36

THE BABY NEARLY BURNED TO DEATH

Around two in the morning, my phone rang with a desperate call to come pray over a one-year-old baby girl at the Cornell Burn Center in New York City. I was told she had been burned over 90% of her little body in a horrific accident inadvertently caused by her father. The medical staff did not expect the baby to survive through the night.

On my way to the Burn Center, I prayed to Saint Anne and the Blessed Virgin Mary and asked them to join me in my prayers to God, to help me comfort and encourage those involved. As I prayed from the inner recesses of my heart and soul, I envisioned myself standing in front of Saint Anne's Shrine in St. Jean the Baptiste Church.

When I arrived at the Burn Center, the head nurse told me, "The baby is so badly burned, we don't think she is going to make it to dawn. But she is not the one we are so concerned about; we are worried about the father who caused the accident."

She explained, "Earlier, when he learned how badly the baby was injured and that she was not likely going to survive, he collapsed, sobbing uncontrollably. Sometimes, when something like this happens, the one causing the accident cannot deal with the guilt, and so they think about ending it all!

"When a friend of his said he knew someone with a powerful healing ministry, the father begged her to have that person come right away to pray over his baby.

"That is when you were called."

In order for me to go in and join the father and injured baby, I had to put on sterile clothing – literally, head to toe – in order to protect the baby from possible infection. When I entered the slightly darkened room, I went straight over to stand on the opposite side from the father as he stood over the fully-enclosed incubator that contained the little baby girl lying on her back. She was unconscious and encased in white gauze from head to toe with a number of tubes protruding from her little body.

The father was hunched over with his head hung low. His eyes were swollen and red from extensive crying. His hands were resting on top of the incubator as if he was praying over his little daughter. He looked up and greeted me with a nod. Since he was expecting me to come pray over his baby, I made the Sign of the Cross and began by encouraging him to pray with me as he had never prayed before.

I told him that the very first thing Jesus tells us we must do is to forgive everyone, everything … and that includes forgiving ourselves.

I stressed how important this is, "In your case, that means you must forgive yourself for the accident that happened! I cannot stress this enough … for the love of your daughter … Jesus tells us that you must forgive yourself before we pray for your baby's healing!

"Please nod when you have been able to forgive yourself."

As the father silently prayed, I again envisioned myself in front of Saint Anne's Shrine as I begged Saint Anne and the Blessed Mother Mary to implore Jesus to hear our prayers and heal this little baby … and her father.

After a while, the father was able to nod that he had, indeed, forgiven himself for the accident that he caused.

"Wonderful! Now we must ask God to heal your baby … and don't limit what you ask God to do! In the Bible, Jesus often asked people what they wanted Him to do … even though He already knew what they wanted! So, don't limit what you ask of Him. Tell Him that you want your baby healed … totally and completely!

"And remember, Jesus also asked people if they believed that He could do what they were asking of Him! (Matthew 9:28) Then He said, 'According to your faith, let it be done!'

"So believe with all the faith that you are capable of that Jesus can heal your baby! After all, Jesus did say that 'With God, all things are possible,' didn't He?"

Nodding his head repeatedly, he prayed much like, I imagine, many of the people we hear about in the Bible.

As I joined him in prayer, I remembered that the only one who ever got Jesus to change His mind was a mother … the Blessed Mother at the marriage feast of Cana! And so, I asked Saint Anne AND the Blessed Mother to go directly to Jesus … as mothers … and ask Him to please intercede and heal this poor little baby.

As we prayed, I felt a familiar exhilarating, tingling sensation shower down from above and cascade over and through my entire being.

Before I left, I encouraged the father to continue praying and thanking God for whatever He does on behalf of the baby. Outside the room, I asked the nurse to please let me know how things go the following day.

Late into the following day, I had not heard from anyone at the Burn Center, and so I continued to pray to Saint Anne and the Blessed Mother. I asked them to please go to Jesus … AS MOTHERS … and ask Him to please heal the little baby. I call such persistent prayer, "soaking prayer."

Well, late the next day, the nurse at Cornell's Burn Center called. She was quite emotional as she told me that the baby was not only still alive, but when they removed the bandages covering her entire body, there were no burn scars on the baby's body … there were no scars anywhere!

The following day, the little baby girl was carried happily out of the Burn Center nestled in the arms of her loving father whose faith in God was rewarded as Jesus says in Matthew 19:26, "With God all things are possible!"

Chapter 37

SINGING IN THE RAIN

After praying over a group of sickly men and women at Saint Anne's Shrine, a crippled, elderly lady came over and asked me to pray over her the same way I did for those in our group. She explained that she was crippled from birth, and wanted God to heal her so she could walk "like everyone else."

We immediately formed a circle around her as I led the group in healing prayer. When it came to forgiving others, however, the crippled lady she said that she could not forgive some people who had done "terrible things" to her.

I explained how Jesus calls us to forgive, and shows us how. Hanging in agony on the cross, He forgave everyone, everything, when He said, "Father, forgive them; for they do not know what they are doing!" (Luke 23:34)

If they did understand how wrong their actions were, or, if they fully understood the consequences of their wrong-doings, perhaps they would not have done so. After a pause, the crippled lady … with tears streaming down her face … told us that she would forgive those who had hurt her. At that very moment, I felt the familiar, spiritual tingling sensation pour over me. God had just done something good … something very good for her. I hoped that it included physical healing for her.

The lady looked stunned as she just stood there motionless and speechless. After a while, I invited her to join us at a restaurant a block away but she shook her head no. The rest of us made our way in torrential rain to the nearby restaurant.

Standing under the restaurant's canopy, I held the entrance door open for our group until the last person entered. Then I heard the sound of someone running in the rain behind me. Before I could fully turn around, there was a hard tap on my shoulder.

When I turned around, I saw the elderly, handicapped lady standing out there in the pouring rain … dripping wet and smiling broadly!

She exclaimed, "Look, I am healed; I am healed! Look! My legs are perfectly straight and normal now! God healed me!" Now I can walk like everyone else!"

Indeed, she was miraculously, completely healed of her life-long affliction!

Without hesitation, the thought came into my mind to tell her, "How wonderful! Praise be to God! Now you must go and tell everybody you know what God has done for you … and don't forget to thank Him like the one leper did!"

This lady was so excited, she turned and literally began singing and dancing in the rain … much like Gene Kelly in the famous movie, "Singing in the Rain."

Thank you, Saint Anne, and praise God!

Chapter 38

CATCHING THE GIANT

There was a giant of a man with faith as big as the rest of him … nearly seven feet tall and quite husky! Respecting his privacy, we will call him, Tony.

Unfortunately, Tony was diagnosed with late-stage prostate cancer that had metastasized. The oncologists said they would try chemo and radiation to perhaps give him more time but it was likely he had less than a year left to live.

Tony's response was to tell the doctors they could do their job … and he would do his, "I am going to pray to God for a miracle to heal me of the cancer!"

One of my friends, Kevin DeBear, is one of those wonderful people in life who always does what he can to help others. He is a living example of the "Good Samaritan" Jesus tells us about in the Bible (Luke 10:30.)

When Kevin heard of Tony's illness, he told him about me, a fellow Catholic blessed with healing ministry. Tony asked Kevin to contact me right away to arrange a healing prayer session for him. I recommended that Tony first go to Confession and then we could go to Saint Anne's Shrine at St. Jean the Baptiste to attend Mass, the perfect healing prayer, and venerate Saint Anne's relic and pray for her help. Tony was absolutely thrilled, and so arrangements were immediately made.

On the next Tuesday, we attended the 5:30 p.m. Mass at St. Jean the Baptiste Church. Afterward, we lined up in the center aisle to process up, as was the custom, to have the priest place Saint Anne's relic on our forehead or heart. As we moved up in the long line of people toward the priest up front, Kevin stood directly behind Tony … just in case Tony might be "slain in the spirit" (fall down) when the relic was placed on his forehead or heart.

I placed a hand on Tony's shoulder and stood next to him when we finally reached the front of the line. As soon as the priest placed Saint Anne's relic on Tony's forehead, Tony was slain in the spirit as he fell heavily backward … into the arms of Kevin, a much-smaller man! Kevin caught him but was nearly knocked off his feet in doing so. Tony might have been seriously injured if Kevin was not there to break his fall.

Alarmed, Kevin laughed out loudly, "Sure … I come here to see a miracle, but what do I get? I get to catch a giant instead!"

Little did Kevin realize at the time, but when he "caught the giant," he did, in fact, share in an utterly remarkable miracle.

The very next week, Tony, the "giant," discovered that he was miraculously healed of the prostate cancer … before any chemo or radiation was done! The malignant cancer had literally disappeared! The doctors at the cancer center were so amazed, they repeated their tests a number of times … and then declared the amazing fact that Tony was, in fact, now completely free of the cancer!

Thank you, Saint Anne, and praise God!

And thank you, Kevin … for catching the "giant!"

Chapter 39

SHIRT WITH THE BLOOD OF CHRIST

In July 1998, I underwent extensive surgery at Long Island Jewish Hospital on Long Island in which one-third of my large intestines had to be removed due to damage caused by diverticulitis.

Immediately following the long operation, the surgeon, Doctor Leroy Levin, came out to speak with my wife, Margie, who was surrounded by friends and family members.

"Mrs. Walsh, your husband is doing well ... he's in recovery right now. He'll be fine but I must tell you, when we first opened him up, we were shocked to discover that he had a large, significant hole in his intestines!"

"It was so bad," he laughed, "it was as if he had been eating sharp chicken bones! Before surgery, I had no reason to suspect that he had such a serious condition. There was no prior sign, no symptom whatsoever. His temperature and white blood count were both perfectly normal!

"We repaired the damage, of course, along with the large section of the colon that was destroyed by diverticulitis. He should be fine now … but I'll never understand how he survived with that hole in his intestines. He should have died from peritonitis!"

Some family members giggled. Margie shushed them and explained, "Thank you, doctor, for everything you did to help Bob. In terms of him living with a hole in his intestines, nothing about Bob ever really surprises us! You see, his life has been filled with miracles of every kind imaginable. God has blessed him in so many ways like no other person we've ever heard of."

Doctor Levin nodded, "Well, thank you for sharing that with me. I tell you, that is the ***only thing*** that makes any sense to explain what I and the other doctors saw in the operating room."

Days later while I was recovering in the hospital from the surgery, I was trying unsuccessfully to encourage the fellow sharing the room with me, Michael. He had far more serious, extensive surgery than I had. The surgery saved his life but it left him physically compromised in many ways. He was so depressed, he spent most of the time sitting quietly and occasionally crying.

At one time, Michael vehemently complained to me about people like me not needing miracles, "People like me do!" he shouted.

So I asked him what it would take for him to trust God.

"A miracle," he quickly answered. "A physical miracle, something that unmistakably can only be from God. That's the only way I can place my trust in a God … a physical miracle!"

I asked, "Michael, have you ever, in fact, asked God to allow you to see a miracle?"

"No, I haven't."

"Well, you can't expect something from God if you don't at least ask Him! What do you say we pray right here, right now, for God to let you see an unmistakable physical miracle?"

"Sure. Please help me say the prayer, Bob."

I led Michael in a heartfelt prayer in which we called out to God and asked Him to please allow Michael to see a physical miracle - one that Michael could not refute.

"Please allow this, Lord, to bolster Michael's faith … and help him to carry his heavy cross."

The moment we finished praying, Michael pointed to the T-shirt I was wearing and shouted, "Oh, my God, Bob, you're bleeding!"

I looked at the front of my shirt and was greatly surprised to see bright red blood splattered near the bottom front area. A group of doctors and nurses "happened" to be making their rounds when they heard Michael's alarming words.

They came rushing into our room led by a doctor who came right over to me and lifted up my shirt because there was bright red blood on the bottom. Holding up my shirt, all he and the others could see was the white adhesive bandaging covering the entire front of my torso from my chest to my groin. The entire area was spotlessly white … no blood was anywhere on the white bandaging!

As everyone looked on, a small drop of blood came floating down from somewhere above … in slow motion! When it landed on my shirt being held outward by the doctor, it caused the shirt to suddenly move as if the drop of blood weighed a ton!

I joined the doctors and nurses in immediately looking up at the ceiling to see where that drop of blood came from. To everyone's confusion, there was absolutely no blood or anything else coming down from the ceiling above!

However, as we all looked on, another drop of blood appeared in mid-air and floated down in slow motion until it landed on my shirt causing it to move as if it was hit by something very heavy!

Then another drop of blood appeared in midair and did the same thing as the others. Then another drop appeared, and another!

Everyone present was so stunned, no one said a word over the two or so minutes as this breath-taking miracle continued to unfold before everyone's eyes. Other nurses and doctors soon hurried in to the room to see what was happening. One nurse stood motionless as tears silently streamed down her face.

By the way, the image on my shirt was that of Jesus Christ bent over carrying His cross. The blood that miraculously landed on the shirt appeared to be dripping from the wounds in Christ's Head. Perhaps most stunning was the puddle of blood that formed on the shirt at the feet of Jesus. The pool of blood formed an image that reflected Christ's face as if He was looking down into it!

The saying on the shirt below the miraculous image was from the Bible, Philippians 4:13, which states, "I can do all things through Christ who strengthens me!"

I broke the heavy silence in the crowded room by simply saying, "Michael … it looks like God heard your prayers for a physical miracle. You just got your very own physical miracle!"

Chapter 40

"YOU ARE GOING TO DIE!"

Following the miracle of the shirt while I was hospitalized at Long Island Jewish Hospital in July 1998, I was released but returned two days later close to death from some unknown internal blood loss.

The doctors could not determine what was causing the internal loss of blood but they said I must immediately have several donations of blood to save my life. However, I did not want to risk getting HIV, Aids or hepatitis from donated blood so I staunchly refused.

I was admitted to the hospital and once I was settled in a room, one doctor after another came in to tell me how urgent it was that I have emergency blood transfusions. I repeatedly refused for the same reasons I stated earlier.

Around midnight, a young, resident doctor came and stood in the doorway of my room and bluntly said, "I know you are concerned about getting Aids or Hepatitis from donated blood, but unless you immediately begin getting massive infusions of blood, ***YOU ARE GOING TO DIE!*** Do you understand me? As it is, it may already be too late to save you!"

With that, he turned and walked quickly away. His words hit me like a ton of bricks; they were exactly what I needed to hear to convince me that I had to proceed! I immediately summoned the nurse and asked her to do whatever was needed to begin giving me blood transfusions. Within a short time, doctors and nurses arrived, quickly placed me flat on my back, tightly tied each arm onto long wooden boards, then started an infusion of donated blood into each arm at the same time.

I was in absolute physical agony from the major surgery I had only days before. They said they couldn't give me pain medications because they didn't know what was causing my internal loss of blood. Pinned to the wooden boards while blood was flowing into each arm, I couldn't move. I suffered greatly with one spasm after another ripping across my back, surgical area and both legs. Then the torture of itching began on my face and neck. It was from beads of sweat … and I couldn't relieve it! I felt so weak and miserable that even taking little breaths was difficult and very painful.

Suffering like this reminded me of what it must have been like for Jesus to be nailed to the wooden cross with far worse pain and agony than what I was experiencing. I thanked Jesus for enduring such terrible suffering for me and everyone else. Following His example, I offered up the agony I was suffering to God the Father to help the poor souls in Purgatory.

After doing so, I begged God to please take away the unbearable pain … or help me to deal with it. As soon as I cried this plea, I had a powerful sense that a large group of special, loving people had entered my room to keep me company. I opened my eyes but no one was present … that is … no one I could see **physically** present. I understood. God sent these holy souls to be with me and to comfort me with their holy presence … much like the holy men and women who stayed by Jesus while He was suffering on the cross at Calvary.

My spirits were raised … but my pain only grew worse. When the doctors checked my blood levels, they told me the two simultaneous blood transfusions I received did NOT work in building up my blood supply! With a sense of urgency, they immediately began a second set of blood infusions into each arm at the same time.

"Pray this helps," one doctor ominously said. "If this doesn't work, it may be too late!"

His blunt comment along with the physical agony I was suffering would have terrified me if it had not been for the holy souls surrounding my bed in the hospital room. Nevertheless, I realizing that I might, indeed, die, I made a good confession directly to God and begged Him for mercy and forgiveness for all the sins I had committed in my life.

Then I asked Him once again to heal me, only this time, I renewed the promise I had given twice before in my life when I was in the process of dying.

"I promise to continue my life doing anything I can to lead others to Heaven."

Later when the dual blood transfusions were completed, the doctors once again checked my blood levels. Unfortunately, they said there was only a minimal improvement in building up my blood! Accordingly, they began yet another set of simultaneous blood infusions in each arm!

As the light of day flowed into my room signaling the beginning of another day, I sensed the holy souls in my room depart. This indicated to me that I would be okay. Almost on cue, a group of doctors entered my room and happily informed me that the ongoing blood transfusions finally worked to bring my blood levels to a safe level!

The head of gastroenterology at Long Island Jewish Hospital then came in and conducted an endoscopy right there at my bedside. This made it possible for him to clearly identify the cause of my internal blood loss. I had a bleeding traumatic ulcer in my stomach that was caused by the horrific physical pain I suffered after major surgery a few days before. They knew I did not have a bleeding ulcer before surgery because an endoscopy done just before the surgery showed that I did not have any stomach ulcers at all!

I explained to the doctor what must have caused this. I remembered waking up in recovery after the operation … feeling the excruciating pain of radical surgery because the epidural that was supposed to administer pain medication was dislodged from my spine when I was moved from the operating table onto the gurney taking me to my hospital room! The doctors in recovery confirmed that the epidural was, in fact, dislodged from my spine requiring that they begin administering conventional pain medication via IV.

My wife, Margie, and family members felt badly hearing that I had no pain medication and was alone all night close to death while getting one blood transfusion after another.

I smiled and reassured them, “Don’t feel badly … I actually had a lot of great company all night!”

Chapter 41

COUSIN LOUIS AND THE BUTTERFLY

This reflects the painful reality of life for so many in today's society who struggle with the cross of an addiction.

At the center of this story is my wife Margie's cousin, Louis. Our story finds him suffering terribly from the ravages of a life of alcoholism and now … terminal cancer. Sadly, Louis was only in his mid-sixties when the effects of his life-long addiction finally caught up to him. At times along the way, he was able with the wonderful help of Alcohol Anonymous to stay sober but once he stopped attending meetings, he fell off the wagon and into the bottle.

Louis was baptized in the Catholic faith and had received all the sacraments. He held a strong belief in God and all that he had been taught, but unfortunately he did little to practice his Catholic faith throughout his adult life. And so it was that Louis struggled through life with the disease of alcoholism but without the strength and support of his Catholic faith. Sadly, along the way he hurt and offended a great many of his family and friends.

One day, Margie and I met Louis' mother, Aunt Dot, for what we all realized was likely to be a last visit with Louis since he was then in the Hospice program at Good Samaritan Hospital in West Islip, Long Island, New York. The cancer had spread to his brain.

Knowing that Louis had very little time left before God called him home, I asked him - as I often did over the years - if he would like me to arrange for a priest to come and administer the Church's Sacraments of Reconciliation, Holy Communion and Anointing for him. Over the years, Louis consistently had declined my invitations for him to make peace with God and family but under his present dire health condition, I felt strongly that it was my responsibility to at least try one more time before he died.

I went over to his bedside, held his hand and looked straight into his eyes. To my great surprise, Louis squeezed my hand and looked back deeply into my eyes. It was clear that I had his undivided attention, and he actually appeared eager to hear what I had to say.

I spoke softly, "Louis, you and I both know that you will soon be finally free of this terrible disease. And … you will soon be meeting God."

Louis immediately teared up and whispered, "I know."

His eyes appeared to plead for some comfort and reassurance as he added, "After the life I've lived, Bob, I'm afraid of what is going to happen to me when I stand before God."

"Don't be afraid, Louis … God is a God of love, mercy and forgiveness way beyond our human understanding! You are one of His beloved children whom He loves completely. He knows all that you have done and been through, and yet, He still loves you and wants you to come home to Him where He can forgive you and comfort you!

"Listen to what Jesus tells us in the Bible. He tells us of Dismas, the 'good thief' who was being crucified on the cross next to Him. Dismas actually said that he had lived such a terrible life that he deserved to be crucified! Can you imagine what kind of life he must have lived? But then Dismas asked Jesus to forgive him. That is when Jesus told Dismas that he would be in Heaven with Him that day!

"What Jesus is telling us, Louis, is that no matter how bad a life we have lived, He will forgive us as long as we are sorry and ask for His forgiveness."

Louis asked, "But how can I do that now … I am about to die. Isn't it too late?"

"It is never too late, Louis. You have until your very last moment of life to simply call out to God and ask Him to forgive you … and He will! But before your dying moments, you can have a priest come here to hear your confession and have all your sins forgiven and receive special graces from God to comfort and strengthen you."

"How is that possible, Bob?"

"Jesus tells us how, Louis. He tells us in the Bible that whatever sins a priest forgives, they are forgiven in Heaven as well! In fact, Jesus says that when we go to Confession, our souls become 'white as snow'!"

With a far-away look in his eyes, Louis softly said, "I remember that now. I was taught that when I was a kid before I made my first Confession."

"So, what do you say, Louis, how would you like me to get a priest to come here so you can confess your sins … and be 'white as snow' again?"

To my surprise and delight, Louis smiled mischievously and said, "Sure, Bob … but can you get a priest to come here?"

I answered, "Does a rabbit have ears? You bet I can get a priest here! Now, don't you go anywhere!"

I left his room listening to Louis' laughter at my last comment as I prayed that I could find a priest on duty at that time at the hospital. My good friend, Father Paul Dahm, was the Catholic Chaplain in Good Samaritan Hospital but I didn't know if he was there and available.

I called Father Paul's number and he answered! I briefly explained the circumstances of the troubled life Louis had lived, and that he was going to be meeting God very soon. I also explained how his mother, Aunt Dot, was a good Catholic who had never given up on her deeply-troubled son. She had prayed for him throughout his entire life, and forgiven him countless times no matter how cruel and hurtful he had been.

I added, "In so many ways, Father, she has lived a life like St. Monica with her wayward son, St. Augustine. And look at how that turned out! St. Augustine went on to become a Doctor of the Church … one of the greatest Catholics who ever lived!

"For Aunt Dot to see you enter Louis' room, Father, and bring him the mercy and love of God's sacraments will be a great comfort for her … and for me."

A short time later, Father Paul entered Louis' room wearing his full clerical clothing.

He looked directly over to Louis as he introduced himself, "Hi. My name is Father Paul **Dahm**. Now don't you go around telling everyone that the **DAMN** priest came to hear your Confession!"

Louis burst out laughing! That was exactly what he needed to relax and welcome Christ's personal representative of love and mercy. The rest of us left the room as Father Paul administered the sacraments to Louis.

After a while, we returned to see a noticeably different looking Louis than the one we left only a short time earlier. There was a remarkable, unmistakable, aura of peace and joy about him. Aunt Dot was so taken back by all this, she cried tears of relief and joy as she hugged her now "white as snow" son.

Even Father Paul appeared emotional as he watched mother and son crying in each other's arms. Aunt Dot then turned and hugged Father Paul and profusely thanked him.

Father Paul soon turned to leave but paused at the door and said to Louis, "Save a place for me, Louis!"

"You bet I will, Father! Thanks again," Louis cheerfully replied.

Before I left, I asked Louis if he would do me a favor when he crossed the lifeline. I asked him if he would ask God to send me a beautiful butterfly as a sign of new life … from his physical life to spiritual life. I explained that this wasn't to bolster my faith, it was simply a request for what I call a "spiritual vitamin pill" for me.

Louis answered in his inimitable, confident way, "Hey, Bob, if anyone can get you a butterfly, I will!"

Well, not too long afterward, Louis died at peace with the world and with God. At his wake, our entire family … and I … began watching to see if a butterfly would appear. We were all disappointed that none appeared during the wake and funeral Mass. However, something quite extraordinary did happen at Louis' gravesite.

A long line of family members were gathered by their cars about to leave the cemetery when a large, magnificent monarch butterfly appeared at the beginning of the line. It circled around the heads of each and every person present as it moved from car to car! Unfortunately, Louis' mother, Aunt Dot, had already gone inside the first car, the limousine, so she didn't see the butterfly.

Eventually, the butterfly made its way up to the car Aunt Dot was in. To every one's great surprise, the butterfly flew into the car through an open window and circled around Aunt Dot's head as well! After a while, it came out of the car and circled around my wife's head … and then it flew around mine in full view of all the family members looking on. Finally, it flew off gracefully upward into the sky and soon disappeared.

The miraculous manner in which this happened left no doubt in anyone's mind that Louis had, indeed, become our family's very own modern-day version of Saint Dismas, the "good thief" on the cross next to Jesus on Calvary. Thank you, Jesus.

Chapter 42

THE GIUSEPPI VERDI

As often happens, my day started with the distinct feeling that someone I was going to meet that day would need spiritual comfort and encouragement. I soon discovered who it was.

My wife, Margie, and I were visiting her mother, Ethel Holly, at a nursing home where she was temporarily staying while recuperating from a broken femur. Since it was a beautiful summer day, we sat outside on the patio and caught up on things.

Suddenly, someone behind us began sobbing deep, soulful cries. It was another resident, a 98 year-old man by the name of Julius. I rushed over to his side and asked what was wrong, and if there was anything I could do for him.

Julius vigorously shook his head no, but after a while, he explained what was upsetting him so badly.

Amidst his sobs, he explained, "I am the only one who is left alive in my family! Everyone else has died before me.

"I don't have anyone; they're all dead and gone!

"I will never see them again.

"I have no one; I am all alone."

As he cried, I prayed silently to Saint Anne and pleaded with her to ask God to give me the words to comfort poor Julius. What came to mind surprised even me.

I put my arm around his shoulders, and said, "Julius … Julius … listen to me! Your family is not dead and gone! Jesus tells us they are all more alive than ever! They are in Heaven waiting for you, and someday, you will see them all again!"

Julius stopped crying for the moment and looked deeply into my eyes as he searched for comfort … and hope.

"Julius, it's like this. Picture that you and your family are back in Italy when you were a little boy. One day as you stand on the pier, you watch your family get on a ship … let's call it … the **'Giuseppi Verdi.'"**

"Then you watch as the Giuseppi Verdi sails off into the sunset with your family on board on their way to America. When you see the Giuseppi Verdi cross the horizon, it appears that it has disappeared forever. But it hasn't! The Giuseppi Verdi, in fact, sails to the other side of the world where other family members and friends are there to welcome them on their arrival.

"Well, Julius, picture that same ship, the Giuseppi Verdi, comes back to Italy to bring you to America where all your family and friends are waiting on the shore to welcome you there.

"Julius … that is what Jesus tells us happens when we cross the life-line. Jesus IS going to call you one day to come join your loved ones where they are living in Paradise. Then you will be with your family and friends forever … never to be separated again."

To my great surprise and embarrassment, Julius began to cry out loudly … very loudly! He was practically inconsolable. I felt so badly for him and wondered what I said that was so terrible to upset him this way.

After a nurse and others were able to calm him down, Julius smiled and said, "I am okay!"

Turning to me, he said, "Now I know that my family is REALLY still alive and they are waiting for me in Heaven just like the story you told me. You see, when I was a little boy, I really did live in Italy, and my family really did go off to America in a ship as my aunt and I stood on a pier and watched the ship sail out of sight with all my family.

"A year later, my father saved up enough money so my aunt and I could also get on a ship and sail to America to join them. When we got to America, my family was there to greet us … just like you said! Now I know that my family REALLY IS still alive, and although they are far away from me right now … I know I will be joining them someday in Heaven."

"How can you be so sure," one of the other seniors blatantly asked.

Julius smiled and answered confidently, "I am sure because only God knew the story of how when I was a little boy a ship carried my family away but it did come back later to get me and bring me to where my family was!

"The name of the ship was the **'Giuseppi Verdi!'**"

Chapter 43

MIRACULOUS AWAKENING

One of my wonderful prayer-warrior friends, Gino Calaci, appeared uncharacteristically upset this one day.

Shaking his head, he explained, "It just doesn't seem fair, Bob. There is a good, wonderful young man, only 17 years old, who's been in a coma now for two years! He was badly injured in a terrible car accident."

I replied, "Well, why don't we borrow Padre Pio's glove from Grace Begley (the caretaker for the holy relic) and go pray over the young man. You know, Padre Pio looks one way and sees God; he looks the other way, Gino, and he sees us! So let's ask him to go with us to pray over that young man, and join us in our prayers to God to bring the young man out of that coma!"

After retrieving Padre Pio's glove from Grace, Gino and I went directly to the hospital where the young man's family had given permission for us to pray over him. A nurse escorted us into a special room where the young man was located all by himself. The nurse said he had been unchanged in a deep coma ever since the car accident years ago. He was lying on his back, perfectly still, hooked up to all kinds of wires and tubes.

"There's occasional signs of brain activity but little else," the nurse explained.

I placed Padre Pio's glove right over the area of the young man's heart then Gino and I began fervently praying for his healing. As we did, I felt the distinct presence of Padre Pio standing to my right at the bedside. As part of my prayers, I implored God to allow me to serve as a "Centurion" for the young man so I could beg God's forgiveness for any wrongs the young man had ever done and not confessed.

We placed our hands on the young man's arms, as I said,

"Now we will say the perfect prayer ... the one You taught us, Jesus … the Our Father."

As we began to pray, the young man shocked us by joining us as he prayed aloud! Medical alarms began ringing. Soon a doctor and nurse rushed into the room where they observed the young man praying out loud with Gino and me!

His eyes remained closed, and his body remained perfectly still. However, the moment we finished saying the Our Father prayer, the young man opened his eyes and turned his head in my direction.

"Thank you for praying for me," he said matter-of-factly. "When I heard your voice praying for me, it led me back!"

To this day, much later, the young man remains perfectly healthy and is enjoying life. As you might expect, he is quite religious and often tells people how God sent two strangers to lead him out of the coma as they prayed.

You never know how important it is to be a "Good Samaritan" ... to take time to do whatever you can to help someone … even a perfect stranger.

As Jesus says in Matthew 5:7, "Blessed are they who are merciful."

Chapter 44

HEALING RELIGIOUS PREJUDICE

"Hello, my name is Irene. Mr. Walsh, I need you to come to the hospital to pray over my daughter, Sharon. She was in a terrible car crash and is now paralyzed from the neck down! I got your name from one of your fellow church-goers who told me you have a healing ministry. Please call me as soon as you can."

This mother's desperate message was left on my answering machine; it was the beginning of another profound way God intervenes to comfort us, to heal our sufferings … and at times ... to mend our ways.

When I called the mother, she was quite emotional as she explained how the accident happened … and how the doctors say that said her daughter's spine was severed in the accident leaving her paralyzed from the neck down.

Sobbing, she added, "Sharon is only thirteen years old, Mr. Walsh; her whole life may now be over. Her only hope is that God will heal her. She needs a miracle. That is why I called you. We need you to come pray over her."

Irene paused and sounded nervous as she said, "Before we go to the hospital, Mr. Walsh, I am afraid there is something I must tell you. It is not something you're going to like hearing."

After a dramatic pause, she continued, "All my family will be at the hospital to pray with us."

"Okay," I laughed, "that's wonderful. Why in the world would you think I wouldn't like that?"

"Well, you see, we are all Protestants, and ... none of us have any use for Catholics!"

"Oh, I see."

Irene quickly added, "It's very difficult for us to have you come pray with us. In fact, many in my family tried very hard to talk me out of bringing you but I was told you are blessed with a powerful gift of healing.

"So out of love for Sharon, I am willing to put aside the fact that you are Catholic."

I thought to myself, "Apparently, Sharon and her relatives need healing prayer as much as the paralyzed daughter!"

When I arrived at the hospital, Irene met me in the lobby and escorted me directly up to the large, special room where Sharon was located. As I entered the room, I was amazed to see the room jam packed from side to side with Sharon's relatives! There had to be more than twenty of them squeezed into the room! It looked like an over-crowded New York City Subway car during peak rush hour.

Each of Sharon's relatives cast a cold, unfriendly stare in my direction. No one said a word, and not one of them smiled or greeted me. I felt like an unwelcome outcast … a spiritual leper!

So I did what I thought Christ would like me to do … I smiled and warmly greeted each one of them as I made my way through the crowd of unhappy relatives. Soon, I reached Sharon who was located in the far corner of the room firmly secured in an upright seated position in a large, special wheelchair.

I smiled, politely greeted her, kissed her on the cheek, sat down next to her and thanked her for inviting me to come pray with her. Leaning forward, I placing my hands over her folded, unmoving hands, then spoke loudly for the benefit of her relatives in the room.

"Sharon, my name is Bob Walsh. Like you and your family, I am a devout Christian who believes what Jesus says in the Bible is true … that "With God, ALL things are possible!" Our faith tells us that He can even heal the kind of injuries you have.

"Since I was a little boy, I have prayed for people and then watched God heal all kinds of things for those people who called out to Him in faith. That is why your mother asked me to come here today … to lead you and your family in praying that God will shower you with His healing graces.

"Now, you know that I am not a Protestant; I am a Catholic but that is okay. You see, Jesus tells us in the Bible in Mark 9:38 how the apostle John told Him that the apostles saw someone casting out devils in His name so they tried to stop the man because he was not following them. That sounds a little like me being a Catholic … and you being a Protestant. But listen to what Jesus told the apostles … and us.

"Jesus said, '**Do not stop him … for whoever is not against us is for us!'** In that light, Sharon, you and I - and your entire family gathered here - are brothers and sisters in the family of God. I wouldn't be surprised if that is why God brought us all here today … to pray **together** for you."

Sharon teared up and acknowledged my comments with a beautiful smile as she enthusiastically nodded agreement. I turned to her family members and invited them to join Sharon and me in our prayer to God.

"Jesus once said that when two or more of us gather in His name, He is with us. Surely He is with us … right here … right now … since we **are** gathered here in His Holy Name. Let's take a moment to acknowledge His presence here among us."

The room was immersed in a blanket of warmth, peace and comfort as I opened all my sensitivities to the presence of God.

"The first thing Jesus tells us we should do is to forgive everyone, everything … and that includes forgiving ourselves … sometimes that is the most difficult forgiveness to give but Jesus tells us that is what we should do. Please nod, Sharon, to let me know when you have done this."

I turned to discover that all her relatives had their eyes closed and were apparently joining us in this moment of prayerful forgiveness.

After a while, Sharon nodded so I proceeded, "In the Bible, we see how Jesus often asked people what it was that they wanted Him to do for them. Jesus obviously wants us to say what it is that we need and what we want. So please tell Jesus what you want Him to do for you, Sharon, and don't limit what you ask for!

"Please let me know by nodding when you are finished telling Jesus what you would like Him to do for you."

With tears flowing down her face, Sharon took quite a bit of time as she silently spoke with Jesus about what she wanted. While she did, I could hear some family members crying as they also spoke privately with God telling Him what they wanted.

After Sharon finally nodded, I said, "Scripture also tells us, Sharon, about how Jesus asked two blind men if they believed that He was able to heal them. When they said 'Yes,' Jesus then said, 'Let it be done to you ACCORDING TO YOUR FAITH!' Can you imagine! In this scripture, Jesus is showing us how very important it is to express our belief in Him … and in His ability to heal us.

"And so, Sharon, allow me to ask you, do you truly believe that Jesus can heal you?"

Sharon vigorously nodded her head and sobbed, "Yes … I do believe Jesus can heal me. I do believe."

Her soft cries mingled with those of other relatives in the room. After allowing a few moments for all to regain their composure, I invited everyone to come stand around Sharon in the wheelchair and lay hands on her as we pray that God would send His healing graces down upon Sharon.

As we prayed, an electrifying, powerful tingling sensation came surging down upon me from above and raced across my arms before exploding onto my hands and Sharon's hands! She also apparently felt this; her eyes burst wide open with a look of amazement on her face!

Without commenting on this, I instead reminded Sharon - and her family - how pleased Jesus was when one leper came back to thank Him for healing him.

"Now it is time **for all of us** to follow the example of that one leper; let's thank Jesus for what He is doing for Sharon."

I gave Sharon a kiss on the cheek, and encouraged her to stay strong and to talk God often. As I made my way to the door, I thanked Sharon's relatives for joining us in prayer. As soon as I got home, Irene, Sharon's mother, called with exciting news.

"As soon as you left today, **Sharon began to move both of her arms and legs! It's a miracle! It's a miracle!"**

God never ceases to impress me in terms of how and when He chooses to perform miracles of love and mercy. This time, He did so in the presence of people who strongly resisted being led in prayer by ***"someone who does not follow us!"***

Chapter 45

DEVIL ON THE LONG ISLAND RAILROAD

Due to the extreme nature of the events involved in this story, the names of the individuals have been changed to respect their privacy.

Running like a New York Giants' running back through crowded Penn Station in New York City during the rush hour, I barely made it onto the Long Island Railroad (LIRR) train on the Ronkonkoma mainline. The doors closed right behind me.

While I tried to catch my breath, I looked about the train car and, as usual, it was very crowded with other travelers heading home from the city. To my surprise, I saw an empty seat right between two very attractive ladies. Not seeing any women standing who needed a seat, I was quite happy to go over and take the empty seat.

Once I was seated, I nodded to the two young ladies sitting opposite me in a two-seater. As the train started rolling out, I suddenly began to feel ill at ease, almost as if I were being watched by someone who greatly disliked me … and wanted to harm me!

What a silly, strange way to feel, I thought, but my uneasiness steadily increased. I realized this uncomfortable feeling was being directed at me from the well-dressed, attractive lady who was sitting next to me on my right. I soon realized why.

This very attractive lady nudged me and boldly introduced herself, "Hi … my name is … ***Lilith***. I am married … but I'm quite available for a handsome man like you!"

I couldn't believe the lady said that in full hearing and amusement of all the passengers surrounding us on this crowded LIRR train! I immediately felt embarrassed and ill-at-ease.

Before I knew it, she snuggled up against me, wrapped her hands around my right arm and leaning against me, she said, "Why don't you take me home with you!"

The screeching noise of the train suddenly pierced my ear drums! It was unusually loud and had an alarming sound to it. In all my years riding the LIRR, I had never heard such a loud, disturbing noise!

Soon I could hear the laughter of other passengers as they were reacting to the lady's highly-inappropriate comment … and my obvious uneasiness.

I told her, "I don't think my wife … or your husband … would like that!"

It was then that I realized that Lilith was serious – dead serious as she began saying highly-inappropriate sexual things to me … at the top of her voice!

One of the ladies sitting across from us chided Lilith, "Hey, that's enough now! Leave that poor fellow alone."

Lilith ignored her and continued her outrageous sexual comments about what she and I could do together! Soon, some of the people standing near us in the aisle also chastised Lilith and told her to stop. Others, however, were greatly amused by her lewd remarks.

I repeatedly told Lilith, "You've got to stop what you are saying! It isn't funny; it is terribly inappropriate!"

Rather than stopping, Lilith persisted in saying even more explicit, sexually inappropriate things to me. It was then that I first noticed that her voice had become unnaturally louder.

To my surprise, Lilith suddenly stood up and began shouting at the top of her voice, "Ss. Cyril and Methodius Church in Deer Park doesn't allow anyone into their church unless they are perfect! Handicapped people are not welcome!"

I was mystified and wondered why in God's name this wild lady was now saying something so bizarre - and untrue - about my parish, Ss. Cyril and Methodius.

I recognized some of the people in the LIRR train car were from my parish and just heard what Lilith said.

Feeling obligated to correct what Lilith had announced, I stood up and as loudly as I was able to speak, I said, "What she just said is not true … absolutely EVERYONE is welcome at Ss. Cyril and Methodius Church. I know because I am from that parish."

I turned to see Lilith smiling with a really sick, demented, twisted look on her face.

I sat down next to her and asked, "You knew that I was from Ss. Cyril and Methodius, didn't you? Have I met you before?"

Still looking at me, Lilith lowered her head but only half of the pupils of her eyes could be seen at the very top of her eyes! A barely audible, unnatural sound came from her. For a second it sounded like a growl.

I persisted, "Lilith, how did you know that I come from Ss. Cyril and Methodius Church? How do you know me?"

Lilith's countenance and appearance now completely transformed into something quite horrifying and ugly. The lines on her face disappeared … and her eyes changed color from hazel to lifeless looking light grey!

Her lips barely moved but a powerful-sounding man's voice came booming loudly out of her and reverberated throughout the entire LIRR car, **"We know EVERYTHING about you! This is the Devil you are talking to! This one is ours!"**

In that moment, everyone around us realized what was happening right there on the LIRR! We were all in the very presence of a person who appeared to be possessed by the Devil!

The people sitting and standing in our immediate area scrambled wildly to get away from where Lilith was located. Most of these petrified people gathered in the small area by the train doors about eight feet away where they could watch and listen to what Lilith would do next.

Other people who were sitting farther away in the car stood up and joined the others looking on in disbelief. I, too, was startled, and at first, was terribly frightened. But then, I quickly composed myself and drew on the unique training and instruction I had previously received in deliverance ministry to deal with such issues involving the devil.

Reminding, myself that I was anointed in the healing ministry including deliverance of evil spirits, I prayed out loud, "Dear God, please protect me … and free this poor lady from the Devil!"

In addition to the hoarse, disturbing male voice coming out of her, I sensed the intimidating presence of a powerful demon that had gained an ungodly hold of Lilith.

The demon defiantly snarled, **"He cannot help her! She is ours!"**

I immediately, firmly countered, "**No! She's not yours!** She is a daughter of the most high; she belongs to Almighty God, and God alone!"

"No, she is ours!" the demon defiantly screamed.

I again directly confronted the demon, "**No!** This lady is a daughter of Christ; she belongs to Him and to Him alone! She is NOT yours!"

"She is ours," the devil bragged. "She gave herself over to us … she is ours! There is nothing HE can do!"

Relying on what I was taught, I firmly addressed the demon, "I command you in the Holiest of Names, the Name of Jesus Christ, to stop tormenting this daughter of Christ and leave her right now … and do not return!"

The demon inside Lilith began growling words in a language I did not understand.

I ignored this and continued confronting the demon with words of deliverance, "In the Holy Name of Jesus Christ, I command you to leave and not return! In the Holy Name of Jesus Christ, I command you to leave and not return! In the Holy Name of Jesus Christ, I command you to leave and not return!"

I repeated this command over and over while the demon in Lilith emitted a ferocious, unearthly growl. Then as suddenly as it all began, the Devil ceased its verbal assaults as Lilith's face returned to natural color and appearance.

While all this was happening, the ladies standing nearby were praying out loud.

To my surprise, Lilith said to me, "Where was I? Oh, yeah, I was talking about what you and I can do together!"

She apparently was not aware of the terrible thing that had just transpired!

When I told her what happened, Lilith slowly put her head down and sobbed. I stayed focused on what was happening and worried that the Devil might again suddenly confront me. However, I still felt confident that God would protect me … and help this poor tormented soul.

After a short time, Lilith leaned over and whispered in barely audible words, "Please help me."

I told her to go to Confession, Mass and Communion, cease any and all actions that are not pleasing to God, stay away from anyone who is sinful, rid her home of anything not of God … and as soon as possible, go see her parish priest. In time, I would be able to help Lilith … but not that night on the crowded LIRR train.

I later learned that ***Lilith*** in Hebrew-language texts translates as a "night creature" … a mythological female demon thought to be a bearer of disease, illness and death.

I also learned that the lady's true name was not Lilith!

God help unsuspecting people who come into direct, personal contact with the Devil itself.

Chapter 46

BABY TEETH

I was at home when I received a phone call from a distraught couple whose two-year old child was about to have his teeth removed because they had become blackened by chemo and radiation treatments.

The hospital was too far away for me to travel there, so the parents begged me to give them words to comfort them in their grief for their child who had already suffered so greatly.

As I do in such difficult, painful situations, I quickly called out to Saint Anne and asked her to please ask the Holy Spirit to give me the words to comfort the parents. After all, God does tell us in the Bible that we should not worry about what to say … that He will give us the words.

The words came right away.

I told them what came into my mind at that very moment, "When parents cry for their child, God the Father sends the Cherubim Angels down to catch the tears of the parents. The angels then carry those tears right up to God the Father where the angels pour the parents' tears into the loving Hands of God the Father.

"When God the Father looks down upon the parents' tears in His Hands, they remind Him of the time the Blessed Mother cried for her Child, Jesus. And so, God the Father blesses those parents' tears and turns them into Holy Water!

"Then … God the Father turns His Hands over so that the parents' tears rain down as Holy Water upon the parents and their child!"

These words comforted the couple as they requested that I pray for their baby at that very moment since he was then being taken into the operating room where the doctors were going to remove his teeth.

I asked Saint Anne and the Blessed Mother – as mothers – to join me in my prayers as I begged God the Father from the very depths of my heart and soul to please heal the child's teeth. And if that is not to be, then I asked that God shower them with the graces to endure such terrible suffering.

A little more than an hour later, the mother called but she was crying so pathetically I could not understand her words. The father took the phone sounding out of breath; he also sounded like he had been crying. I feared for what I might hear him say.

Finally, the father composed himself enough to say, "Bob, the doctors just came out of the operating room and told us that a miracle happened! They didn't have to remove any of the baby's teeth … ALL HIS TEETH TURNED TO NORMAL SIZE AND COLOR!"

Praise God, and thank you, Saint Anne and the Blessed Mother!

Chapter 47

PADRE PIO AND I VISIT MY SISTER

Although she was only in her early sixties, the oldest of my seven sisters was in a deep coma on life-support in a hospital located several states away from where I lived on Long Island in New York.

Her doctors said she was in the process of dying, "She is in hospice. There is nothing we can do to help her except to keep her comfortable until she goes."

I was filled with great sorrow – not only because of her suffering, but because she had led a violent, sinful life ... and to my knowledge had not made peace with God.

Even though she was dying, her family members did not want me to come visit and pray over her even though they knew I was blessed with healing ministry. In fact, many of them had followed her unchristian ways in life, and considered me to be "too religious" despite all the stories they heard of miracles that happened when I prayed over someone.

They might not have felt that way if they saw what I did in a terrifying vision. However, out of respect for her and her family's strong feelings, I do not use their real names in sharing this important story. The fictitious name I use for her is Marie.

One day following mid-day Mass at St. Patrick's Cathedral in New York City, a vision filled my mind showing Marie surrounded by a wild group of small, frightful-looking, hate-filled demons clawing at her in their violent attempt to drag her off into the depths of the eternal abyss. As she struggled to fend them off, Marie frantically cried out for help but no one could hear her … except me.

I witnessed this terrifying scene and heard her soulful cries to God to forgive her and save her from the marauding devils. Believing the reality of what I saw happening, I knelt down before the tabernacle and begged God to allow me to go spiritually to my sister's aid to protect her from the demons … and to get her back to the sacraments! An inspiration led me to ask Padre Pio to personally ask Jesus on my behalf to let him go with me to my sister's bedside to save her from the devils.

Knowing the demons would be there waiting for us, I asked Padre Pio to bring St. Michael the Archangel and the Angels of Dominion with us to chase the demons away. I felt Padre Pio by my left side and St. Michael the Archangel and many other angels to my right. In the next instant, I felt us rush off through time and space to the hospital room where my sister was struggling with countless little, black demons as they violently pulled at her.

When these evil creatures saw St. Michael and the Angels of Dominion, they momentarily froze before turning all their hatred and fury toward them.

In a flash of a moment, St. Michael and the Angels of Dominion in the form of glorious, bright lights charged at the demons surrounding Marie. In that instant, the demons were vanquished, cast away in the blink of an eye as St. Michael and the Angels of Dominion stationed themselves around Marie's bed.

With Padre Pio at my right side, I stood by Marie's bedside, held her right hand and confidently encouraged her, "Marie, keep your eyes and faith on Jesus … and do so the same way St. Peter did when he was able to walk on the water!

"And have a priest come right away to hear your confession and receive the Sacrament of Anointing!"

The vision then quickly faded in a blur of brilliant white light. As soon as I could, I told family members about what happened, and asked them to pray every day for Marie's safety and salvation.

Weeks later, one of Marie's adult children surprised me

with a call. He said a miracle had happened … Marie had a miraculous recovery from what doctors considered certain death!

He then provided even more amazing information, "When she came out of the coma, the first thing she told the doctors was that she was awake in the coma! She said there were little black devils trying to drag her off with them into Hell! She said she cried out to God and begged Him to save her … to give her another chance at living properly. That's when she said she saw her brother, Bobby, approaching off in the distance … surrounded by brilliant white lights … and a little bearded man in a brown robe.

"She said the lights rushed past her bed and chased all the devils away. Then Bobby came over, held her right hand and told her to do as St. Peter did when he was able to walk on the water … to keep her eyes on Christ! Then he told her to get a priest to come right away so she could go to confession and be anointed.

"With all the doctors and nurses fussing over her, she kept demanding that they get a priest to come right away! Then she insisted that the family have you come see her.

"Oh … and she wants to know who is that little bearded man in the brown outfit who came with you."

Chapter 48

DOUBLE BLESSING

For ten years, a young, faith-filled couple tried unsuccessfully to have a child. In time, their doctors said they did not think it was possible for them to conceive. Someone who knew of my devotion to Saint Anne and the many miracles that happened through her intercession, referred the couple to me for healing prayer.

When I met them, I suggested that they follow the example of Jesus' grandparents, Saint Anne and St. Joachim, who were childless after 20 years of marriage.

"Do as Saint Anne and St. Joachim did … turn ever more so to God," I encouraged them. "Let's start by attending Mass, the greatest healing prayer of all. Afterward, we can pray in front of the tabernacle and ask Saint Anne to intercede on your behalf with her Grandson, Jesus, for the gift of life."

And so, after attending Mass, I prayed over them as they knelt in front of the tabernacle. I felt the presence of countless, holy souls encircle us. When I asked Saint Anne to intercede on their behalf, an exhilarating, familiar tingling sensation swept over me. I knew this indicated that something good was going to happen for them but I did not know what it might be… or when it might come.

Only God knew.

At the next Sunday Mass, I saw the young couple sitting together, devoutly praying in the middle of the church. It was dark and overcast outside … when something quite extraordinary happened. Two beams of translucent light suddenly shone down upon the young couple from somewhere above! They didn't appear to see or otherwise notice these lights. I told my wife, Margie, about the two beams of light, but she said she didn't see any lights at all.

No one saw them … except me.

The lights stayed there shining down upon the couple for a few moments before the lights simply disappeared.

I surmised that those two translucent lights were a sign from God that He had, indeed, blessed the couple with the gift of life, a child. I, of course, said nothing to the young couple because only God knows what, when, where and how it is that He may do something in answer to our prayers.

A few weeks later, the couple told me that God had blessed their efforts to conceive … they were going to have twins!

Thank you, God, and thank you, Saint Anne and the Blessed Mother, for interceding on our behalf.

Chapter 49

LIGHT OF CHRIST IN THE EUCHARIST

My wife, Margie, and I joined other family members to attend a funeral Mass for one of Margie's cousins, Jimmy Hogan, at Mary Gate of Heaven Church in Ozone Park, Queens, New York.

Moments before the Mass was to begin, I approached a statue of Saint Anne and the Blessed Virgin Mary located in the rear corner of the Church near the entrance. As I stood in front of the statue studying it, it began to turn a bright, pink color … exactly like what happened to the same type of statue in St. Jean the Baptiste Church in New York City years earlier!

As the vibrant pink color brightened ever more, I felt surrounded by a vast array of holy souls. I was mesmerized admiring the sheer beauty and grace displayed before me … and around me. A quick glance around the area disclosed that I was quite apparently the only one who was blessed to see this startling miracle.

Since the Mass was just about to begin, I had to leave this remarkable experience and go sit up front with the rest of my wife's family. I was so thrilled by what I just witnessed, I excitedly whispered to Margie what happened at the statue of Saint Anne and the Blessed Mother in the back of the church.

"You are so fortunate," she replied with a mischievous smile. "Saint Anne must really like you to follow you all the way out here to Queens from Manhattan!"

I had little time to reflect further on the miracle since the Mass then started. Then, at the consecration of the Mass, a far greater miracle happened … in fact, the most breath-taking miracle of my life!

As the priest held the Eucharist high up in the air, the Host instantly turned into a brilliant, glorious burst of dazzlingly white light emanating from the Host in the priest's hands! I could no longer see the Host; I could only see the glorious white light in the hands of the priest. He held the consecrated Host up an unusually long time. As he did, the bright, glorious white light remained glowing. Once again, I was the only one who saw this miracle take place as the light of Christ glowed magnificently outward from the Eucharist.

Later that day, I checked the Bible to see the connection between Jesus in the Eucharist and the brilliant, white light shining out from It. There were many such references, of course, but there was one in particular that resonated.

It is in John 8:12, where Jesus tells us, "I am the Light of the world. Whoever follows Me will never walk in darkness but will have the light of life."

I later called the priest who celebrated the Mass, Father Matthew J. Considine, and described the miracle of the light of Christ in the Eucharist that happened during Mass earlier that day. He thanked me for "having the courage" to tell him. Then he shared with me that he felt something quite extraordinary was happening at the very moment he held the Eucharist up in the air.

"In all my years, I have never felt such an exhilarating … ecstatic joy! I will always remember that experience every time I celebrate the Eucharist the rest of my life."

This miracle of the light of Christ is especially interesting to me because one of my favorite readings is what Christ tells us in Matthew 5:16, "Let your light shine before others, so that they may see your good works and give glory to your Father in Heaven!"

I hope that you, my readers, will also remember this Eucharistic miracle **every time** you receive Holy Communion.

Chapter 50

BELLY-BUMP WITH THE MONSIGNOR

My wife, Margie, and I rushed to Good Samaritan Hospital emergency room late one night to visit her elderly Aunt Dot Primavera who was taken there by ambulance. She was so gravely ill, we worried she might not survive.

At her bedside, I told her how important it was to have a priest come by to hear her confession and to administer the healing Sacrament of Anointing.

"Jesus says that you will be 'as white as snow' after confession," I told her.

I asked her if she would allow me to get a priest to come to her bedside right then to administer the Sacraments of Reconciliation and Anointing. To my great joy, she said yes! I was exhilarated but then I realized that it was after midnight!

"Where will I be able to get a priest to come to this busy emergency room at this hour for Aunt Dot?" I worried.

As I walked out of her cubicle, I called out to God to please help me quickly find a priest, "Please send me a priest real fast!"

Turning a corner in the emergency room, I slammed right into someone going the other way; I did a belly-bump right into Monsignor Jim Vlaun! He is the same Father Vlaun who is well-known on Long Island for his popular television show that deals with cooking! Monsignor looked as surprised as I was that we had collided!

I said, "Wow, God works fast! You are not going to believe this, Father, but I just prayed a second ago that God would send me a priest for our Aunt Dot. She is here, very sick and has just agreed to have a priest come. She has been away from the sacraments for quite a while. And here you are! I guess God wanted to make sure I realize that He has answered my prayer."

Father explained that he normally would not be at the emergency room; however, someone he knew called for him to come there. He then visited with Aunt Dot and administered the Sacraments of Reconciliation and Anointing for her.

Afterward, Father Vlaun told me this is what he enjoys most as a priest … administering to those who are spiritually ill … even in an emergency room in the middle of the night.

Chapter 51

"WITH GOD ALL THINGS ARE POSSIBLE!"

My good friend and fellow prayer warrior, Gino Calaci, received some sad news from his next door neighbors, Janet and Bob. They were told Bob had inoperable brain cancer.

The two of them were good Catholics who regularly attended Mass every week. In addition, Janet was a devotee of Padre Pio, the priest who has been blessed with the Stigmata - the bleeding wounds of Christ on his hands, feet and side.

Over the years, Gino shared with them many of the miracles that happened when he and I prayed over people. Not surprisingly, when they received the bad news about Bob's terminal cancer, Janet asked Gino and I to come pray over Bob while he was still at Good Samaritan Hospital in West Islip, Long Island, New York.

On our way, we stopped first at Grace Begley's home to borrow Padre Pio's glove so we could bring it with us when we pray over Bob. Grace was the caretaker for this precious relic which was one of a set of gloves was once worn by Padre Pio when he celebrated Mass. He wore the gloves so he would not distract people who were attending the Mass.

Once we had Padre Pio's glove, we went directly to Bob's room in the hospital. Janet was already there waiting to pray with us for Bob's healing. As soon as we walked in with the glove, Bob began loudly weeping. While Bob held Padre Pio's glove close to his heart, Janet, Gino and I prayed earnestly for God's healing graces to come down upon Bob and heal him of the cancer.

As I held my hand on top of his head, deep, penetrating heat formed.

It became so intense, Bob cried out, "Oh, my God … I

think God is burning the cancer right out of my brain!"

Immediately following our prayer, Bob said the pain he had been experiencing was gone. A follow-up MRI the very next week showed he was right! God had miraculously removed all the cancer from Bob's brain! No more tumors could be seen anywhere.

Shockingly, a few years later, Janet learned she had pancreatic cancer. By the time I heard about this, her condition had deteriorated so quickly she was being treated at home through hospice care.

As we had done for her husband years earlier, Gino and I brought Padre Pio's glove to her bedside and prayed with her. Her husband, Bob, joined us as we beseeched Our Lord for His healing graces. We could easily see the terrible effects the cancer had taken on her body. She was barely able to speak and was down to less than 80 pounds!

When our prayer session came to the part where she is supposed to tell God what it is she wants Him to do for her, Janet surprised all of us.

"I've had a very good life. All I ask of God now is that He allows me live long enough so I can attend my daughter's wedding in three months."

Bob sadly explained, however, "The oncologists have told us Janet only has at most … a week or two left."

Putting on my cloak of faith, I prayed out loud the words that came to mind, "Well, Jesus **DID SAY** didn't He - that all things are possible with God! So let's pray that **BOTH OF YOU** get to attend your daughter's wedding!"

As we prayed, I implored Padre Pio, the Blessed Mother, Saint Anne (Jesus' grandmother), and all the angels and saints to join us at Janet's bedside to pray with us that God would grant Janet's wish to live long enough to attend her daughter's wedding in three months.

Looking at Janet's weakened, debilitated condition, I thought, "Dear God, I know this is really going to take a miracle but I place my friend and her request in your loving Hands."

As each day went by, I inquired of Janet's condition and was pleased to hear she was unchanged. Then one week led into another as each of my calls and visits received the same surprising, remarkable news that she was still holding her own. The oncologists treating her were at a complete loss for words to explain how she it was that she was still alive!

The closer we got to her daughter's wedding date, the tougher it became for everyone - family, friends and doctors alike - to realize Janet was still alive and might actually live long enough to attend her daughter's upcoming wedding.

When three months had passed since we prayed over Janet asking God to allow her to live long enough to attend her daughter's wedding, she was miraculously still alive!

Then one day, when Bob answered the door bell, a flood of family and friends flooded into Janet's home and crowded around her bedside. Last to enter, were her daughter and future son-in-law followed by a Catholic priest! God had rewarded Janet and Bob's faith by allowing her to miraculously live long enough to attend her daughter's wedding - in her home and at her bedside!

Following the wedding, Janet lived to take her daughter's phone call every day while her daughter was on her honeymoon. It was only after her daughter returned home that Janet did finally go - quite joyfully - to Heaven where I am sure she personally thanked Jesus.

In so many ways, Janet and Bob showed us all how very real Christ's words are that "With God, all things are possible."

Chapter 52

"THE STATUE OF MARY IS CRYING!"

On occasion when I brought people to Saint Anne's Shrine for healing prayer, the statue of the Blessed Mother Mary has cried real tears! When this has happened, I would later learn that some of the people were miraculously healed. In other cases, the people - or their family members - were greatly comforted … even though those who were ill later died.

I believe in the cases when the statue of Mary cried real tears, she was indicating that she hears the prayers of her children who are suffering … and she suffers with her children … just as all mothers do. Here are a few examples I have witnessed.

My sister, Geri, asked that I lead a healing prayer service for one of her sons and her daughter. They were both suffering with illness at the time. And so, I arranged for Geri and several other family members to join me at Saint Anne's Shrine for healing prayer.

As we prayed before the statue of Saint Anne and the Blessed Mother at the Shrine, a six year-old member of our family noticed that tears suddenly appeared on the right cheek of the statue of Mary! Upon close inspection, we all saw that the tears solidified into a quarter-inch wide, glossy, stream of tears that ran from Mary's right eye all the way down her cheek. Each of us thoroughly rubbed the stream of tears but this had had absolutely no affect whatsoever on the tears!

Greatly inspired, we resumed our fervent prayer for the healing of our family members. Days later, Geri told us that her son and daughter awoke the following morning completely healed for the first time in years!

Another event in which the statue of the Blessed Virgin Mary cried real tears involved a very courageous, holy lady, Mary

Averna. Mary was fighting fourth-stage colon cancer, was a good Catholic, a lawyer, in her late forties and was married with two young boys. After I met with her and her family, she requested that I arrange for us to go to Saint Anne's Shrine to pray for healing.

Since I was already in New York City this one day, I asked my holy, elderly friend, Gino Calaci, to accompany Mary to New York City where she was to receive her next chemo treatment for the late-stage colon cancer that had metastasized. Gino who carried with him a relic of the True Cross of Jesus allowed Mary to venerate the holy, precious relic.

Afterward, we all met at St. Jean the Baptiste Church to venerate Saint Anne's relic and to ask for her assistance in battling Mary's cancer. As we stood before the statue of Saint Anne and the Blessed Mother, glistening tears suddenly appeared and rolled steadily down the face of the statue of the Blessed Mother!

I told Mary and Gino that this miracle was a gift from God to let us know that the Blessed Mother is looking over Mary.

"The tears flowing down the Blessed Mother's face on the statue is a sign that she hears our prayers. Like all mothers do when their children are suffering, the Blessed Mother is saddened to see her beloved children suffer."

Afterward, the three of us went up to the front of the church and knelt at the altar where the Blessed Sacrament was on exposition in a monstrance. As Mary and Gino looked upon the Eucharist, both saw the face of Padre Pio appear within the Host! I was not so blessed to see what they did … but I did feel the holy presence of countless angels and saints surrounding the sacred Host in the monstrance. Mary, of course, was greatly moved and comforted.

In turn, she was an great inspiration to other cancer patients. She encouraged everyone to turn to God, fight the illness and make the very best of every moment they had. As happens with many who are fighting a terminal illness, there came a time when Mary was worried about how her family would do without her if she lost her battle with cancer.

I told her, "Mary, just because you die, it doesn't mean you are dead! When you cross the life-line, you don't stop being mother … wife … daughter … friend; in fact, you are more so than ever! In Heaven, you can intercede for your family by going directly to Jesus, Saint Anne, Padre Pio and all the angels and saints … face to face!

"Mary, you can do more for your family in Heaven than you can actually do here in physical life!"

Those words brought peace and comfort to Mary as she nodded, "'I've never thought about it that way, Bob. Of course, that's right. When I am in Heaven ... I will be able to look over my family even better than I can here!"

Mary continued to stay close to the sacraments and attended Mass until a short time later when she got to personally meet Jesus, Saint Anne, the Blessed Mother and Padre Pio when God called her home.

Soon after Mary's funeral, Gino lost the Holy Relic of the True Cross of Jesus! It had been in his safekeeping for many years. It was a small reliquary that contained a tiny piece of the true cross of Jesus as confirmed on a certification from the Vatican attesting to its authenticity. Gino was distraught but he believed wherever the relic of the cross was, it was then blessing the lives of those who had it.

Soon afterward, Gino became seriously ill and was hospitalized at Good Samaritan Hospital in West Islip, New York. He was diagnosed with cancer, heart failure and kidney failure requiring dialysis three times a week. Throughout his suffering, his greatest comfort was remembering the miraculous events he witnessed with me when we prayed over people.

I told him, "You may not be able to go pray OVER people, Gino, but you can still pray FOR people … and you can offer up all your sufferings for the poor souls in Purgatory.

"I am sure when Jesus, Saint Anne, the Blessed Mother and Padre Pio look upon you, Gino, they are quite pleased because of your faithful devotion and the loving way you have ministered to so many people."

In so many wonderful ways, Gino was much like Mary in that they both ministered to others while courageously fighting cancer and suffering with the related hardships that come with serious illness. People like them are truly among the richest people I've known because of the treasures they have gained in Heaven.

Thank you, God, for the gift of holy, wonderful, inspiring people like Mary and Gino.

Chapter 53

THE PERFECT GIFT

Patrick has been an usher at Ss. Cyril and Methodius Church in Deer Park, Long Island, New York for many years. After Mass one Sunday, he asked if I would join him in a visit to his mother-in-law whose husband had recently passed away. He told her that I was a good, fellow Catholic who had experienced quite a few miracles, and perhaps could offer some words to comfort her grief.

When we arrived at her home, we exchanged greetings and then followed this wonderful Catholic matriarch to her formal dining room. Patrick and I politely waited for her to sit at the head of the table before we sat opposite each other on either side of a large table.

The matriarch spoke briefly and lovingly about the good life she and her husband had enjoyed before God called him home. He, in particular, had lived a very good and noble life.

Patrick said, "Momma, I'd like Bob to tell you now one of the amazing miracles he has experienced."

She nodded politely yes, and waited for me to share something she assumed might provide comfort for her feelings of loss.

What immediately came to mind was a vision I once had involving Purgatory, and so I shared this with her and Patrick.

"I'd like to share with you the remarkable experience I once had during a visit my wife and I made to the National Shrine of the Immaculate Conception in Washington, D.C. At Mass in the lower Crypt Church, I offered the Mass for my paternal grandpa who had died under uncertain circumstances years before. I did so in case he was in Purgatory and needed a Mass to aid his purification.

"After Mass, I was puzzled to see a vision of angels bowing in reverence behind the altar as they knelt facing the back wall of the Church! I told my wife, Margie, what I saw so we agreed to go back there to see what, if anything, could explain this. When we arrived there, we immediately discovered why the angels were prostrating themselves in reverence.

"There in the center of the wall was a Tabernacle containing the Eucharist! As we then moved to the right, I noticed that the next area with a Tabernacle was devoted to one of my beloved patron saints, Jesus' grandmother, Saint Anne.

"At that very moment, I felt my spirit suddenly and forcefully rise straight up out of my body! I was whisked at a herculean speed across the life-line into another dimension of life. I thought this must be what it is like when we die physically and cross the life-line into the next realm of existence. I was soon suspended, motionless, in a place I instinctively recognized was Purgatory.

"I was immersed in warmth that permeated my very being and the entire area. The refreshing fragrance of purifying incense filled the air. The area in which I was suspended resembled a vast ocean. There were various shades of grey incense representing separate levels in Purgatory reflecting the gravity of stains of sins to be removed. The farther down I could see, the darker the grey color.

"Looking upward about ten feet away was a surface composed of a brilliant, white light. I understood this to be the light of God emanating from above in Paradise, the full presence of God, the angels and saints.

"Looking downward, I saw countless souls being purified. To my surprise, alongside every soul in Purgatory was their guardian angel still ministering to them as they did in physical life!

"Looking upward once again, I saw two magnificent

angels stationed just below the brilliant white surface. They were looking downward and had one hand extended in that direction as if to welcome someone. Their other hand was extended upward toward God in Paradise in the light above."

I paused at this point and asked the matriarch if she was interested in hearing more of this vision. She rather calmly nodded yes so I continued.

"Curious to see what the angels were looking at, I looked in the same direction and was surprised to see a young man being escorted by two angels upward in the direction of the brilliant surface above."

"Who was it?" the matriarch wanted to know.

"I didn't recognize the young man as he rushed past me but I will never forget the incredible expression he had on his face. His eyes, fixed at the area above, sparkled with a look of incredible joy and ecstasy! The young man and the angels quickly disappeared into the light of God above.

"My attention was then immediately drawn to a dazzling sight. There, stationed high up in the center of Purgatory where all the souls could see her, was a beautiful 'lady in blue.' Although she was at a distance from me, I could clearly see that she was smiling at me!

"It was the Blessed Mother!"

The matriarch was so impressed hearing this was the Blessed Mother, she made the sign of the cross.

I continued, "The Blessed Mother was so far away, I just assumed that I wouldn't be able to hear anything she said. However, to my great surprise, I could hear her beautiful voice clearly across the great distance between us!

"She said, 'The last vestige of purification that man needed to be freed into the fullness of God's presence in Paradise was the Holy Sacrifice of the Mass you offered for your grandpa!'

"Hearing this brought me great joy because I realized that

this meant my grandpa must ALREADY have been in Paradise. You see, he didn't need the Mass I offered for him so it was given to the young man whom I was allowed to see!"

The matriarch and Patrick smiled and nodded their heads in agreement.

"Wow," Patrick exclaimed. "That's incredible!"

The matriarch agreed and then surprised me by asking if anything else happened.

"Oh, yes," I answered, "the Blessed Mother then told me one of the most profound things I have ever heard! She said, 'If you add up all the people who have ever lived, are living now, and will ever live … and add up all their prayers and sacrifices … they do not equal the benefit of just one Mass. That is because your prayers are united with the infinite value of my Son's Holy Sacrifice!'

"Then Our Lady added, 'As you have seen, if the person you offer a Mass for is already in Heaven, my Son in His infinite love and mercy allows that person to give the benefit of that Mass to someone he knows who is still in Purgatory!'"

All of this has greatly impressed the matriarch and Patrick so I immediately seized the opportunity to say to the matriarch, "Hearing how wonderful and important it is to offer a special Mass for our loved ones … have you offered one for your husband in case he is in Purgatory?"

This gentle lady's friendly demeanor immediately changed as it became quickly apparent that my suggestion greatly offended her!

Composing herself, she answered as politely as she could, "My husband was a good and honorable man who lived a good life. He certainly is in Heaven … and does **NOT** need a special Mass to be said for him!"

At that moment, a loud crashing noise alarmed us all! It came from the far corner of the dining room we were in so Patrick quickly got up to see what crashed. Whatever it was, he fixed it and returned to his seat but strangely didn't explain what happened.

When the matriarch asked, Patrick would only say, "It's okay, Momma; it's nothing. I fixed it. Everything's okay."

She shrugged then tried to change the subject of a special Mass for her husband. However, I felt so strongly about it that I repeated my suggestion that she have a special Mass celebrated for her husband.

She again bristled at my suggestion and leaning forward for emphasis, she sternly said, "I told you … my husband was a good man. He's in Heaven so he does **NOT** need a special Mass said for him!"

Another loud crashing noise again came from the far corner of the room! Patrick got up once again and fixed whatever had crashed. When he returned, he simply said that he had taken care of what fell. Oddly, he refused again to say what caused the loud, disturbing noise.

Despite the matriarch's strong objections, I still felt that I should pursue the subject of having a special Mass said for her husband. In fact, I actually felt obligated to do so.

This time, I said, "I can tell that you have great love and reverence for the Blessed Mother. Please consider what she told me about offering a special Mass for those we love who have crossed the life-line before us. It is the perfect gift!"

The matriarch emphatically shook her head no!

In that instant, the loudest, most alarming crash noise yet wickedly resounded throughout the room!

Patrick jumped up and tended to whatever caused the terrible crashing noise. This time, however, he brought something back with him and stood right next to the matriarch holding a large picture in front of her.

"Momma," Patrick said dramatically, "Look at what was

causing all that noise! Look!"

Seeing what it was caused her to lower her face into her hands as she began to weep.

"Momma, I want to show Mr. Walsh what was causing the noise. Is that okay?"

She nodded yes so Patrick held up for me to see a large, glass-covered, framed picture containing a photo of the matriarch's late husband! And the glass cover was not shattered!

Patrick added, "Momma, every time you said no to Mr. Walsh's suggestion to have a special Mass said for Poppi … his picture went flying off the shelf and crashed! Each time I put it back on the shelf, I put things in front of it so it couldn't possibly fall off the shelf!

"Momma, all the big things I put in front of Poppi's picture are still there … unmoved!"

Realizing what this represented, the matriarch sobbed, made the sign of the cross … and finally agreed to have a Mass said for her husband!

She had a special Mass said for her late husband … and his picture never flew off the shelf again.

Chapter 54

THE BREAKING OF A DEMONIC CURSE

"Curses invoke evil … and the origin of all evil is demonic.

These words were spoken by Father Gabriele Amorth who was Chief Exorcist of the Vatican at the time. The reality of his comments were further supported by other exorcists.

In fact, Father Gabriele Nanni, an exorcist, further explained that, "Curses are the main cause of suffering for so many people who go to exorcists!"

The victims of a curse can experience unexplained problems and sufferings in their lives including attacks on their physical and mental health, employment, finances, relationships, personal anxieties and much, much more.

Both exorcists point out that those who wish a curse upon others, **always** have the demons attack them as well!

Another exorcist, Father Jose Antonio Fortea, confirms this, "Without a doubt, they will suffer some type of demonic influence, possession or sickness! The evil they wish upon others will come back to them. **A demon is never invoked in vain!"**

It is noteworthy that these exorcists conducted countless exorcisms that had their origins in curses wished upon the victims.

Surprisingly, Father Amorth once said, "In cases where a curse is spoken with true treachery, especially if there is a blood relationship between the one who casts them and the intended victims, the outcome can be quite hellacious, more so, if the curse is wished by a family member against other relatives … and especially if the curse is wished on a special occasion … such as a wedding!"

That is exactly what happened in the following true story. An innocent Long Island, New York family had a hate-filled curse wished upon them by their in-laws at the wedding. And the curse was wished upon their offspring for generations to follow!

The main character in this story is a member of the victimized family - a middle-aged Roman Catholic woman who eventually stood up to the forces of evil torturing her family. Fortunately for her, she was well-founded in her faith and quite courageous. To respect the privacy of all those involved, all the names in this story have been changed … but not a single detail in the nightmarish events. We will call the brave lady, Judy.

I am the other central character in this story. Although I am a lay person, a Roman Catholic who was not ordained, I was anointed in the healing ministry including deliverance of evil spirits. That anointing was conducted years ago by one of the holiest Roman Catholic priests in the twentieth century, Father John Lazanski, at St. Anthony's Shrine on Arch Street in downtown Boston.

An elderly priest, Father Lazanski was blessed with a remarkable healing ministry in which he prayed over tens of thousands of people over the course of his priesthood. He and I were graced by God to pray over countless people – often resulting in a miracle of every kind.

A significant difference between us was that I was periodically called upon to lead a deliverance prayer in fierce battles to free people who were held in the clutches of the Devil. In time, I came to realize that the Holy Spirit calls lay people like me in every age to serve in deliverance ministry when an ordained exorcist is not available.

While I am not allowed to say the official prayers of exorcism strictly reserved only for ordained priests. I may only say prayers of deliverance. Having said that, Exorcists and deliverance ministers are merely intermediaries; in all cases it is God - and God alone - who drives out devils.

This last fact was crystalized in an amazing experience I once had. As always in preparation to pray deliverance prayer over someone troubled by the Devil, I had fasted and prayed for days and then went to Confession in preparation to help Judy.

On this particular day, I happened to stop by the Church of Holy Innocents located on 37th Street, west of Broadway in Manhattan. It was mid-afternoon as I entered the darkened, silent and completely empty church. I was surprised to see a young priest I had never seen before in the church suddenly appear by the Confessional booth located in the back right of the church. Without saying a word, he quickly entered the booth and waited to hear my Confession!

I thanked God that I would be able to go to Confession in preparation for the upcoming battle with the demons. Without hesitation, I eagerly went over and entered the Confessional.

I began by briefly explaining to the priest that I was anointed in the healing and deliverance ministry, and that my confession today was critical for me since it was in preparation for another dangerous confrontation with the Devil.

The young priest's response was surprising and highly-encouraging, "I understand … and I commend you for using the gift God has entrusted in your hands.

"But be careful. You must strictly follow the Church's teachings in such cases. Do not allow yourself to be distracted by anything the Devil might say or do. You must keep your focus on saying the prescribed prayers of deliverance, and under no circumstances, are you to say the prayers that are reserved only for those who are ordained."

I thanked him for his advice, and then, guided by Padre Pio's words that there are no such things as unimportant venial sins, I confessed all the transgressions I could recall.

When I completed confessing everything, the young priest surprised me by asking, "What was your reaction when you didn't receive the help you expected from clergy?"

I realized that I had overlooked confessing the sin of anger I felt toward Catholic clergy who failed to fulfill their duties to help people tormented by the Devil.

"When I suspected the Devil was entrenched in someone, I always did what the Church tells lay people like me to do. I reached out to cardinals and bishops and asked who the exorcist was so I could turn everything over to him. But no one would tell me who the exorcist was so I was filled with anger because they left me to proceed alone on my own.

"I am sorry for this anger, Father … but I still want to know who the exorcist is!"

At that moment, I clearly heard the voice of God speak directly into my right ear, "**I AM**!"

I understood immediately what I heard was the voice of God Himself telling me that **HE** is the ultimate exorcist! Ordained exorcists and lay deliverance ministers like me are merely intermediaries! I excitedly told the young priest how God just spoke in my right ear and told me who the exorcist is … HE is the exorcist!

Very calmly, the young priest replied, "Yes, that's true. Now, God has greatly favored you by personally giving you the answer you've been seeking. So now you should thank Him … and be faithful to the ministry He has called to."

After receiving absolution, I thanked the young priest, went right outside the confessional booth where I said my prayers of penance only a few feet from the confessional. After saying my prayers, I waited for the young priest to come out so I could speak further with him. No one else had gone into the confessional after me.

There still was no one in the church except the young priest and me, so I patiently watched, prayed and waited for a long time. Finally, I went over to the confessional booth and gently knocked on the door, and waited for a response. When no sound was heard within the booth, I knocked again and waited a few more moments hoping the young priest would answer. Once again, there was no reply … only dead silence in the confessional.

Wondering if the young priest might have fallen asleep, I called out loudly, "Father, I am going to open the door. If you are in there, please say something."

Again, no sound came from inside the confessional so I slowly opened the door and was shocked to see that the young priest was not inside the confessional! How is this possible, I wondered. The confessional had only one door which I was blocking! The young priest had literally vanished!

I quickly went to the front of the church and knelt before Jesus in the tabernacle as I thanked God for what just transpired. God had given me the answer I so desperately had sought for so many years … He told me who the exorcist is.

He, God, is the exorcist! Ordained exorcists and anointed lay deliverance ministers like me are only the intermediaries.

Before I proceed with Judy's plight, allow me to provide some additional, important background on the reality of curses. Catholic exorcists tell us that those of us who are still physically alive can wish a curse upon others … but no living person can actually carry out a curse. However, the Devil can and often does take up a curse and carry it out with a fierce, diabolical force and violence against the unsuspecting target of the curse … the victims.

There are countless cases where it was later learned that a curse wished upon someone and/or a family resulted in terrible misfortunes and suffering of every type. These can last until an exorcism or deliverance is performed to break the curse. Sometimes, the victim dies before this can be achieved!

We have all heard people say, "Things are so bad, I feel like I've been cursed!"

In many cases, this is exactly what has happened as curses are carried out by demons filling the lives of victims at times with suffering in which nothing ever seems to go right. Misfortunes of every type can include endless “bad luck,” violent physical and emotional attacks, strange accidents, serious health issues, sudden unexplained deaths, relationship problems, loss of employment, and much, much more.

Interestingly, exorcists tell us that the one who wishes a curse upon someone else also winds up being tormented by the Devil! When it comes to a curse being wished, clearly no one escapes unscathed … everyone suffers … and suffers badly.

The Vatican’s chief exorcist, Father Gabriel Amorth, once said this of curses, “It is almost as if the demon persecutes a family from without … without taking possession of any of its members!”

To discover who wished the terrible curse against the family in this chapter, we must go back in time past a number of generations. It all began in the late 1900’s when Judy’s great grandmother emigrated from Ireland and settled in Boston. She worked as a waitress in a restaurant and soon fell in love with a fellow worker, a waiter. She was Roman Catholic; he was Jewish.

When they were married in the rectory of a local Catholic church, the Jewish man’s family was enraged that he married a non-Jew! Their outrage was so great, they actually sat in “Shiva” as if he were dead! Shiva in Hebrew literally means seven representing the week-long mourning period in Judaism for first-degree relatives, that is, father, mother, son, daughter, brother, sister, and spouse. This is often referred to as “sitting Shiva.”

These hate-filled family members wished a curse upon the newly married couple … and on all their descendants! They decided that the specific object of their curse would be the wedding ring worn by the Catholic bride.

From that time on, Judy's great grandparents and their descendants have suffered endless tragedies and misfortunes of every type. The family stories abound with horrendous events that included the death of several babies, mysterious illnesses, mental illness in family members, horrific accidents, financial disasters, broken relationships and more.

Over the years, it became obvious that whoever had responsibility for the great grandparents' wedding ring suffered far more than others. As the years rolled by, the mysterious misfortunes continued, and ... several younger adults in the family became Satan worshippers.

It was then that Judy was named executrix of her great grandparent's wedding ring which had been kept locked up in a bank safe deposit box for many years. Knowing the history of the ring, no one in the family dared to go anywhere near it. Even workers at the bank who were familiar with the ring's history would not go anywhere near the safe deposit box that held it.

In 2007, as accidents and tragedies fell ever more heavily upon Judy and her family, she realized she had to do something to get rid of the cursed ring ... and all the evil that was linked to it. That was when she reached out to Father James J. LeBar, the chief exorcist and foremost authority on such matters at the Catholic Archdiocese of New York in residence at St. Patrick's Cathedral. Cardinal Egan at the time headed up the Archdiocese.

After Father LeBar and his support team of five conducted a thorough discernment of the terrible events, it was decided that a formal exorcism was justified to break the curse. Cardinal Egan then granted the required permission. In an extraordinary act of faith and love, Judy agreed to serve as the subject of the exorcism - representing all the members of her family.

The exorcism to end the curse on the family began well but things soon turned quite badly. The comments and actions of the Devil were so vile, Father LeBar collapsed and had to be rushed to the hospital. He soon lapsed into critical condition and despite the very best medical care, Father LeBar shockingly died soon afterward!

Since no other exorcist was available at the time, the exorcism was indefinitely suspended. In the weeks following Father LeBar's death, Judy and her family members suffered even greater, unrelenting attacks by demons. More desperate than ever, Judy tried without success to find another exorcist. Everywhere she turned, she was told no one knew where to find an exorcist who could resume the exorcism. She assumed the news of what happened to Father LeBar made it virtually impossible for her to find another exorcist.

Just when everything seemed hopeless, a Catholic priest friend of hers called with encouraging news. He knew of a fellow Catholic, a lay person, who was anointed in deliverance ministry. The priest was convinced this man could help.

He was speaking of me.

"He is an extraordinary man of God who is anointed with a remarkable healing ministry that includes deliverance! And he lives right here on Long Island. I and other priests have sent people to him whom we believed were under attack by the Devil … as you and your family are. He helped to free those people, and I think he can help you. I have arranged for you to meet right away."

Surprisingly, Judy was at first hesitant to contact me since - like most Catholics - she knew little about the critical role played by lay deliverance ministers in the spiritual battle against Satan and its legions of devils. However, considering her dire circumstances, Judy felt she had no other choice.

At our very first meeting, Judy told me she felt as comfortable with me as she did with Father LeBar. She poured out her heart about everything that had transpired up to that time including the cursed ring and how Father LeBar, the chief exorcist in New York, collapsed during the exorcism and soon thereafter died!

After carefully listening, I agreed to help Judy find another ordained exorcist to help her and her family. The first thing I did was call the Archdiocese of New York but was unable to speak with Cardinal Egan who was thoroughly familiar with what happened. I asked the Cardinal's secretary to ask him who was going to replace Father LeBar as the exorcist in New York so I could take Judy to him to resume the exorcism.

After speaking with Cardinal Egan, his secretary called back and told me, "Cardinal Egan has "emphatically" decided **NOT** to appoint another exorcist at this time given the terrible circumstances of what happened to Father LeBar."

She quickly added that the Cardinal had no idea where I might find another exorcist!

Frustrated, I asked, "Well, what am I to do? I cannot just desert this poor lady and her family; what am I to do? Please ask the Cardinal to give me his advice."

The Cardinal's secretary soon called back with Cardinal Egan's advice, "You should seek assistance from the Ordinary (Bishop) of your diocese in Rockville Centre since that is where you and the lady both live. That's the proper protocol in this situation."

I found myself, once again, angry and terribly frustrated by the inability to get Catholic clergy to fulfill their duty in this critical area of ministry.

With no other choice, I followed Cardinal Egan's advice and called the Bishop of Rockville Centre, Bishop William Murphy. I explained Judy's dilemma including the disturbing news of what happened to Father LeBar during the exorcism at St. Patrick's Cathedral in New York City. I also explained that Cardinal Egan advised me to call the Bishop regarding the matter.

After conferring with the Bishop, his secretary called and told me, "Although the Bishop is 'deeply concerned about such matters,' there is no priest in our Rockville Centre Diocese at this time who feels called to serve as an exorcist."

I replied that I understood but added, "Please ask the Bishop to tell me where an exorcist is located in another diocese so I can take Judy there for help."

Surprisingly, the answer came right back, "The Bishop said to tell you that he doesn't know where you might find another exorcist."

I was stunned, "Well, what am I supposed to do then? I cannot just leave this poor woman and her family. I feel obligated to do something to help but I am only a lay person. Although I have been anointed in healing and deliverance, I know the Church teaches that cases possibly involving possession, only an ordained exorcist should lead the prayers. So what am I supposed to do?"

The next words I heard were shocking, "We don't know what to tell you; all we can say is that there is nothing **WE** can do!"

I strongly disagreed, "That's not acceptable! Jesus tells us in the parable of the 'Good Samaritan' in the Bible (Luke 10:29) that both the Bishop and I cannot just go on our merry way without doing **something** to help!"

"The Bishop said to tell you to do what you can," his secretary said matter-of-factly … then she abruptly hung up!

I felt so lost and abandoned by the very ones, our Catholic clergy, who are empowered by God to deal with attacks by the Devil. In Matthew 10:7, Jesus tells us, "As you go, proclaim the good news, 'The kingdom of heaven has come near.' Cure the sick, raise the dead, cleanse the lepers, **and cast out demons**!"

I was stunned to realize that these powerful leaders of two massive Roman Catholic dioceses in New York and Rockville Centre were not going to do anything to help the poor tormented soul for whom the chief exorcist in New York, Father James LeBar, had been conducting an exorcism!

I could not understand how they could be so lacking in compassion to turn away and do nothing to help the least of our brethren … someone the chief exorcist, Father LeBar, believed was being tormented by the Devil.

I also found it quite disturbing that neither Cardinal Egan nor Bishop Murphy, nor their staff, ever inquired about the well-being of the poor woman for whom Father LeBar was conducting the authorized exorcism.

They were behaving much like the uncaring priest Jesus tells us about in Luke 10:29, "Now by chance a priest was going down that road; and when he saw him (the poor man who was badly beaten and needed help), he passed by on the other side!"

Chills ran up and down my spine as I wondered, "If this can happen here in these two great centers of Roman Catholicism, in how many other dioceses across America is the same thing being done? How many other poor souls are being ignored by Roman Catholic clergy when it comes to dealing with demonic torments?

My subsequent attempts to find a Catholic exorcist anywhere in America failed. Ultimately, I realized that the Catholic Church in America was not going to divulge where the reported 17 ordained exorcists were located. Having fulfilled my duty to try to find one, I realized that it remained my responsibility to do whatever I could to help free Judy of her generational curse in keeping with Christ's words in the "Good Samaritan" and in Mark 9:38 where Christ clearly approves of lay people helping to free people besieged by the Devil.

In Mark 9:38, Jesus tells us, "John said to him, 'Teacher, we saw someone casting out demons in your name, and we tried to stop him, because he was not following us.' But Jesus said, **'Do not stop him**; for no one who does a deed of power in my name will be able soon afterward to speak evil of me. **Whoever is not against us is for us!"**

And so, after much prayer, I told Judy how my efforts to find an exorcist to finish the exorcism were unsuccessful. I explained, however, that under these circumstances, I would step in as an anointed lay deliverance minister to pick up where the exorcist, Father James LeBar, left off.

I explained how I could conduct a "private exorcism prayer" as compared with a Church authorized "public exorcism prayer" to break the curse. I added that since I was not ordained, I was NOT permitted to use the official prayers of exorcism used only by an ordained priest.

However, I was allowed to use proper deliverance prayers using the Holy Name of Jesus to cast out the evil spirits. I also explained that, as an anointed lay deliverance minister, I was not required to obtain the permission of the local Bishop.

Having said that, I comforted Judy with the words Christ gives us in Mark 9:38, and assured her that I would be strictly following the guidelines provided by Roman Catholic exorcists in terms of how lay deliverance prayer should be conducted.

Judy put her face in her hands and wept with tears of hope. When she told family members that a lay person was going to conduct a private deliverance prayer to break the demonic torments their family had suffered for generations, they all laughed and scoffed saying it was all "utter nonsense."

In particular, younger adult family members who were involved in Satan worship jumped about the room in celebration and maniacally laughed, "The Devil is going to eat his soul alive! The Devil is going to eat his soul alive!"

They were referring to me.

Judy's older brother, a Harvard professor and avowed atheist, scoffed the loudest at such a silly idea that a lay person was going to conduct what he called "medieval voodoo nonsense." The next day, he collapsed and slipped into a coma as he was rushed unconscious to a local Boston hospital. Startled doctors watched as the skin all over his body mysteriously began to peel off!

They were at a loss to understand why this was happening so they placed him in insolation. Infectious disease specialists were called in but they, too, were not able to diagnose what was happening as Judy's brother slipped into an even deeper coma. He was kept in isolation while many other tests were ordered.

When I heard this latest disturbing news, I immediately thought of what happened to Father LeBar, and prepared myself for what I was sure would be a fierce, hellacious confrontation with the Devil and its entrenched horde of evil spirits. I went to Confession, prayed fervently and fasted for days.

Armed with more confidence in God's love and majesty than I had fear of the Devil, I set out to do battle with the creatures from Hell.

After explaining the Church approved process to Judy, I and two other Catholic prayer warriors first accompanied her to the bank to get the cursed ring where it had been stored for years in one of the bank's safety deposit boxes. Under the nervous view of bank employees, I used a pair of metal tongs to carefully remove the cursed ring and then I submerged it in a thick, black metal pot, a cauldron that I had filled with holy water. I did this as exorcists caution us to do … and under no circumstances to come into direct contact with any objects that have been cursed.

The next prescribed step was to have an ordained priest bless the cursed ring with prayer and more even holy water. As prearranged, we drove to a Catholic parish located all the way out east on Long Island. There, the young priest waited for us. He was surprisingly familiar with such things when I explained all that was involved.

When we arrived at the Church, the young priest led us directly to the tabernacle where we stood closely together while he said several prayers over the cursed ring. Then he asked God to protect us and everyone else who is involved. When he finished praying, he blessed us and sprinkled holy water on us and the pot containing the cursed ring.

Since exorcists tell us that cursed objects should be burned and/or melted, we carefully transported the cursed ring in the small cauldron of holy water to a car repair shop where a friend of mine, Gary, was a mechanic. Using a commercial blowtorch, he tried to melt the ring while it remained submerged in the holy water at the bottom of the pot.

Amazingly, the holy water did not boil … and the ring did not melt despite the intense heat from the blowtorch! As soon as I began to pray, however, the submerged ring at the bottom of the pot began to melt into liquid gold right before our very eyes.

The holy water in the pot never boiled!

Next, as exorcists tell us, I had to cast the cursed, melted ring as far as I could into running water like that of a river. So much time had been taken to remove the ring from the bank, have it blessed by a priest and then melted by my friend, Gary, it was quite late at night.

At two in the morning, there was no one available to go with me as I drove along the Belt Parkway with the cursed, melted ring still submerged in the pot of holy water. My destination was the walkway immediately adjacent to the East River in Brooklyn by 18th Avenue near the Verrazano Narrows Bridge.

When I arrived there, the entire area leading up to the river was shrouded in pitch-black darkness. It was eerily silent and completely deserted where I parked the car. Other than myself, no one was there … that is, no one human.

As I got out of the car with the melted ring submerged in the pot of holy water carefully balanced in my hands, I was suddenly surrounded by hundreds of little black, screeching birds swarming in the air all around me! At the same time, a powerful wind began blowing against me so strongly that I had to struggle to take every step!

It was obvious the Devil was behind what was happening. As the screeching of the birds and howling of the wind intensified, I felt slightly alarmed. I realized that I was now in mortal danger … physically and spiritually.

The Devil was doing everything it could to frighten, intimidate and stop me from getting to the river's edge where the Devil knew I needed to throw the cursed ring far out into the depths of the East River!

I called out the name of Jesus as the ultimate exorcist and begged Him to help and protect me from the Devil, the black screeching birds, the howling wind, the raging river and the unseen demonic creatures I sensed swirling madly around me.

Struggling mightily against the howling winds, I finally reached the short railing positioned right in front of the East River only a few feet below. Looking out upon the dark, thrashing waves of the river, I implored God once again to bless my efforts and protect everyone involved … including me!

With all the force I could muster, I raised up high the pot containing the cursed ring still submerged in holy water and flung it as far as I could out into the East River. As soon as the pot splashed down into the East River, the water appeared to swirl wildly around the pot until it was suddenly violently sucked down into the depths!

At that very moment, the screeching birds disappeared and the winds died down. The sense of utter chaos and mayhem was gone.

In Boston, Judy's atheist brother abruptly awoke from the deep coma he was in at the hospital. Medical staff rushed into his insolation room and watched in disbelief as all the areas on his body that had been peeling transformed into blisters, burst, oozed and disappeared before their very eyes!

The family curse had finally been broken … made possible by the remarkable faith and perseverance of Judy … and carried out by the ultimate exorcist … Jesus.

Chapter 55

WARREN'S MIRACLE

My sister, Mary Ann, and her wonderful husband, Warren, were enjoying young married life together when they were hit with devastating news. Warren was diagnosed with late stage malignant intestinal cancer. The oncologists said there was nothing they could do to help except to "keep him comfortable." They estimated Warren had about three months left. Warren was only 33 years old.

His illness was so advanced, Warren was immediately placed in Hospice care at home with Mary ever at his side along with highly-skilled, compassionate medical care.

I was on the other side of the world in Taiwan, China on business when doctors told our family to come right away to say goodbye to Warren because he was about to cross the lifeline. As family members joined Mary standing around Warren's bed, I walked quite a distance from the Grand Hotel on Zhongshan N Road to St. Christopher's Catholic Church in Taipei City. I was determined to attend a Mass to pray for Warren and Mary.

When I arrived, I went directly to the sacristy where I was told a priest was about to arrive to celebrate Mass. I wanted to ask him if he would pray for Warren and Mary. I assumed the priest would be Chinese, so I wondered what I would do if the priest didn't speak English. I was worried about how I would be able to communicate with him, so I asked the Blessed Mother and Saint Anne to help me.

At that moment, a young, red-haired priest briskly walked in and introduced himself in English … with an Irish brogue!

"Hi, I am Father Tom; it's nice to meet you!"

"Hello, Father; my name is Bob Walsh."

Then before Father could say anything, I quickly blurted

out, "You're not Chinese!"

Laughing, he said, "Yes, that's true. As a matter of fact, I am a Missionary priest here on assignment from Boston! You, too, are far away from home. What brings you here to beautiful, downtown Taipei?"

"I am here on business, Father. I have a favor to ask of you. Unfortunately, at this very moment back home, my sister's husband, Warren, is at home dying from cancer. The family is gathered around him and Mary right now but I am here on the other side of the world in China. So … I know the closest I can be with them is here where the Eucharist is celebrated at Mass."

"That's true," Father said with confidence.

"Father, would you please include Warren in your prayers at this Mass?"

"Yes, of course, I will," he said in his lyrical Irish brogue. "What's more, I will ask our congregation to join us in that prayer!"

"Back home, Father, I serve as a Eucharistic Minister at my parish of Ss. Cyril and Methodius on Long Island. Is there any chance I be allowed to assist at this Mass as an EM?"

"Yes, that would be wonderful. However, it is the tradition of our parish here that all those who assist at Mass wear a white robe. Is that all right?"

"Yes, Father, of course."

This requirement actually stunned me. It was the fulfillment of a lifelong vision I had from my earliest days of life. In the vision, I am wearing a full length white robe as I assist on the altar of God at Mass.

During Mass, Chinese was spoken but I somehow, miraculously, understood Father Tom's words when he asked the congregation to pray for Warren. A powerful, exhilarating feeling flowed over my entire being as congregation said Warren's name.

At that moment back home in America, our family was

gathered around Warren's bedside praying for him since the doctors said he surely would pass away then. The Hospice aide checked Warren's vital signs and frowned. Before she could say anything, Warren suddenly sat bolt upright, practically jumped up out of bed, briskly walked through the rooms to the kitchen, sat down then loudly invited everyone to come play cards with him!

He was speaking and acting as if there was little wrong with him! When a doctor arrived, he and the aide said they had never seen anything like it remarking, "It's a miracle that he is still with us!"

Our family's prayers joined with Father Tom and the congregation in St. Christopher's Church in China, were rewarded with a startling miracle.

My brother, Paddy, was so shocked, he exclaimed, "Oh, my God, Warren, you are a modern-day Lazarus!"

When I returned from my trip to China, I asked Warren, an agnostic, if he wanted a Catholic priest to come administer the Sacrament of Anointing. Countless times before when I asked him this, he would always refuse saying that he just wasn't sure. This time, however, Warren smiled and nodded yes!

It was then that I realized that Warren's miracle wasn't just that he was able to get up off his death bed and live for weeks more. It was also that God allowed him to live long enough to more fully understand his feelings toward God.

That was Warren's miracle.

I quickly made arrangements for Monsignor Brendan Riordan from our parish, Ss. Cyril and Methodius, to come by and administer the sacraments. When Father Riordan arrived and joined us in Warren and Mary's crowded apartment, we all felt reassured and comforted by his very presence and demeanor.

Of all the good and wonderful priests I have had the good fortune to know, Father Riordan is one of the most loving and in so many ways … Christ-like. He not only ministered to Warren and Mary, he ministered to all of us as if he were a member of our close family.

After Warren received the sacraments, we all sensed that Warren would now cross over the lifeline. As we stood around his bedside praying, he finally peacefully went to God … with a smile on his face.

Just then, one of our younger sisters entered the room. She didn't realize that Warren had just gone to God. She walked right past us all and leaned over Warren so she could place a beautiful red rose in his right hand which was resting on his chest.

As we watched, the petals on the head of this delicate little flower gently opened up and rose toward the heavens as if it was being raised by an unseen hand.

Warren's miracle was made possible, first of all, through God's love for him. But the miracle was also accomplished through the ardent love and prayers of his wife, Mary, our entire family and friends, Father Riordan, Father "Boston" Tom, and the many men, women and children filling St. Christopher's church on the other side of the world in China.

Chapter 56

BABY BRENDAN

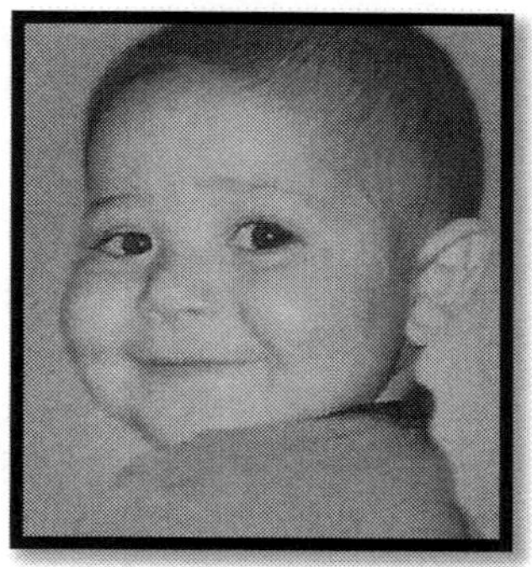

Brendan William Pio Caselli

This is a very special love story - the kind of love that parents and siblings have for a child suffering with terminal illness. This is also a story of God's love for all of us, His children.

After Mass one Sunday, my wife, Margie, and I met Mike and Tracy Caselli and their three adorable children - Michael, Sarah and baby Brendan. Mike was a New York City police officer at the time, and Tracy a nurse at a local Long Island hospital. They were a beautiful, young family were often seen attending Mass at our parish, Ss. Cyril and Methodius Catholic Church in Deer Park, Long Island, New York.

Together with relatives and close-knit friends, they were enjoying all the joys and challenges of young family life until the day they received some devastating news. Baby Brendan was diagnosed with a terrifying, fast-growing, lethal form of childhood cancer, "Acute Lymphocytic Leukemia (ALL)," also known as "Acute Lymphoblastic Leukemia."

ALL is a cancer that starts from the early version of white

blood cells called lymphocytes in the bone marrow (the soft inner part of the bones where new blood cells are made). The blood cells divide too quickly and form too many immature "myoblasts" which fail to mature into normal, functioning blood cells. As the myoblasts multiply, they crowd out remaining normal blood cells and quickly spread to other parts of the body including the lymph nodes, liver, spleen, central nervous system (brain and spinal cord) and testicles in males. What exactly causes this cancerous change is not yet known.

Baby Brendan was only a year old.

As this terrifying journey began, Mike and Tracey prayed fervently while struggling to understand this terrible illness and get medical help to treat baby Brendan.

Along the way, God sent wonderful, caring people to help them carry this terrible cross. These modern-day" "Simons of Cyrene" included members of Mike and Tracy's family, friends, fellow parishioners at Ss. Cyril and Methodius Church and the medical staff at Columbia Hospital Cancer Center for Children in upper Manhattan.

Since I was a Catholic Eucharistic Minister at our parish, I decided one day to bring Holy Communion to Mike while he was with Brendan following a treatment at Winthrop University Hospital in Mineola, Long Island. (In the Catholic faith, I and other Eucharistic Ministers are allowed to bring Holy Communion to those who are at the hospital or are otherwise unable to attend Mass.)

At that time, it seemed that nothing could comfort poor little Brendan as he cried from the pain and discomfort of the medical treatment. Since his room was located right outside the nurses' station, nurses periodically came in to check on him. After giving Mike Holy Communion, I held out the open, now empty, Pyx toward Brendan. Only moments before, the Pyx held Holy Communion.

To our great surprise, Brendan immediately crying and eagerly reached out to take the Pyx in his little hands. He then held it against his heart and began to rock back and forth smiling at the Pyx. It appeared to Mike and me that baby Brendan was seeing something we could not see. It became so quiet, so suddenly, in Brendan's room, a nurse came rushing in to see if everything was okay.

Softly, she asked Mike, "Is everything all right? Why did Brendan stop crying? What is that he is holding?"

Mike explained, "Bob gave him the Pyx which had Holy Communion in it."

"Oh … my God," she exclaimed.

With tears welling up, she went out to tell other nurses who then came in to see baby Brendan still sitting there, gently rocking, smiling and staring into the open Pyx in his little hands.

Weeks later, Brendan was being treated at the Columbia cancer hospital in upper Manhattan. Mike was alone with him when suddenly, Brendan sat up with an expression of great surprise and joy while he pointed to the far side of his room and shouted, **"Jesus! Jesus!"**

Astonished, Mike asked, "Brendan, do you see Jesus?"

Still pointing, Brendan enthusiastically nodded his head and excitedly answered, **"YES! Jesus!" Jesus!"**

"Where is Jesus?" Mike asked. "Where do you see Him?"

Brendan continued to point toward the same area of the room as he emphatically shouted, **"There! Jesus! Jesus!"**

For the next five minutes, Brendan remained sitting up in the hospital bed staring and smiling in the same direction where he said Jesus was standing. Occasionally, Brendan giggled and nodded his head as if he was responding to something Jesus was saying to him!

Every time Mike asked Brendan if he was still seeing

Jesus in the room, Brendan enthusiastically nodded yes and replied, **"Jesus,"** as he pointed to the part of the room where he apparently saw Him.

Jesus had personally come to visit baby Brendan in the room at the Columbia Hospital Children's Cancer Center! What a remarkable blessing this was for Brendan … Mike … Tracey … and for all of their family, friends and staff at the cancer center.

One of the very special family members who helped from the very outset was Brendan's maternal grandmother, Monenna Kennedy, a wonderful, Irish lady of enormous faith. She did everything she could to help - cooking, babysitting, chauffeuring, shopping, cleaning, doing laundry and most importantly, storming Heaven with her prayers.

Throughout their ordeal, Tracy's good friend since childhood, Jenn, and her husband, Pete, took loving care of Brendan's siblings, Sarah and Michael, enabling Tracy and Mike to spend as much time as needed with Baby Brendan in the hospital. Jenn and Pete often had the children stay at their home where they spent time with their own four children. In addition, Jenn and Pete frequently made the trip from Long Island to the cancer hospital in upper New York City to visit with Brendan and the family. They made themselves available every day and did whatever they could to help their beloved friends.

Another childhood friend, Tina Lewis, and her husband, provided ongoing emotional support, chauffeuring, cooking and child care. During the summer months, Tina shared their pool with Michael and Sarah. A number of times when Brendan had to be rushed to the hospital in the middle of the night, Tina came right over to stay with Michael and Sarah.

In the midst of all their suffering, a construction contractor was hired by Mike and Tracy to make changes in their home to make it possible for Brendan to come home from the hospital for short visits. Unfortunately, the contractor was a heartless, dishonest individual. He disappeared with their money without doing any of the needed construction!

At the time, Brendan was undergoing chemotherapy to prepare his body for a possible bone marrow transplant. To bring him home, Mike and Tracy needed to prepare their home by removing all the carpeting and then installing new wood flooring. This was necessary in order to provide a sterile environment. Otherwise, baby Brendan would not be able to come home for a short visit with his family.

That is when I and my wife, Margie, our daughter, Peggie Murano, our daughter-in-law, Barbara Jean, our five teenage grandchildren and five of their teenage friends from our community went to Brendan's home and worked hard all day long in sweltering heat and humidity to prepare Brendan's home to make it possible for him to come home.

In part, this required pulling up and removing all the carpeting and padding throughout the second level of the home. Then we had to cut and roll all the carpeting and carry it all out to the curb. Next, we had to carefully remove all the staples in the floors before sweeping and vacuuming every bedroom in Brendan's home.

All that hard work and sacrifice by the teenagers and adults made it possible for Mike and Tracy to bring baby Brendan home to be with his family for that weekend before he had to return to the hospital. Young Michael and Sarah were as thrilled as little Brendan when he was able to come home and play with them.

So often in our American society we hear negative things about our youth; however, watching these teenagers work so hard, so unselfishly, to help Brendan's family restored our faith in the goodness of young people. Grandma Monenna rewarded all the laborers with a delicious pizza party.

Mike, meanwhile attended as many Masses as he could

for Brendan. At the Church of the Holy Innocents on west 37th Street in Manhattan, Mike spoke with an elderly, 90-year-old priest and asked him to pray for his son, Brendan. Mike explained that Brendan was being treated at Columbia Hospital for leukemia.

The elderly priest obviously had a hearing problem because he wanted to know why Brendan was in "Columbia, South America" rather than in a New York City hospital! No matter how many times Mike tried to explain that Brendan was, in fact, in Columbia Hospital in New York City, the priest persisted in asking why Brendan was in Columbia! This humorous exchange was just the kind of comic relief Mike needed.

A good friend of ours, Grace Begley, had the privilege of having one of the precious gloves once worn by Padre Pio, the saintly priest who was blessed with the stigmata, the wounds of Christ. Grace often allowed my wife, Margie, and me to bring Padre Pio's glove to Brendan's hospital room to pray over him with his parents.

Neighbors and friends cooked meals and sent them to Grandma Monenna for Sarah and Michael. Friends Jenn, Pete and Nancy cared for Michael and Sarah while other friends arranged play dates for the kids. A neighbor, Charlie, helped by mowing and raking Mike and Tracy's huge lawn.

While Brendan was being treated at the cancer hospital in Manhattan, Mike and Tracy took turns staying overnight with him in the large, special room specifically designed to accommodate families. Baby Brendan was never alone.

It was during especially difficult days that God sent several other people to visit and comfort Mike and Tracy. This included, in part, a holy man of God by the name of "Pastor Tim Fauvell."

Pastor Tim was a deeply-religious, licensed counselor who advised and comforted the Caselli family. He had a great sense of humor and was greatly admired by all including Brendan's sister, Sarah, and brother, Michael. Pastor Tim was personally familiar with the kind of heart-breaking suffering parents experience when a child suffers with leukemia … he lost his own two-year old son 10 years earlier to the same illness.

One day when Pastor Tim was on his way to the hospital to once again comfort Brendan and his family, God suddenly called Pastor Tim to Heaven! He had a massive heart attack in a taxi and died at the age of only 42. How wonderful it was that God allowed Pastor Tim to befriend, counsel and comfort Mike and Tracy before calling him home!

Another person sent by God was Mary, a loving, sensitive, prayerful, Christian nurse at Columbia Hospital who helped to care for Brendan and his parents. She was joined there by other wonderful, caring medical professionals including Nurse Sheryl and Doctor Diane George, a very spiritual woman who frequently prayed with Mike and Tracey.

Through these difficult months of pain and suffering, Mike went to nearby churches to attend Mass and pray for his baby boy. He asked everyone he met to pray for Brendan. Returning to the hospital one day, Mike stopped to speak with an obviously despondent, homeless man by the name of Anthony.

This day, Mike saw Anthony sitting slumped on the corner right across the street from the hospital.

"Hey, Buddy, are you okay?" Mike asked. "Do you need some help?"

Looking down at the ground, Anthony answered, "I've wasted my life; I've accomplished nothing. I'm a nobody; nobody cares if I live or die. There's no one in the whole world who loves me."

Mike corrected him, "Anthony, don't talk like that! You have a lot to live for! You are a child of God, a son of the most high! Don't you forget that! You should be rejoicing!"

Anthony looked up in amazement as Mike continued, "My little boy is in that hospital over there across the street fighting for his life at this very moment like so many other poor kids there. And all we parents can do is to be there with them, to pray for them and hope that God will heal them. Think of all the good **YOU** can do every day by praying for all those poor little kids and their families!"

Mike helped Anthony stand up, hugged him and gave him a set of rosary beads to use when praying for others. Weeping, Anthony thanked Mike and promised him he would be there every day at that corner to pray for all the sick kids in the hospital and all the people going to be with them.

Every day thereafter when Mike entered and left the cancer center, he would look across the street and often see Anthony standing there, smiling and waving the rosary beads high in the air.

Several volunteers came from our parish to do whatever they could to help: cooking, cleaning, arranging play dates for Sarah and Michael, contributing funds to offset the enormous medical expenses and more.

Students from Ss. Cyril and Methodius parish school went to Mike and Tracy's home to rake the front and back yards. The property looked immaculate whenever the school kids finished. The outpouring of prayer, love and Christian spirit from our church community was wonderful to behold.

Our beloved pastor at Ss. Cyril and Methodius, Monsignor Frank Gaeta, often made the long journey from Deer Park, Long Island to the hospital in New York City to visit Mike, Tracy and Brendan. His loving presence, prayers and spiritual guidance were a great comfort.

Father Donald Johnson, the chaplain at the cancer hospital, had become a daily visitor to spend time with Brendan and the family in Brendan's room. One day, he suggested that

Brendan be confirmed to receive the strength and graces of the Sacrament of Confirmation. Tracy and Mike immediately agreed and made arrangements to have Brendan confirmed right there in his hospital room.

The Confirmation name they chose for Brendan was "Pio" in honor of their family's close saintly friend, Padre Pio. As Father Donald confirmed Brendan in his hospital room, present were Tracy, Mike, Pete, Jenn, Monenna, Sarah, Michael and Nurse Mary.

After recuperating from foot surgery, my wife, Margie, would drive Grandma Monenna, brother Michael and sister Sarah, to spend time with Brendan at the cancer hospital. I would later join them after finishing work in downtown Manhattan. Margie often brought meals she prepared for everyone to enjoy while visiting Brendan. According to Tracy, these visits were like celebrating Thanksgiving together with Brendan as the family sat together and enjoyed the meals.

One Monday in late November began as usual for Tracy and Mike as they comforted, caressed, kissed and blessed Brendan, their little, beloved gift from God. This day, however, was to be different from all others … quite different. This was to be a sacred day.

As the day unfolded in what had become a holy place, Brendan's room at the cancer hospital, Pete, Jenn and Nurse Mary were present for a day of prayer and spiritual encouragement. Joining us were four holy, deeply-faithful women who knelt around Brendan's bed while they prayed. Mike, Tracy and I joined them in praying the Rosary. One of the ladies, a visionary, said that she saw a beautiful blue light appear above Brendan. That light, she explained, represented the "Lady in Blue," the Blessed Mother Mary.

Tracy was lying on the hospital bed cuddling Brendan next to her right side when our lovable pastor, Monsignor Frank

Gaeta, arrived. Joining him this day was a young, newly-ordained priest, Father Lee Descoteaux. Their presence brought an aura of peace and goodness. After greeting everyone - especially Brendan - Monsignor Gaeta sat by Brendan's bedside, closed his eyes and prayed silently for his youngest parishioner.

After Monsignor Gaeta and Father Lee left, Father Donald arrived and proceeded to bless Brendan, his parents and the faithful friends gathered there. After he departed, Father Portugal then arrived from St. Michael's Parish in Farmingville, Long Island.

It was then that I felt moved to say to everyone present that we were in the presence of a living saint - someone who had never sinned … baby Brendan.

Hearing this, Father Portugal smiled and began to recite soulful prayers in Latin as he sat close to Brendan. After giving a blessing to everyone, he departed. As he did, a powerful feeling of finality descended upon me.

It was about 6 p.m. as I watched Mike walking around the room splashing holy water everywhere especially on Brendan, Tracy and the area surrounding them. At that moment, an exhilarating sensation swept over me as I sensed the room being transformed into an utterly holy environment!

I realized this was related to Brendan … and his appointed time.

As Mike continued going about the room splashing holy water everywhere, I watched as a large area of the wall adjacent to Brendan's bed began to open wide! Through it billowed grey incense filling the room and immersing everyone in its beautiful, heavenly fragrance.

Then as I watched, two lines of majestic angels descended from above and glided through the opening and filled the room surrounding Brendan and the rest of us. The room was now fully immersed in absolutely brilliant, white light. I instinctively understood why these angels had come … they were here as an honor guard for some holy entity.

In the next moment, I discovered who.

I watched as remarkably beautiful Blessed Mother Mary gracefully entered the room and went directly to Brendan's bedside where she stood smiling lovingly down upon him. She exuded pure love and grace as she smiled upon baby Brendan.

Brendan quite apparently could see the Blessed Mother since he was smiling at her as he stared right back up into her loving eyes! Judging by the incredible look of joy and love on his little face, it was clear to me that he knew who exactly who this beautiful lady was.

I felt as if time stood still as the Blessed Mother, dressed in a full-length blue robe, stood by Brendan's bed and continued to gaze lovingly upon him. I realized that some communication was taking place between them but it wasn't for me to hear or understand.

Brendan now had a special light all around him … and he clearly no longer appeared to be suffering! Snuggled up close against his mommy, he looked up at her. The look of love and appreciation on his face was such as I have never seen before on a child's face. Turning his head, Brendan then looked over to his father, Mike, who was standing at the foot of the bed at the time. Brendan smiled as he watched Mike still spraying the room with holy water. The look on Brendan's face reflected such love and appreciation for his faith-filled father.

Mike and Tracy apparently were not aware of what was happening.

With her back to me, the Blessed Mother Mary leaned over slightly toward Brendan and extended her arms in a gesture that invited him to come to her. With his eyes fixed on hers, Brendan's spirit gracefully flowed up into her embrace.

In that moment, baby Brendan had gone from the loving

arms of one mommy to those of another.

All his terrible suffering was replaced with indescribable love, peace and happiness as he wrapped his little arms around his heavenly mother and rested his head on her left shoulder. The Blessed Mother slowly drew slightly back from the bed, turned into the opening and ascended upward toward the Light of God in Paradise escorted by the majestic honor guard of angels.

As they were departing, baby Brendan still resting his head on the Blessed Mother's shoulder, his eyes locked onto mine. He was communicating a powerful, exhilarating love and appreciation to me. Brendan then looked over to his mommy and daddy with a love now perfected in the presence of Almighty God. He and the Blessed Mother soon rose out of sight followed by all the angels.

After the last two angels ascended through the opening, it closed. The fragrance of roses and the brilliant light were gone. It was then that Tracy realized little Brendan had just died. The tears and sorrow that followed were what I imagine it must have been like at the foot of the cross on Calvary when Our Lord finally gave up His spirit.

Later that evening, I had a vision of Brendan standing in the midst of a breath-taking, never-ending gathering of saints of all sizes dressed in brilliant white robes. It was easy to recognize which one was Brendan. For my benefit, he was the little one wearing a police cap standing next to the Lady in Blue, the Blessed Mother, on one side, and on his other side was a short saintly priest in a brown robe … Padre Pio.

Brendan's funeral Mass was celebrated by our pastor at Ss. Cyril and Methodius Church. Nearly one hundred police officers attended from Mike's precinct in New York City. After the Mass, the police officers lined up in the street in front of the church and served as an honor guard for Brendan. Each saluted him as his tiny hearse passed by.

A few days later, Margie and I were waiting for the Thanksgiving Day Mass at our church to begin. As I sat praying for Mike and Tracy and their family, a vision of Brendan suddenly appeared in front of the altar in the sanctuary! He was dressed in a brilliant white robe and was playing around the altar area with countless other children who appeared to be his age … and they were all dressed in the same type of white robes!

My sense was that all these children had suffered in some similar way as Brendan did in physical life … but they were all now enjoying great joy and happiness together in Heaven. Just then, as a bell rang indicating that the Thanksgiving Mass was to begin, Brendan and all his little friends abruptly stopped playing and quickly lined up in front of the Communion rail and directly faced me.

Staring right at us, each one of these blessed children cast a look of consummate love upon Margie and me. My innermost being was filled with an exhilarating, ecstatic sensation of love and appreciation for all the prayers and things we did to comfort Brendan and his family during their time of suffering.

I understood that the children wanted us to know they are more alive than ever in Heaven with God, the angels and all the saints where they no longer suffer but rather, enjoy never-ending, indescribable, love, peace and happiness far beyond our understanding.

Brendan in particular wanted his parents, siblings, family and friends to know how grateful he was for how they all loved and comforted him during his suffering … and that he certainly is all right.

As the procession of altar servers and clergy then approached the altar, Brendan and his many friends joyfully rushed off together into the glorious white Light of God.

After Mass, I shared with Brendan's parents and siblings how I had a vision of Brendan before Mass running around the altar area playing with lots of kids in white robes.

Tracy and Mike were overjoyed to hear this.

Mike was especially interested in hearing more details as he fired off several questions, "How did Brendan look? How was he playing? Who was he playing with? What were the other kids like? Did Brendan say anything?"

I described everything I saw in the vision then I explained that although Brendan didn't speak words to me, I clearly understood what he wanted me to convey to his parents and family.

"Brendan expressed great love and gratitude for all those who cared for him, and he wanted in particular to let you and his siblings know how happy he is in Heaven. He stressed that I should let you know that he is having fun playing with so many new friends in Heaven! He indicated that you, his mother and father, would understand why he conveys that."

Tracy smiled and nodded, "One of the many things that has greatly saddened us is that Brendan's illness denied him a normal childhood. He was always so sick, he couldn't play with other children his age. Now we know that he is finally getting to play with his friends."

Mike was also quite emotional, "Brendan wanted us to know that he is all right now so God allowed him to send us a message about him playing with other kids. Only God knew how much it hurt us that he couldn't play with other kids.

"God is so beautiful. Thank you, God. Thank you."

Just then, a young girl from our church's children's choir, Theresa, came literally running over from the other side of the church.

Catching her breath, she said, "I've got to tell you about a dream I had involving Brendan last night! I saw him wearing his pajamas that have police motorcycles on them. He looked so happy and healthy as he and I played so happily together!"

Tracy and Mike smiled. They knew what Theresa didn't know. Brendan's favorite pajamas were his ones with the police motorcycles on them. Their spirits were so uplifted to hear another miraculous story describing how their baby Brendan was finally able to play and have fun … and was free from all the suffering he endured!

AUTHOR'S NOTE: Over the course of my life, I have witnessed events like this touching story where God in His infinite love and mercy reached out in some miraculous way to comfort and assure us that life does, in fact, continue after physical death.

Sometimes, this can be in the form of some sign that is meaningful to us - a butterfly, a familiar song, a meaningful expression, a dream of a departed loved one … or even … a group of white-robed children playing joyfully together.

For those of us who are Christian, we believe that our very best days are truly yet ahead in Heaven where we will be reunited with our loved ones forever. Our great comfort comes, in part, from the many promises God makes for us and for our loved ones in the Bible.

For example, the remarkable promise Jesus gives us in John 14:1, "Do not let your hearts be troubled. Believe in God, believe also in me. In my Father's house there are many dwelling places. If it were not so, would I have told you that I go to prepare a place for you? And if I go to prepare a place for you, I will come again and will take you to myself, so that where I am, there you may be also."

Amen.

Chapter 57

ST. MATTHEW'S ROSARY ALTAR SOCIETY

On November 3, 2016, the Rosary Altar Society of St. Matthew's RC Church in Dix Hills, New York, arranged for me to conduct a special presentation on the life of Saint Anne, the grandmother of Jesus Christ, and the mother of the Blessed Virgin Mary. I was delighted to speak about Saint Anne since she was one of my patron saints since early childhood.

The mid-week, evening event was surprisingly well attended by a large number of parishioners. Following my presentation, a long line of people spontaneously formed as people requested individual healing prayer. I listened with a heavy heart as many described the heavy crosses they carried, often for a loved one.

I prayed to the Holy Spirit for inspiration as I encouraged each one to stay close to God through Confession, Mass and Holy Communion; forgive everyone - everything; tell God exactly what they need; and steadfastly maintain faith that He will answer their prayers in the very best way and time.

When I extended my hands over each and prayed for God's blessings, the familiar, tingling surge of the Holy Spirit's exhilarating love came pouring down upon me and the person crying out to Him. Some commented how they felt a wonderful, "tingling sensation."

I, of course, have no way of knowing how or when God will bless those who reach out to Him - but sometimes He allows me to learn afterward. Over the weeks following my presentation on Saint Anne, I heard how God answered the prayers of many who cried out to Him that evening. Time and again, I am blessed to witness how God's love, mercy and compassion is so far beyond our human understanding.

Later that November, the Rosary Altar Society also organized a spiritual pilgrimage for their parishioners to visit Saint Anne's Shrine in St. Jean the Baptiste Church on Lexington Avenue and 76th Street in New York City. I joined them and provided further details on the Shrine and the Church itself.

After arriving at St. Jean's, parishioners went to Confession, attended Mass and received Holy Communion. Following Mass, everyone lined up in the center aisle where the pastor, Father John Kamas, placed Saint Anne's relic on each person's forehead or heart.

A long line then formed in the back of the Church in front of Saint Anne's Shrine for people who wanted me to pray over them. There were so many people on line, it stretched all the way over to the other side of the Church.

In the middle of the long line was an older man who had not come with St. Matthew's group. He waited patiently on the line as each person was prayed over in front of Saint Anne's Shrine.

When it was finally his turn, he eagerly stepped right up to me and smiling broadly, he mysteriously said, "You don't remember me … do you?"

I confessed, "I'm sorry, I don't recognize you. Please understand, I have prayed over thousands of people in my life."

"That's all right; I am not surprised to hear that. Let me tell you, I was here ten years ago and saw you standing right here at this very same spot in front of Saint Anne's Shrine. You were praying over people … just as you're doing today.

"I didn't know who you were but I asked you to pray over me because I had just come from Sloane Kettering's cancer center where they told me I had inoperable brain cancer! They said there was nothing they could do for me, and that I had about a year to live. That's when I came here and asked you to pray over me for a miracle; I didn't want to die so I wanted God to take away the cancer and let me live.

"I've never forgotten what you said to me. You said the very first thing I had to do was to forgive everyone, everything! And that included forgiving myself!

"After that, you said I had to tell God what it was that I wanted Him to do for me. When I told you I wanted Him to take away my cancer, you said I had to express faith in His ability to do it! I did … and said so loudly!

"You put your hands on my head and prayed out loud to Saint Anne and the Blessed Mother to carry my request to Jesus. While you were praying, my head tingled wildly."

His voice trembled with great emotion as he continued, "The next time I went to Sloane Kettering, they had to conduct more tests including an MRI of my brain because symptoms of the cancer were gone. The tests showed that a miracle had taken place … all the signs of the brain cancer were gone!

"I went back to St. Jean the Baptiste Church to tell you about the miracle but you weren't here - and no one knew who you were - or how I could contact you.

"Here it is ten years later, and I had a powerful urge this morning to go to St. Jean's; I had the strongest sense that you might be here. And here you are!"

I thanked him for letting me know how God had blessed HIS faith so long ago. We said a prayer of thanksgiving to God, Saint Anne and the Blessed Mother for his miraculous healing so long ago.

Next on the line to be prayed over was a wonderful lady of great faith from my parish, Ss. Cyril and Methodius in Deer Park, Long Island. She had arranged to come with St. Matthew's Rosary group.

Quickly stepping up to me, she closed her eyes and began

to pray aloud asking God to heal many of the people in her life. She implored Saint Anne and the Blessed Mother to go to Jesus on her behalf. As she prayed, I had the strong inspiration to put my hands over the sides of her face and gently place my thumbs over her closed eyes. As I did, that familiar, ecstatic tingling of the Holy Spirit descended upon both of us.

She exclaimed, "Oh, my God, do you feel that?"

In the next instant, she began to shake all over. Pulling away, she stepped over to the right and opened her eyes.

Crying out loudly, she proclaimed, "Oh, my God … I can see through my 'bad' eye! I can see! I can see!"

The first thing she saw with her fully healed vision was the statue of Saint Anne and the Blessed mother. How appropriate, I thought, that a lady of such great faith was aided by two of the most faithful, loving women who have ever lived.

Over the following weeks, I heard how others who made that spiritual journey to Saint Anne's Shrine in New York City had their prayers answered … some in miraculous ways.

Thank you once again, Saint Anne and the Blessed Mother for interceding on our behalf with Jesus.

Little did I know at the time, I would soon be at the center of yet another utterly amazing intercession by Saint Anne and the Blessed Mother. Only this time … I would be the one in need of serious healing prayer.

Chapter 58

MIRACLE OF DIVINE MERCY

In early February 2017, my regularly scheduled donation of blood every eight weeks was not allowed because my hematocrit blood level was way too low. In the past, this indicated there might be a silent, deadly buildup of iron in my liver from a condition I had called Hemochromatosis ("iron overload"). Accordingly, my primary care doctor, Howard Hertz, Babylon, New York, prescribed that an MRI using a MRCP T-cell be taken with and without contrast to scan my liver and entire abdomen to see if there was any iron buildup.

This special MRI was completed the next day at one of the finest radiology groups in America, Zwanger-Pesiri Radiology in Massapequa, Long Island. Interestingly, the MRI was scheduled to be done at three o'clock, the hour of Divine Mercy.

Afterward, the radiologist reported some surprising, terrible news. While there was no sign of iron buildup in my liver, there was strong evidence that I had cancer located near my pancreas and a few other areas in my gastrointestinal system in addition to a "pre-cancerous" lesion in my stomach!

I was shocked.

Two weeks later, again at three o'clock, the hour of Divine Mercy, Doctor Rajiv Bansal, a highly-regarded gastroenterologist, conducted a special endoscopic procedure (Endoscopic EUS and ERCP) at North Shore University Hospital on Long Island. He took several biopsies along with color pictures of a tumor he saw located on my Ampulla of Vater next to the pancreas. He also took a number of biopsies of the suspicious looking lesion in the antrum (bottom) of my stomach.

Two different pathologists later reviewed the biopsies and agreed that there was a rare, malignant neuroendocrine (NET) tumor located on my Ampulla of Vater near my pancreas. They also concurred that the growth in the antrum of my stomach was a "pre-cancerous lesion."

The rest of my digestive system was in very bad condition since the NET tumor had closed off the common bile duct resulting in a serious backup of digestive fluids and a grotesque distension of the gallbladder and entire biliary tree. To say the least, I was quite seriously ill.

Weeks later, special blood tests and a whole body PET/CT "Dota-tate" scan was conducted using "gallium 68" contrast at Northwell Labs in Bay Shore, Long Island. The pathologists who reviewed the results of the Dota-tate scan agreed it confirmed the earlier findings of my biopsy slides … I had the rare, malignant NET cancer.

It appeared that extensive, radical surgery was needed to deal with the cancer. I followed up with a renowned surgical oncologist who specialized in treatment of the rare NET cancer. My wife, Margie, and I travelled in to New York City for a consult with the doctor at his midtown office. We were hoping to hear something more promising about what might be done to treat the NET cancer. What we heard confirmed our worst fears.

This oncologist explained how he was convinced I needed the "Whipple" surgery which involved removal of the cancerous NET tumor, ampulla of vater, the gallbladder, about 40% of the pancreas, part of the duodenum, and part of the common bile duct. What remained in the area would then have to be surgically reconstructed.

Just when I thought things couldn't get much worse, the doctor ominously added that "given my other conditions and age," patients like me sometimes do not survive such traumatic surgery! He provided several reasons for this dire possibility in my case: because of where the NET cancer tumor was located in my body; many other serious health issues I had; and, many complications presented by prior extensive surgeries I had in the past.

Needless to say, my wife, Margie, and I left that meeting terribly depressed and worried.

It was three o'clock, the hour of Divine Mercy, when we walked directly across the street from the doctor's office and entered St. Jean the Baptiste Church on Lexington Avenue and 76th Street. That is where Jesus is always present in the Eucharist in a monstrance on the main altar when Mass is not being celebrated. And … that is where there is a shrine dedicated to Saint Anne, Jesus' grandmother - unchanged for over 100 years.

To my great surprise, Margie stood in the middle aisle and promptly began complaining to Jesus, **"Are you kidding me? You didn't answer my prayers and now Bob has to have life-threatening surgery!"**

While Margie continued her "discussion" with Jesus, I quietly walked over to the beautiful, pure white marble, life-size statue of Saint Anne and the Blessed Mother located in an alcove in the right rear (southwest) area of the church. Standing there, my mind was filled with frightening thoughts of the terrible pa*t*h before me. I felt so vulnerable, so down, my thoughts turned to how Jesus suffered in the Garden of Gethsemane.

Envisioning Him kneeling there in the Garden of Gethsemane, suffering terribly, I pleaded, "Dear Jesus, You asked the Father if the cup of suffering might pass from You without having to drink from it. I, too, ask the Father - through You, Jesus, to let this cup of suffering pass from me."

After a pause, I reluctantly added, "But as You also said, I, too, say, 'Your will be done, Father … not mine.' If I am not to be healed of this cancer, then please bless me with the graces I am going to need to endure the agony I see coming my way."

I then asked my beloved patron saint, Saint Anne, and her daughter, the Blessed Mother, to intercede on my behalf with Jesus. At that moment, my guardian angel encouraged me to use my cell phone to take a photo of the statue of Saint Anne and the Blessed Mother. After taking the picture, I was urged to take yet another picture of the statue. When I looked at the photos I had taken, I was amazed to discover a remarkable miracle was captured in the pictures!

In the first photo I took depicted here, you can see that Saint Anne's head on the statue is clearly looking downward off to her right side as it has for well over 100 years since it was installed at Saint Anne's Shrine in St. Jean the Baptiste Church.

In the second photo, Saint Anne's head can be seen looking directly at me! Also quite noticeable is the fact that there appears to be far more stars in the background behind the statue! As captured in these two remarkable photos, it is clear that Saint Anne wanted to comfort me … and make sure that I knew she and the Blessed Mother heard my cries for their help interceding on my behalf with Jesus. This extraordinary miracle greatly lifted my spirits for the difficult times ahead for me.

A few weeks later, I was

laying on the operating table at St. Francis Hospital in Roslyn, New York about to go under general anesthesia for another endoscopic procedure on the cancer. The same specialist who found the cancerous NET tumor weeks earlier, Doctor Rajiv Bansal, was ready to proceed.

Before beginning, he said, "I am going to do my very best to take out as much of the tumor as I can. If this doesn't work, you might have to go for the more extensive 'Whipple' surgery. "

In the operating room, just as I was about to go asleep from the anesthesia, I looked up and saw a large digital clock hanging on the opposite wall facing me. The very last thing I remember seeing as I began to whirl off into unconsciousness from the anesthesia was that the time was about **three o'clock ... the hour of Divine Mercy!**

When I awoke in the surgical recovery room much later, my wife, Margie, and my daughter, Peggie Murano, joined me as Doctor Bansal came in to tell us how the surgery went.

Looking mystified, the doctor shook his head and stated, "The tumor is gone! It's gone! There's nothing there now! And, all the other damage I saw in your system weeks ago is also gone! I took many biopsies."

When those biopsies were analyzed, the pathologists confirmed that the cancerous NET tumor was, indeed, truly gone. The tumor quite apparently just disappeared. All the doctors familiar with my condition are at a loss to understand how this could happen. Doctor Bansal personally saw the tumor in my body only weeks earlier, used special equipment to photograph it in living color, and the biopsies he took were clinically confirmed by different pathologists as a cancerous NET tumor.

In early June 2017, I participated in an ongoing medical research project on NET cancer at the National Institutes of Health (NIH) in Bethesda Maryland. For one week, some of the world's leading oncologists who specialize in the research and treatment of NET cancer conducted extensive testing on me and one of my sisters who was also diagnosed with NET cancer.

In studying us, NIH oncologists hope to learn more about this rare, deadly cancer including genetic implications. In my case, the NIH oncologists hope to gain a better scientific understanding of the following:

1. What, if anything, may have contributed to the disappearance of the malignant ampulla NET tumor that was seen and clinically confirmed in my body; and,
2. What is the biological nature and behavior of the rare, malignant NET cancer in my body.

The NIH oncologists could not provide a scientific explanation for how the malignant NET tumor in my body disappeared … but they were able to confirm that the underlying NET cancer was still present elsewhere in my body. In fact, they identified two new NET tumors - one in the vicinity of the original tumor, and another NET tumor located in a lymph node in my diaphragm. They expect other tumors will likely appear in time since there are NET cancer cells microscopically present throughout my body.

I truly believe God miraculously removed the malignant tumor … but not the underlying cancer. People who heard how God miraculously removed the cancerous tumor from my body during the hour of Divine Mercy have returned to the sacraments.

That provides light for the path before me leading to cancer treatment and research centers … where I can encourage other cancer patients to turn to God. What a beautiful silver lining.

Chapter 59

A SECOND DEADLY TUMOR APPEARS!

On July 25, 2018, a sharp, excruciating pain radiated across the center of my digestive system like a bolt of lightning doubling me over. "God help me; here we go again," I lamented. This sudden, unexplained physical pain ebbed and flowed throughout the night until the early morning hours of the next day.

Fortunately, I was able to get an appointment with my primary care physician, Dr. Howard Hertz. After examining me, the doctor ordered a number of tests including a MRI with MRCP of my abdomen to determine the source of my pain. He was concerned as I was that the neuroendocrine cancer was the cause of my suffering.

The very next day, a MRI with MRCP was done at Zwanger-Pesiri in Deer Park, Long Island. The radiologist who reviewed the MRI compared it to the MRI that had been done a year earlier on February 10, 2017.

His report stated, in part, **"the common bile duct still abruptly tapers at the ampulla but no discrete ampullary mass is appreciated."**

I thought his report required additional information so I called the radiologist and asked him to state in an amended report exactly how "abruptly narrowed my common bile duct was at the ampulla." It seemed only obvious to me that oncologists treating me would need a relative number to gauge the seriousness of the narrowing.

I also asked why he failed to recommend that I

follow up with my doctors regarding the abrupt narrowing at my ampulla especially since he knew I was already diagnosed with ampulla cancer at that specific site.

His answer surprised me, "We simply disagree, Mr. Walsh. I do not think it is necessary to recommend any follow up!"

"Why?" I asked.

"Because you already know you have neuroendocrine cancer at the ampulla. Besides, I don't see any tumors; I only see an abrupt narrowing!"

After further discussion, this radiologist eventually agreed to provide an amended report that contained a number describing just how narrowed my common bile duct was at the site of my ampulla. He stated my common bile duct was virtually closed but he just couldn't bring himself to write zero. Instead, he listed the opening of the narrowed area as being 1 mm.

His amended radiology report on my patient portal at the Zwanger-Pesiri website stated in an addendum, "The common bile duct narrows approximately 5 mm upstream to the ampulla and measures less than 1 mm in diameter following its abrupt narrowing. No discrete ampullary mass is identified that would correspond to the known neuroendocrine tumor."

Research I conducted on neuroendocrine cancer indicated that such abrupt narrowing in the common bile duct at the ampulla may indicate the presence of an aggressive malignancy.

On August 25, 2018, I made an appointment with a local oncologist for her advice. My wife, Margie, and I visited Dr. Mary Puccio, oncologist, in her Bay Shore, Long Island, New York office. After thoroughly reviewing my medical history including all recent MRI reports, Dr. Puccio prescribed a 68-gallium Dota-tate full body CT/PET scan be conducted as soon as possible to determine what role neuroendocrine cancer may be playing in my common bile duct … and possibly elsewhere.

Accordingly, on August 27, 2018, a 68-gallium Dota-tate scan full body CT/PET scan was done at the Northwell Imaging Center in Bay Shore, New York. Two days later, we met with Dr. Puccio who told us what radiologists at Northwell Imaging had to report. She began by telling us they compared their findings with those Northwell reported on another CT/PET scan done more than a year earlier on March 27, 2017.

This report stated there was tracer uptake in my common bile duct at the ampulla "consistent with the known neuroendocrine tumor. Alarmingly, the SUV (standard uptake value) of that area was 19.1; the SUV a year earlier was only 14.9. A higher SUV level is known to indicate a highly aggressive malignancy.

As a next step, Dr. Puccio recommended I have an endoscopy with EUS and ERCP of my abdomen … as soon as it can be arranged. And so, I made an appointment for a consultation with Dr. Raj Bansal, gastroenterologist who was familiar with my medical condition since he twice before conducted an endoscopy with EUS and ERCP a year earlier.

In making this appointment, I explained to his secretary why I needed this consult so that an endoscopy with EUS and ERCP could be done as soon as possible. Despite explaining the circumstances of my present medical condition, his secretary said I would have to wait a few weeks before I could see the doctor!

Those weeks passed very, very slowly for me as I prayed and worried, prayed and worried, prayed and worried, and then prayed and worried some more. Living with a terminal, incurable cancer has a way at times like these of dramatically slowing the passing of time.

Then, unfortunately, a few days before the consult was to take place, his secretary called to tell me the doctor had to cancel the appointment. Under the circumstances, I requested the next earliest appointment for a consult. She shocked me by saying quite matter-of-factly that the next available appointment was several more weeks from then! I implored her under my dire circumstances to please give me an earlier appointment.

"My recent scans clearly show how the malignant neuroendocrine cancer in me is growing and the only way oncologists can determine what steps to take requires that an endoscopy be done as soon as possible."

It was as if she wasn't listening as she said "the best she could" do was to give me an appointment three weeks away! No amount of explaining could influence her to give me an earlier appointment. Under the circumstances, I had no choice but to wait … and pray … wait and pray … wait and pray … wait and pray.

When that second appointment finally approached, Dr. Bansal's secretary called a few days before and once again cancelled the appointment! This second time left me completely stunned and disturbed.

I could only assume Dr. Bansal was not aware his appointments secretary was doing something I felt he would never approve. Her actions were simply outrageous. Waiting to see him had cost me two valuable months in my struggle with a rare, incurable, malignancy growing inside me. For patients like me with an incurable cancer, every day is critical to us.

As soon as I hung up with Dr. Bansal's secretary, I immediately called for a consultation with Dr. Myron Schwartz, the director of surgery at the Neuroendocrine Cancer Center at Mount Sinai Hospital in New York City. Unlike dealing with Dr. Bansal's staff, Dr. Schwartz' representative patiently and efficiently gathered all pertinent information related to my health issues … and scheduled an appointment for me to see Dr. Schwartz the very next week!

Although Mount Sinai and North Shore Hospital are part of the same Northwell System, it was quite apparent that Dr. Schwartz and Mount Sinai Hospital maintained a much higher standard in handling quality of care issues in support of medical services. This may not seem very important to most people, however, to cancer patients like me dealing with an incurable malignancy it makes a great deal of difference.

Administrative and clerical issues matter. North Shore Hospital would do well to learn how Mount Sinai Hospital is able to maintain such a high quality of care … and follow their example!

On September 19, 2018, my wife, Margie, and I attended a consultation meeting with Dr. Schwartz and his staff at Mount Sinai hospital in New York City. After thoroughly reviewing my scans, pathology and radiology reports, Dr. Schwartz focused on the recent 68-gallium Dota-tate CT/PET scan of my abdomen. He advised us that he concurred with the radiology findings that indicated there was an ominous area where neuroendocrine cancer was situated in the very bottom of my common bile duct right at the ampulla.

I asked him to explain what the tumor's SUV (standard uptake value) indicated on this recent scan.

"Well," he began with an ominous tone in his voice, "I am afraid the higher SUV on this scan unfortunately indicates the tumor is now much larger - and more aggressive than what was seen on the CT/PET scan last year."

Without further comment on this, he added, "It might be possible for us to do an 'ampullectomy' during an endoscopy to remove the cancerous tissue. This can only be done if the cancer has not spread into the surrounding area.

"In an ampullectomy, the doctor removes the ampulla and as much of the surrounding cancerous area as possible. The remaining area is then closed off by carefully attaching what is left together."

"How effective is this," Margie wanted to know.

"We have found this procedure is quite effective. However, every patient is a unique physical environment therefore specific circumstances always dictate what can be come and affect results. Having said that, I can tell you we have had great experience performing ampullectomies … and patients typically recover quite well following the procedure.

"To determine whether or not an ampullectomy may be done in your husband's case, an endoscopy is needed with EUS and ERCP. This can be done here at Mount Sinai if you wish."

I asked Dr. Schwartz how capable and experienced the Mount Sinai doctors were who wound be performing the procedure. I was concerned because I knew the procedure came with some very real, serious risks.

One of Dr. Schwartz' colleagues surprised us by calling out his confident reply, "Mr. Walsh, we do ampullectomies all the time; they are actually quite fun to do!"

Dr. Schwartz added, "Doctor Christopher DiMaio, head of our gastroenterology department, has extensive experience with this procedure and can do the endoscopy here at Mount Sinai if you would like. Would you like me to speak with him and have him call you to make arrangements?"

"Yes, please do," I quickly answered.

Margie and I asked several questions related to this procedure and my particular case of neuroendocrine cancer. The doctor listened carefully and patiently answered our questions and concerns. We left this meeting feeling highly confident we were in the hands of highly capable medical professionals who were thoroughly familiar with neuroendocrine cancer.

I immediately called and made an appointment to have the needed endoscopy done by Dr. DiMaio on October 2, 2018 at Mount Sinai Hospital in upper Manhattan in New

York City.

On that day just prior to the procedure, Dr. DiMaio spent considerable time with Margie and me thoroughly reviewing my health issues, and explaining the endoscopy procedure.

In particular, he stressed, "The principle purpose of this endoscopy is to identify if the cancer we see on your recent CT/PET scan has spread to the surrounding area. That will help us determine whether or not an ampullectomy may be done at a later date.

"To be sure you understand, Mr. Walsh, I am **NOT** going to do an ampullectomy today … even if it appears one may be done at this time. I **AM** planning to take several biopsies throughout your system, and I will also take a number of photos.

"When our pathology department reports their findings on the biopsies, I will confer with Doctors Schwartz and Wolin and then share with you our observations and recommendations."

Margie said she hoped the results would be the same as what happened a year earlier. "A malignant tumor in that same area had closed off Bob's entire biliary system leaving him in danger of dying. That is when God intervened and miraculously took the tumor away without surgery or chemo! It was a miracle."

Dr. DiMaio smiled, "Well, from what I read of your husband's medical records, I have to say what happened was really quite amazing. But from what we now see on his recent CT/PET scan, we must deal with this in science … not miracles."

With that, he rushed off saying, "I'll come talk with both of you as soon as I complete the procedure today."

Margie and I were left sitting comfortably in a quiet area not far from the operating room. Not knowing what news this day may bring, we did what came so easily. We prayed. We thanked God for all He had done for us and our loved ones … and we asked Him to pour His healing graces down upon us, the doctors, other patients, all those who suffer and our loved ones. Praying together brought great peace for both of us as I was led off to the operating room.

Once there, Dr. DiMaio again went over everything pertinent for my benefit, the anesthesiologist and other attending staff. When he finished, the anesthesiologist explained that he was going to inject me with Octreotide which he held up for me to see. The Octreotide was in a bottle no more than one inch long.

"Anyone who has neuroendocrine cancer as you do, must receive this Octreotide before general anesthesia is administered," he elaborated before injecting it in my left shoulder. He then said he was going to administer the general anesthesia. Within a few moments, I felt myself gradually drift away from consciousness and bring me to an utterly peaceful state of being.

When I awoke in recovery, Margie came in and greeted me, "Okay, enough of this sleeping in the middle of the day! The doctor is coming in soon to tell us what he saw."

Just as she finished saying this, Dr. DiMaio walked in almost as if on cue.

He looked perplexed as he launched into a report of

what he saw. "I did **NOT** see any sign of cancer … anywhere! I took many biopsies and photos of your esophagus, stomach, common bile duct, ampulla, small intestine, liver, gallbladder and pancreas."

After these wonderful, remarkable words, the doctor fell silent. He literally just stopped talking!

Margie broke the awkward silence by asking a perfectly pointed, frank question, "How can this be, doctor? How can you say there is nothing there when the 68-Gallium CT/PET scan and the MRI clearly shows there is neuroendocrine tumor there with a high SUV uptake indicating it's a highly aggressive malignancy?!"

"I am sorry, Mrs. Walsh, what you are saying is absolutely right! I can't explain it. I am just as mystified as you are," he confessed.

This is not at all what I expected. It just doesn't make any scientific sense! I can only tell you I did not see **ANY SIGN OF THE CANCEROUS TUMOR** … anywhere in your husband's digestive system!"

After a brief pause, he added, "Mind you … this procedure I did today did **NOT** plan to include looking at any other place in your husband's body where other oncologists have previously established clinical evidence of at least one other active neuroendocrine tumor near Mr. Walsh's spine.

"I can only assure the both of you that I very carefully, thoroughly, looked everywhere in the digestive system and took many, many biopsies. I know I saw the presence of neuroendocrine cancer on the recent CT/PET scan but I assure you … I assure you … I did not see **ANY** sign of the neuroendocrine tumor in today's procedure."

As Margie was about to ask another question, Dr. DiMaio quickly added, "Mrs. Walsh … I just cannot explain this."

Margie confidently said, "Well, doctor, we can! This tumor miraculously disappeared just like the first one did a year ago!"

Dr. DiMaio smiled, "As I mentioned earlier, I am guided by science. Let's wait until the biopsies are reviewed by our pathologists who are well-experienced with neuroendocrine cancer. Then, perhaps, we'll have a better understanding of what is going on here. I will call you at soon as the pathology report is available."

Margie and I went home later that day filled with joy, praise and thanksgiving to God who had quite apparently once again had miraculously interceded to cause a deeply entrenched malignant tumor to literally disappear.

My joy didn't last too long. The very next day, I awoke in terrible pain. I was suffering from what appeared to be pancreatitis, an inflammation of the pancreas. That is one of the possible side effects of having an endoscopy done with EUR and ERCP since that procedure includes obtaining a biopsy from the pancreas. The pain I was experiencing felt like a muscle in my upper, middle torso area was spasmodically twisting.

I went to a local health clinic where a doctor conducted blood tests of my amylase and lipase levels. These hormones are created by pancreas. The doctor explained if these two levels are elevated, this usually indicates pancreatitis. The tests later came back negative.

The excruciating pain I suffered lasted five days, and apparently was caused by the many biopsies taken by Dr. DiMaio during the endoscopy with EUS and ERCP.

Chapter 60

GOD DOES IT AGAIN - A SECOND MIRACLE!

A week following the special endoscopy at Mount Sinai Hospital in New York City, Dr. Christopher DiMaio called me to convey the results of the biopsies he had taken during the procedure.

"Mr. Walsh … all the biopsies came back negative! All of them! I do not understand how this can be. Your recent CT/PET scan clearly shows the presence of a significant lesion located in the distal area of your common bile duct. In doing the procedure, however, I did not see anything at all that looked suspicious to me. Now our pathologists have confirmed there was no sign of cancer in any of the biopsies!"

I immediately began to realize that God had just performed a second miracle in removing another deadly NET tumor! Although I have been blessed in my life to witness countless miracles including the disappearance of the first NET tumor a year earlier - I confess this time, I was completely surprised.

While Dr. DiMaio began trying to make sense out of what happened to this second NET tumor, I began to understand why perhaps God did this again. After I told many people how God had miraculously removed the first NET tumor, there really weren't too many people I can say outwardly were impressed. So a year earlier, God performed another, virtually identical, miracle!

I asked the doctor if he could think of any possible

scientific explanation for how this tumor simply disappeared.

His emphatic response was, "No, Mr. Walsh; I cannot. I cannot think of a single scientific, medical basis to explain this! In all my years of practice, I have never experienced anything even close to this. This is truly amazing."

I was so elated to hear this but the thought occurred to me, "Well, what do I so now?"

"You must follow up with Dr. Wolin right away," he advised. "That tumor may have mysteriously disappeared, but the cancer you have has not. It is still in your body."

After a pause, he added, "Doctor Wolin … like the rest of us is now even more anxious for you to continue your care here at Mount Sinai. And now, it is **NOT** just because you have the rarest form of the rarest cancer."

Before hanging up, Dr. DiMaio said, "By the way, Mr. Walsh, you can tell your wife I can no longer disagree with her. It does appear that happened was miraculous."

Never limit the great power of prayer, and what God may choose to do.

Chapter 61

THE GREATEST OF ALL MIRACLES

As beautiful and touching as the miracles are that I have shared in this book, the greatest of all miracles is one that takes place at every Mass all over the world when Jesus becomes miraculously present in the Eucharist. Therein is the secret to living life in peace and happiness no matter how difficult and painful life's journey may be at times.

Truly, the key to achieving happiness in life is to frequent the sacraments, attend Mass, receive Holy Communion and live life in ways that are in keeping with Christ's teachings. When you do, surely the best days of your life are yet ahead.

Also, remember what Christ says in Matthew 5:16 when He tells us, "Let **your light** shine before men so seeing your good works, they may praise your father in Heaven." Notice that Jesus does not say, "Those of you who have a light." He says, "Let **your light** shine!" He is telling us that we have all been given a special light, a gift from God … some blessing that He encourages us to use.

So let your light shine in all you do!

And importantly, we must also follow the example of the one leper who Jesus made sure to tell us about in Luke 17:17. Jesus tells us that He cured ten lepers but only one of them came back to thank Him! Jesus said, "Were not ten cleansed? Where are the other nine lepers?"

Jesus is telling us loud and clear that we should always make time to express our thankfulness to God for all He does for us and for our loved ones. In particular, take notice of what happened after the one leper came back to say thanks. Jesus tells us that the one leper who came back to thank Him was further blessed … but in a far, far greater way.

Jesus said, ***"Arise, go your way, for your faith has saved you!"***

It is when we are thankful to God that the greatest of all blessings come our way. For a suggestion on how to pray for healing, I repeat below what I listed in Chapter 1 of this book. You can consider following this approach to healing prayer which I have used in countless healing prayer services.

When praying for God's help, I have found there are five steps that are absolutely essential. In order of sequence, they are:

1. First, you must forgive everyone, everything … and that includes forgiving yourself which may be the most difficult forgiveness to give. This first step is so important, Christ tells us if we bring gifts to the church but have unforgiveness in our hearts, we should put the gifts down and go make peace!

2. The next step is for you to clearly tell God what it is that you want Him to do for you. In Matthew 9:27, Jesus shows us how important this is. He asks two blind men what they want Him to do for them. Note that Jesus does not ask them if they want to see. Jesus knows what we need but He obviously wants us to express faith in Him by actually saying the words. Make sure to ask for what is most important to you … and don't limit what you ask of Him. While you have the opportunity to ask, consider asking Jesus to help others in your life.

3. The next step in healing prayer is also vital - it involves expressing faith in Him once again. Using the example of the two blind men, Jesus tells us about how He asks both of them if they believe He can do what they ask of Him … cure their blindness. When they said, "Yes, Lord,"

Jesus replied by saying something quite extraordinary in terms of receiving what it is you ask of Jesus. He said, "According to your faith, let it be done to you!" Remember this when you pray to Jesus. Believe with all your heart that Jesus can and will do whatever is best for you and for those you pray for … and that He will do it in the very best way and time.

4. The fourth step involves acknowledging what Jesus does for you by thanking Him. This is so important to Jesus that He gives us an example in Luke 17:11 where only one leper out of ten who were healed by Jesus came back to thank Him. By the way, tradition tells us that the one leper who came back to thank Jesus was further rewarded by having all that he lost to leprosy returned to him! (Leprosy causes the flesh to rot resulting in the loss of fingers, toes, et al.) Make sure to take time to thank Jesus for what He does for you.

5. For Catholics, this final step represents the greatest healing prayer of all - uniting our prayers for healing with that of the Holy Sacrifice of the Mass. At every Mass, a miracle takes place when the priest consecrates the bread and wine into the Body and Blood of Our Lord and Savior, Jesus Christ. Following this most sacred of all moments, is one of the greatest healing prayers we can say … "Lord, I am not worthy that you should come under my roof but only say the word and my soul shall be healed!"

In closing this book, allow me to offer this prayer for you and your loved ones, "May God heal all your wounds, dry every tear, ease your fears, provide what you need, protect you from evil, guide you in all you do, and on some beautiful, glorious day, May He welcome you into Paradise where you and your loved ones will enjoy everlasting love, peace and happiness. Amen."

EXHIBIT A

Letter Sent to Local Clergy Regarding Miraculous Disappearance of Two Deadly Tumors

Robert T. Walsh
162 Liberty Street, Deer Park, NY 11729

October 14, 2018

Most Reverend John O. Barres	Monsignor Robert J. Clerkin
Diocese of Rockville Centre	Ss. Cyril & Methodius
Rockville Centre, NY 11571-9023	Deer Park, NY 11729

Dear Bishop Barres and Monsignor Clerkin:

This letter confirms my recent phone message to each of you regarding a miraculous experience in which a deadly, cancerous tumor literally disappeared from my body … not once … but twice.

The first time this happened was in late February 2017 soon after I was diagnosed with a rare, incurable malignancy, neuroendocrine (NET) cancer. During exploratory surgery at North Shore Hospital on Long Island, biopsies were taken of a tumor that had completely closed my digestive system leaving me in danger of dying. Pathologists at four different cancer centers (Lenox Hill Hospital, Montefiore Hospital, National Institutes of Health and St. Francis Hospital) later examined these biopsies and confirmed it was the rare, incurable neuroendocrine cancer.

Family members, friends and rosary societies in St. Cyril and St. Matthew Churches joined me in praying for God's help. The doctor who first discovered the cancer went in a second time to cut away some of the tumor in an effort as he said, "to give you a little more time." As soon as the surgery was finished, the doctor came out and exclaimed, "It's gone; the tumor is gone!"

Subsequently, extensive tests at six other cancer centers showed the deadly tumor did inexplicably disappear without any chemo or surgery. Brilliant oncologists in cancer research centers studying this rare cancer could not explain how this could possibly have happened. As one stated, "I don't understand how such a tumor could simply disappear. This type of cancer roots itself deeply within the body … like a tree roots itself in the ground."

For those oncologists who still doubted, God performed the very same miracle a second time! In August of this year, CT/PET and special MRI scans showed that the cancerous tumor had returned at the bottom of the common bile duct … only this time it was much larger. Accordingly, on October 2, oncologists at Mount Sinai Cancer Center in New York City conducted exploratory surgery to determine what, if any, surgical alternatives might be done.

The results were precisely the same as the first time 18 months earlier … all the biopsies taken showed the tumor had once again miraculously disappeared. The surgeon who previously said they were all looking for a scientific explanation called with results of the biopsies.

He stated, "We cannot understand what has happened; the tumor is gone. There is no scientific explanation other than it truly is miraculous!"

While everyone agreed the tumors "mysteriously" disappeared, they also confirmed I still have the NET cancer throughout my body. In fact, one of the worst remaining tumors in my body is located adjacent to my spine where they cannot safely get at it surgically. I suffer badly from the terrible effects of the cancer in my body but God gives me the strength to endure this while offering up my sufferings for the holy souls in Purgatory.

My wife, Margie, and I shared with all the oncologists studying me, that the miracle disappearance of the tumors was in response to many rosaries and Masses offered on my behalf. With no scientific evidence to show otherwise, these medical scientists have acknowledged the only plausible explanation for the disappearing tumors can only be miraculous.

I thought you both would be interested in hearing such wonderful news. I have attached copies of the operating, pathology and radiology reports that provide clear, indisputable scientific evidence of what happened – not once but twice. It is like God wanted to make sure we got the message that prayer, especially the greatest prayer of all – the Eucharist, really helps.

May God continue to bless you both for all you do in His Holy Name; I remain, sincerely,

Bob Walsh

Attachment: Copies of related operating, pathology and radiology reports evidencing miraculous disappearance of two deadly tumors

EXHIBIT B

Biopsy Pathology Report Shows 1st NET Tumor North Shore Hospital - March 2, 2017

Northwell Health Laboratories

NORTH SHORE UNIVERSITY HOSPITAL
300 COMMUNITY DRIVE, MANHASSET, NY 11030
(516) 304-7284 FAX (516) 304-7269

ANATOMIC PATHOLOGY SERVICES

Patient Name: **WALSH, ROBERT T**
Medical Record #: **001280523**
DOB: **1/25/1945** Sex: **Male**
Location: **MH END**
Submitting Physician: **BANSAL, RAJIV**
Copy to Physician:

Accession #: **10- S-17-004107**
Account #: **600003685242**
Collection Date: **2/27/2017**
Received Date: **2/27/2017**

S u r g i c a l P a t h o l o g y R e p o r t

Report Date: 3/2/2017 1:21:48 PM

Final Diagnosis

1. Ampulla, biopsy:
- Well differentiated neuroendocrine neoplasm, grade 1, see note.

Note: Tissue is fragmented with marked cautery artifact. The tumor size, mitotic count, margin, lymphovascular invasion cannot be evaluated. Immunohistochemical stains for Chromogranin, Synaptophysin, and Ki-67 confirm the diagnosis. Dr. Fan has reviewed this part and concurred the diagnosis.

2. Stomach, antrum, biopsy:
- Gastric antral type mucosa with intestinal metaplasia.
- Negative for H. pylori (Warthin Starry stain).

Lihui Qin, M.D.
(Electronic Signature)
Reported on: 03/02/17

Clinical History

r/o CBD stone, dilated gallbladder, abdominal pain
Gastritis, r/o adenoma

Specimen(s) Submitted

1 Ampulla
2 Antrum biopsy

Gross Description

1. The specimen is received in formalin and the specimen container is labeled: **Ampulla biopsy**. It consists of six fragments of tan-pink soft tissue ranging from 0.1 cm to 0.3 cm in greatest dimension. Entirely submitted. One cassette.

2. The specimen is received in formalin and the specimen container is labeled: **Antrum biopsy**. It consists

Patient: **WALSH, ROBERT T**
DISCH: 2/27/2017
Printed: 3/3/2017
Page 1 of 2

Physician: BANSAL, RAJIV
2001 MARCUS AVENUE
SUITE E130
LAKE SUCCESS, NY
11042

EXHIBIT C

Biopsy Pathology Report Shows 1st NET Disappeared! Saint Francis Hospital – April 17, 2017

Saint Francis Hospital
100 Port Washington Blvd
Roslyn, NY 11576-
Laboratory Director Jeffrey A. Hamilton, M.D.
Phone Fax Number 516-562-6410 516-562-6427
Ordering Physician BANSAL RAJIV
Consulting Physician

Patient Name: WALSH, ROBERT
MRN: 2237290
DOB: 01 25 1945 Sex: Male
FIN: 1710200522
Location: FEN. ENDO. 02

7-SP-17-003074

Pathology Reports

Accession	Collected Date/Time	Received Date/Time
7-SP-17-003074	04/17/2017 14:46	04/17/2017 19:03

Surgical Pathology Report

Diagnosis

A. Ampulla, biopsy:

- Benign duodenal mucosa with non specific chronic inflammation. The villous architecture appears preserved. There is no evidence of neuroendocrine neoplasm.

B. Stomach, antrum, biopsy:

- Predominantly oxyntic type mucosa with chronic gastritis. Negative for active inflammation, intestinal metaplasia and neuroendocrine tumor. Modified Giemsa stain demonstrates possible luminal bacterial forms, negative for H. pylori by immunohistochemistry.

C. Stomach, body, biopsy:

- Mild non specific chronic gastritis. Negative for neuroendocrine tumor. Modified Giemsa stain for Helicobacter pylori is negative.

John C Chumas, MD (Electronic Signature)
Reported: 04 20 17 08:24
JCC dv

Ancillary Studies
Immunohistochemistry (7SP17-3074 Block B1)

H. pylori: Negative

W. Liu, M.D.

Appropriate positive and negative tissue control slides for this immunohistochemical study have been reviewed and show expected staining patterns. The study utilizes Ventana ultraView detection system.

Technical component performed at Catholic Health Services Regional Laboratory, 70 Jakas Drive, Hauppauge, NY 11788
Professional component performed at Catholic Health Services Regional Laboratory, 70 Jakas Drive, Hauppauge, NY 11788

Clinical Information
Neuroendocrine tumor, ampulla lesion.

Patient: WALSH, ROBERT Report Request ID: 40117638

EXHIBIT D

CT/PET Scan Report Shows 2nd NET Tumor Northwell Health - August 27, 2018

08/28/2018 12:15:05 PM -0400 PAGE 3 OF 4

NORTHWELL HEALTH

Northwell Imaging at Bay Shore

An Extension of Long Island Jewish Medical Center
440 E Main St., Suite D, Bay Shore, NY, 11706 631-414-8000 631-414-8039

Department of Radiology

HEAD/NECK: Unchanged nodule anterior margin left thyroid lobe extending into the isthmus, 1.8 x 1.8 cm and smaller nodule in the lower right thyroid lobe 1.4 x 1.4 cm (both seen on image 190). Physiologic radiotracer activity in pituitary gland, salivary glands, and thyroid gland.

THORAX: Physiologic radiotracer activity.

LUNGS: No abnormal radiotracer activity. No lung nodule.

PLEURA/PERICARDIUM: No pleural or pericardial effusion.

HEPATOBILIARY/PANCREAS: Physiologic activity. Liver SUV mean is 9.8, previously 9.5

SPLEEN: Physiologic activity. Normal in size.

ADRENAL GLANDS: Physiologic activity. No nodule.

KIDNEYS/URINARY BLADDER: Physiologic radiotracer excretion.

REPRODUCTIVE ORGANS: No abnormal radiotracer activity.

ABDOMINOPELVIC NODES: No enlarged or somatostatin receptor-bearing lymph node.

BOWEL/PERITONEUM/MESENTERY: Unchanged radiotracer accumulation in the region of the ampulla (SUV 19.1; image 178), previous SUV 14.9, which is difficult to difficult to delineate on CT and to seperate from adjacent physiologic activity in the uncinate process of the pancreas. Unchanged sigmoid colon anastomosis.

BONES/SOFT TISSUES: Degenerative changes in the spine. No abnormal radiotracer activity.

IMPRESSION:

Since gallium-68 DOTATATE PET/CT March 28, 2017:

1. Unchanged somatostatin receptor-bearing ampullary lesion, consistent with known neuroendocrine tumor.

2. No new somatostatin receptor bearing sites of disease.

3. Unchanged bilateral thyroid nodules. Consider further evaluation with thyroid ultrasound.

Patient: WALSH, ROBERT MRN: [illegible] Patient #: [illegible] Proc Date: 08/27/2018 Ord #: [illegible]

Page 2 of 3 Date Printed: 8/28/2018 12:31 PM

EXHIBIT E

Biopsy Pathology Report Shows 2nd NET Tumor Disappeared!
Mount Sinai Hospital – October 2, 2018

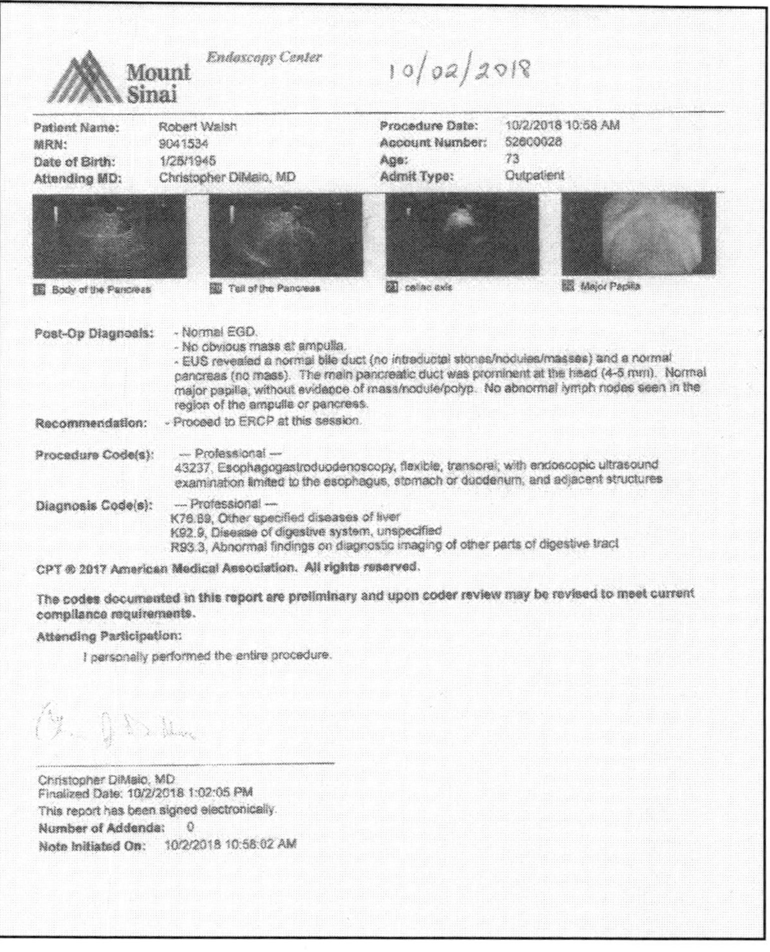

Mount Sinai
Endoscopy Center
10/02/2018

Patient Name:	Robert Walsh	**Procedure Date:**	10/2/2018 10:58 AM
MRN:	9041534	**Account Number:**	52600028
Date of Birth:	1/25/1945	**Age:**	73
Attending MD:	Christopher DiMaio, MD	**Admit Type:**	Outpatient

Body of the Pancreas — Tail of the Pancreas — celiac axis — Major Papilla

Post-Op Diagnosis: - Normal EGD.
- No obvious mass at ampulla.
- EUS revealed a normal bile duct (no intraductal stones/nodules/masses) and a normal pancreas (no mass). The main pancreatic duct was prominent at the head (4-5 mm). Normal major papilla, without evidence of mass/nodule/polyp. No abnormal lymph nodes seen in the region of the ampulla or pancreas.

Recommendation: - Proceed to ERCP at this session.

Procedure Code(s): — Professional —
43237, Esophagogastroduodenoscopy, flexible, transoral; with endoscopic ultrasound examination limited to the esophagus, stomach or duodenum, and adjacent structures

Diagnosis Code(s): — Professional —
K76.89, Other specified diseases of liver
K92.9, Disease of digestive system, unspecified
R93.3, Abnormal findings on diagnostic imaging of other parts of digestive tract

The codes documented in this report are preliminary and upon coder review may be revised to meet current compliance requirements.

Attending Participation:

I personally performed the entire procedure.

Christopher DiMaio, MD
Finalized Date: 10/2/2018 1:02:05 PM
This report has been signed electronically.
Number of Addenda: 0
Note Initiated On: 10/2/2018 10:58:02 AM

OTHER BOOKS BY BOB WALSH

Books written by Bob Walsh may be ordered in paperback and eBook formats through www.Amazon.com.

JIMMY'S BOY
Devils, Angels and Miracles
Bob Walsh shares the true-life story of childhood experiences as a "blessed child of God" endowed with extraordinary spiritual gifts. This first-hand account provides a unique view into the spiritual world surrounding us all. This book chronicles the personal miraculous events and demonic torments exactly as they happened.

STALKED BY THE DEMONS
Based on a True Story
This book provides a chilling, true story of what it is like to be stalked by demons. For those who may not believe that demons exist, or that they can stalk people, be warned … demons do exist and prey upon people … especially unbelievers! As you read this book, you may wish to pray for God's protection … and keep a light on.

MIRACLES AT SAINT ANNE'S SHRINE
At St. Jean the Baptiste Church in New York City
This book tells the remarkable story of miracles occurring at Saint Anne's Shrine in St. Jean the Baptiste Church in New York City. Saint Anne is the mother of the Blessed Virgin Mary, and the grandmother of Jesus Christ. Her story is based upon recorded ancient history, Catholic Church traditions, and visions by the saints. Many of the miraculous events described in this book were personally witnessed by the author.

OTHER BOOKS BY BOB WALSH

Books written by Bob Walsh may be ordered in paperback and eBook formats through www.Amazon.com.

THE DAY THEY KILLED JESUS CHRIST
A Vision of the Passion

Bob Walsh writes of the Passion of Jesus Christ as if the reader was actually present to witness the horrific, heart-breaking events as they occurred. They are graphically described using information recorded in the Bible, Catholic Church teachings, studies of the Holy Shroud, visions by the saints and reported ancient history. To reflect upon the Passion of Jesus Christ in this way is quite disturbing … but at the same time, it also helps reflect how greatly Christ loves us.

MODERN DAY LAZARUS
Raised from Death by God

This book provides a unique view into what it is like to suffer and die a horrific death … and then be brought miraculously back to the fullness of life by God. In this true story, Bob describes the pain and terror he experienced the day he drowned when he was only eight years old. With his spirit hovering above his lifeless body, he called out to God and asked Him to send him back to physical life.

DEMONS, ANGELS AND MIRACLES
Memoirs of a Blessed Child (Three-book Set)

Each of these books provides a "peek behind the curtain" describing the remarkable, often terrifying, true story of a New York City boy blessed by God from birth with extraordinary spiritual gifts involving healing, visions … and the ability to recognize the presence and work of demons.

OTHER BOOKS BY BOB WALSH

Books written by Bob Walsh may be ordered in paperback and eBook formats through www.Amazon.com.

ENCOUNTERS WITH ANGELS AND SPIRITS

Bob Walsh presents true stories of encounters people have had with angels and spirits - both good and evil. Some of these stories are ones he personally encountered. Hearing these stories from the perspective of those who actually experienced them may remind you of similar events in your life. The "good spirits" referred to in this book are angels and glorified souls who are with God … and those souls who are in Purgatory. The "evil spirits" referred to include Satan, fallen angels and those souls who damned themselves to Hell by living out of God's grace during their physical lives.

IF GOD CALLS YOU RIGHT NOW
Will You Be Ready?

In this book, Bob Walsh reminds us that a day is coming for each of us when we will die and find ourselves standing before Almighty God who will judge us according to how we have lived. Will you be ready? While no one knows the very moment when God will call us, we do know from the words of God as recorded in the Bible what is expected of us here in physical life. God's words also tell us of the three possible destinations that await us at the end of our lives. There is the breath-taking beauty of Paradise, the mercy of Purgatory, and the unspeakable agony of Hell for those who follow the wrong roads in life. If God calls you right now … will you be ready?

OTHER BOOKS BY BOB WALSH

Books written by Bob Walsh may be ordered in paperback and eBook formats through www.Amazon.com.

ATTACKS BY THE DEVILS
Exorcists and Survivors Speak Out
This book provides frightening, first-hand accounts shared by Catholic exorcists and by victims of all ages and backgrounds who survived personal attacks by Satan, the demons (fallen angels) and those souls who damned themselves by living out of God's grace during their physical lives. This disturbing "peek behind the curtains" is very disturbing; it shows the reality and hateful work of the Devil and its evil spirits. For those who doubt such things exist, remember Padre Pio's words, "If all the devils that are here were to take bodily form, they would blot out the light of the sun!"

TRUE STORIES OF GHOSTS AND DEMONS
This book presents true stories of encounters people have had with ghosts and demons. Some of these stories I personally experienced. The "good ghosts" referred to in this book include angels, glorified souls who are with God in Heaven and those who are in Purgatory. The "evil spirits" referred to include Satan, fallen angels and souls who damned themselves by living out of God's grace during physical life. This book is not for the faint of heart.

OTHER BOOKS BY BOB WALSH

Books written by Bob Walsh may be ordered in paperback and eBook formats through www.Amazon.com.

MY LIFE OF MIRACLES

In this book, Bob Walsh describes countless miraculous and exhilarating experiences he has witnessed including remarkable healings over the course of his life. He also shares how the Devil relentlessly sought to interfere with God's plans for his life.

Greatly moved by Christ's words in Luke 12:48, "From everyone to whom much is given, much will be required," Bob felt compelled to share what he has been so blessed to witness. Looking back over the years, he provides a first-hand account, a "peek behind the curtain," into the reality of God and the angels, the Devil and its demons, miracles, and the vast spiritual world surrounding us all.

INDEX

A

B

C

D

E

F

G

N

O

P

R

S

T

Made in the USA
Middletown, DE
02 October 2020